World Wide Web Database Programming for Windows NT™

World Wide Web Database Programming for Windows NT™

Brian Jepson

Wiley Computer Publishing

John Wiley & Sons, Inc.

New York • Chichester • Brisbane • Toronto • Singapore

Publisher: Katherine Schowalter
Editor: Philip Sutherland
Managing Editor: Angela Murphy
Electronic Products, Associate Editor: Mike Green
Text Design & Composition: Benchmark Productions, Inc.

Library of Congress Cataloging-in-Publication Data:

Jepson, Brian.
World Wide Web database programming for Windows NT / Brian Jepson.
p. cm.
Includes index.
ISBN 0-471-14930-6 (paper/CD-ROM ; alk. paper)
1. Database management. 2. Microsoft Windows NT. 3. World Wide Web (Information retrieval system) I. Title.
QA76.9.D3J475 1996
005.75'8--dc20

96-14588

Printed in the United States of America
10 9 8 7 6 5 4 3 2 1

CONTENTS

FEAR AND LOATHING ON THE INFOBAHN

We were somewhere around Cambridge on the edge of the 'net when the realization began to take hold. I remember saying something like "Of course . . . it's so simple . . . the answer . . .; maybe I should give you the mouse . . ." And suddenly, there was a terrible roar all around us and the 'net was full of diverse technologies, all swooping and screeching and diving around the heads of developers, who were heading down the path of progress at the speed of light. And a voice was screaming "Yikes! What are we to do?"

– with really, really sincere apologies to Hunter S. Thompson

If you had asked me four years ago whether I could ever see myself writing a serious technical book, I would have laughed you out of the room and sent cious, drunken thugs to follow you home to beat some sense into you.

Nevertheless, I find myself, years later, sitting, somewhat slouched, in an ergonomically correct chair, typing a very technical book into an ergonomically correct keyboard, with the desk just the wrong height, so I have to reach up slightly to type. I've got blisters on my fingers.

I've had a lot of fun in the past year or so. I started out as a humble FoxPro and SQL Server developer, watching Internet technology evolve. I used to sit bolt upright at night, thinking that my skills would be of little use in a market dominated by groovy technology like the World Wide Web. It took me a while, but I finally saw, about a year ago, that I could have an angle in the midst of all this. I realized that eventually people would want to hook their database systems up to the World Wide Web.

Six months before this, I had been wandering around lower Broadway in New York City. I was taking a sanity break by going to Waldenbooks; I decided it would be a good day to add to my book collection. On a complete whim, I purchased Larry Wall and Randal L. Schwartz's *Programming Perl.* After I made my way through some early examples, the book started gathering dust, until about six months later, when I started to learn CGI programming. Desperate to put together what I had learned about Perl and CGI, and what I already knew about databases, I pulled out the FoxPro manuals, turned to the pages where the structure of the DBF file was documented, and started writing a Perl script to read and write DBF files. By four in the morning, I had something working.

Well, it's been about a year since that time, and I'm not using low-level file manipulation to modify DBF files. Now, I use ODBC; you will, too, by the time you are done with this book. There's a lot of information packed into this book; I hope that you will find what you need.

This book could not have gone down without the support and assistance of a lot of folks. I'm going to try to enumerate them here; if I missed anyone, I'll add them to the web page which I have established to support this book (http://www.ids.net/~bjepson/www-database/).

I'd like to thank all the freaks and mutants at AS220 and SMT (http://www.ids.net/~as220/) for providing me with superior social events and moral support. The weekly meetings of SMT at the AS220 Cafe are a blast. If you're ever in Providence, pop in some time. Special thanks also goes out to Prosoft Systems International, who didn't fire me while I was writing this book, despite the gross lack of billable hours during the last few weeks of writing. I'd also like to thank the folks who contributed to the huge supply of free software that made this book possible. Thanks to Larry Wall and the Author of his story, for giving us Perl and also to Hip Communications, for porting Perl to Windows NT and Windows 95 (and to Microsoft, who paid for it). Thanks also goes out to the folks at EMWAC, for a great, free Web server on Windows NT. I'd especially like to thank Lee Fesperman of FFE Software, Inc. for providing Jasmine and IODBC, which was used as the original ODBC engine for the examples in this book. I still use IODBC daily for getting at ODBC data sources from the command prompt. Appreciation also goes out to Shishir Gundavaram, the author of CGI_Lite. Much appreciation goes out to Dan DeMaggio, author of the ODBC extensions for Perl for Win32. These extensions provide the core functionality of the Perl/ODBC connectivity demonstrated in this book.

I'd also like to thank Tim Bunce and Jacqui Caren, both of the Paul Ingram Group for looking at an early draft of this manuscript and Randal L. Schwartz for going over some of the material pertaining to Perl. Thanks also to Joshua Marketos and Shawn Wallace of SMT, who proofread some of the chapters in the book. Thanks goes out to Tim Bunce (again) and Ke Jin of Empress Software for giving me a great deal of insight into the future convergence of UNIX, Windows NT, Perl, and ODBC technologies.

I appreciated the support of my family and friends during this time, especially that of my best friend (who is also my wife) Pam, who put up with me tapping on the keyboard at ungodly hours, muttering curses under my breath. Thanks also goes out to our cat, Oscar, who refrained from biting me, except between feedings.

Every effort has been made to ensure that the information in this book is up-to-date and accurate. However, the technology used in this book is something of a moving target. As a result, a support site has been set up on:

```
http://www.ids.net/~bjepson/www-database/
```

You should check into that site from time to time, as any bug fixes and enhancements will be available there, as well as new goodies as they become available. If you really get stuck, send me some email at bjepson@conan.ids.net. You can send me email even if you're not stuck. Be seeing you!

BRIAN JEPSON
Providence, RI

CHAPTER

1

INTERNET BASICS

Traditionally, initiates to the SMT Computing Society in Providence, Rhode Island, are required to wear the "Golden SCSI Cable" for a week before they can become voting members. Thankfully, this has never been enforced. This humiliating, yet unpracticed tradition, illustrates the necessity of observing certain rites of passage before one can venture forth into new territory. We're going to observe such a rite in this chapter: You will be initiated into the world of the Internet, as it would be advantageous for you, as a reader of this book to have some familiarity with the Internet. If you are not familiar with the Internet, this chapter will make the rest of the book easier for you.

What Is the Internet?

There are three components to the Internet: computers, a networking infrastructure, and a means of making the physical composition of the network a lot simpler to deal with. The computer part is simple; these are box-like appliances which can weigh less than your cat or more than your car, depending on how much you believed of what the computer salesman told you. Generally, computers come with some sort of interface which allows you to put information into the computer, such as a keyboard and/or mouse, and some sort of interface for you to get information out, such as a monitor or printer.

The network portion is a little more complex; a network infrastructure is what physically connects two or more computers together. This is generally composed of metal fibers encased in some sort of plastic-like substance (a wire or cable), but sometimes can involve fiber optic cable, infrared radiation (like your TV's remote control), or radio waves. Another component is some sort of *hardware* which allows your computer to send information over the wire or cables. This is often a *network card*, but can also be a modem, which connects your computer to telephone lines rather than to other sorts of specialized cabling.

The part which concerns you the most is the software portion. This is what makes it easy for the folks who write programs to converse with the network. The actual way your computer converses with the network is far too complex for ordinary mortals to comprehend. A software *networking protocol* is designed to hide the complexity of the physical network. There are many software protocols that can be used over nearly any network card or modem. Windows NT provides protocols with such strange names as IPX, NetBEUI, and TCP/IP. Each of these provides the computer with the ability to address the network in a different way, much in the same way that you can choose various means of travel; you can drive, fly, or swim. Each method has its advantage and its limitations.

The networked computers which make up the Internet share at least one thing in common: They all use the TCP/IP network protocol. It is likely that they are running other protocols in addition to TCP/IP, but the transactions that occur over the Internet use TCP/IP to get the job done. TCP/IP stands for Transmission Control Protocol/Internet Protocol; to a software package, the network looks rather simple.

Each computer on a TCP/IP network is given a four-byte *IP address*. Each of the four bytes can hold a value of 1 to 254. Here's an example of an IP address: 155.212.99.10. When one computer wants to talk to another computer over TCP/IP, a connection is opened to one or more ports on the other computer. The ports are software constructs designed to make the network easier to understand from a software developer's point of view. At any given time, my computer can open up connections to many ports on a remote computer. All of the data that is sent from my computer to the remote computer is organized in such a way so as to know to which port it is going. As a result, one *stream* of data can be devoted to transferring a file to the remote computer and another stream can be used for viewing web pages on that computer.

Although there are many more details involved with this process, the fundamentals of how computers communicate over the Internet were just spelled out. This technology is applied to a worldwide network of computers; hence, you can make a connection from your computer to one half-way around the world just as easily as to one two blocks down the street.

In order to implement the examples shown in this book, you need access to one or more computers running Windows NT with the TCP/IP protocol installed. One of the computers must have a *web server* installed; fortunately, a web server is contained on the CD-ROM. The examples in this book can be adapted to Windows 95 Web Servers, provided they can execute Perl scripts. You will need to contact your vendor for this information.

It Just Doesn't Matter: Internal Networks

You really don't need to be on the Internet in order to put technologies such as the World Wide Web to use. The Internet has facilitated the growth of these technologies, but anyone with a TCP/IP network can take advantage of them. If your organization has a very large network, chances are good that one of the network protocols in use is TCP/IP. Even small Windows 95 networks can use TCP/IP; it is one of the network protocols included with Windows 95.

Even on a large private network with many computers running TCP/IP, the technology demonstrated in this book can provide a solution for those seeking to deliver corporate data to many users on many different platforms. Perhaps the accounting workgroup uses only Windows 3.1; the desktop publishing group uses a combination of Atari STs, Atari Falcons, and Apple Macintoshes; and the custodial staff uses SparcStations. A perverse situation such as this is a great example of how traditional Internet solutions can be used to solve your high-tech conundrums. Imagine that you are saddled with the responsibility of providing access to a data repository to all the users in your company. Well, you could force everyone to use the same OS, but that would be a nightmare and you'd probably lose your job. Since all of the computers in your building are connected using TCP/IP, it is only a matter of installing one Windows NT or Windows 95 computer as a server on your network and installing World Wide Web clients on each person's machine—and *voilà*! you can now implement the techniques illustrated in this book. Since Web clients can generally be gotten for very little cost, and in some cases are free, using the World Wide Web to implement an internal groupware solution is very attractive.

Concepts and Services

Hostnames

The Internet is made up of a great many computers; there has to be some way of naming them if you and your computers are to make any sense of things. Fortunately, the Internet naming conventions are somewhat standardized. Each computer gets a name, called a *hostname*, and large groups of computers are often organized under a *domain*. Let's imagine you are the CEO of Cheezeco, Inc., makers of fine 1970s-style clothing. You've got offices in London as well as New York, and it doesn't simply suffice for you to name your computers cheddar, stilton, brie, and so forth. All of the computers in the main London office are grouped under a domain called cheeze.uk. All of the computers in the New York office are grouped under a domain called cheeze.com. (If any of those domains belong to someone, I formally apologize.) Finally, your research and development computers, situated in Arkham, Massachusetts, belong to a domain called cthulu.cheeze.com, which is a *subdomain* of cheeze.com.

Given these domain name groupings, your main research and development server might be known as

```
cheddar.cthulu.cheeze.com
```

Your corporate web server might be called

```
www.cheeze.com
```

and its UK mirror might be called

```
www.cheeze.uk
```

> A mirror computer is a computer which has a complete copy of another computer's publicly available information, which includes its web pages, its ftp directories, and so forth. These are generally used when demand for a site in another country becomes high. If your main site is in the United States, it might be a little slow for European users to access. This is when you put up a mirror of the site up in another country.

The domain names are used within a complex mechanism called *DNS* (domain name system), which is basically a database of all the hostnames and domains distributed across a lot of computers. When another computer needs to access one of your computers, it will have the host and domain name, but it probably doesn't know the corresponding IP address. A *name server lookup* will convert the host and domain name (such as cheddar.cheeze.com) to an IP address. Once a computer knows the IP address, it can make a TCP/IP connection to a port on that computer.

For example, your name server at cheeze.com (which could very well be a computer named cheeze.com), is the authoritative source for all hostnames which are in the domain cheeze.com. Anyone looking for www.cheeze.com will probably have to ask cheeze.com what the IP address is. For example, before a computer can ask cheeze.com the IP address of stilton.cheeze.com, it must ask its local name server what the IP address of cheeze.com is! If the local name server can't find it, it has to ask elsewhere. The nice thing about DNS is that the process is carried out transparently (behind the scenes). As a user, you just specify the hostname, and your computer will handle finding it. There are times when a critical name server may be inaccessible; this can be frustrating and can often make it impossible to find a remote system until the problem is corrected.

> Configuring DNS can be everything from a pain to a nightmare. Fortunately, you don't always have to do this. Unless you are putting together a really large network, you don't have to deal with it. When you set up an Internet account with an ISP, they will tell you the IP address of the DNS, and you simply tell your computers about it when you configure your Internet access software.

ftp

The acronym *ftp* stands for file transfer protocol and the name just about says it all. It allows you to transfer files between one computer and another over TCP/IP. Although facilities exist to mount drives over the Internet, ftp is usually the common denominator. Many large archives offer access to their files via ftp. Many of these archives are available via *anonymous ftp*, which is a *site* that allows access to anyone. On Windows NT, ftp can be invoked from the command line by typing

```
ftp [host]
```

where *host* is the name of the computer to which you want to connect. A lot of the free software used in this book is available via anonymous ftp. For example, Perl 5 for Win32 is available on an ftp site named ntperl.hip.com. To establish a connection to this site from your computer, you must invoke ftp and log in, supplying the username *ftp* or *anonymous*, and your complete email address as a password (actually, you can stop typing after the @, because most ftp servers can figure out your hostname—so bjepson@ would be expanded to bjepson@bjepson.org).

Here's an example of connecting to and logging into ftp.cygnus.com, the home of the gnu-win32 project (commands you type are in bold—note that your password will not appear on screen, but I show it here for completeness):

```
Microsoft(R) Windows NT(TM)
(C) Copyright 1985-1995 Microsoft Corp.
Command Processor Extensions Enabled

C:\>ftp ftp.cygnus.com
Connected to majipoor.cygnus.com.
220 majipoor.cygnus.com FTP server (Version wu-2.4(3) Mon Oct 2 13:58:01 PDT 199
5) ready.
User (majipoor.cygnus.com:(none)): ftp
331 Guest login ok, send your complete e-mail address as password.
Password: bjepson@
230-          Welcome to the Cygnus Support ftp server!
230-             "We Make Free Software Affordable."
230-
230-
230-    For more information about Cygnus Support:
230-      Send email to........................... info@cygnus.com
230-      Visit our web site at................... http://www.cygnus.com/
230-      Call.................................... +1 415 903 1400
230-
230-    Only anonymous logins are allowed.  Mail problems to
```

```
230-     ftp@cygnus.com
230-
230-   All transfers are logged with your host name and email address.
230-   If you don't like this policy, disconnect now!
230-
230-   If your FTP client crashes or hangs shortly after login, try
230-   using a dash (-) as the first character of your password.  This
230-   will turn off the informational messages which may be confusing
230-   your ftp client.
230-
230 Guest login ok, access restrictions apply.
ftp>
```

Once you are connected over an ftp session, you can transfer files to and from your computer. The ftp protocol recognizes two file transfer types, binary and ASCII. By default, the Windows NT ftp *client* (a client is a piece of software that connects to a server somewhere on the same or on another computer; ftp.cygnus.com is running an ftp server, you use an ftp client to connect to that server) transfers files in ASCII mode. This is perfect for retrieving text files, but you will need to issue the `binary` (you can shorten this to `bin`) command to transfer executables, images, or compressed files. The first command you will find useful is the `cd` command. It functions the same way that `cd` functions in the Windows NT and Windows 95 command shell, but pathnames are separated with a / instead of a \. Let's `cd` to the gnu—win32 directory and use the `dir` command (this should also be familiar) to get a list of files:

```
ftp> cd /pub/gnu-win32
250-Please read the file README
250-  it was last modified on Sat Nov 11 19:39:29 1995 - 1 day ago
250 CWD command successful.
ftp> dir
200 PORT command successful.
```

```
150 Opening ASCII mode data connection for /bin/ls.
total 1454
-rw-rw-r--  1 219      1002       2053 Nov 11 19:39 README
lrwxrwxrwx  1 219      1002         19 Nov 10 18:35 beta-5 -> ../sac/gnu-win32
-b5
lrwxrwxrwx  1 219      1002         19 Nov 10 18:35 beta-7 -> ../sac/gnu-win32
-b7
lrwxrwxrwx  1 219      1002         19 Nov 10 18:35 beta-8 -> ../sac/gnu-win32
-b8
lrwxrwxrwx  1 219      1002         16 Nov 10 18:34 latest -> ../sac/gnu-win32

-rw-r--r--  1 219      1002     605326 Nov 12 07:07 ml-archive
-rw-rw-r--  1 219      1002     160875 Nov 10 18:50 stabs.html
-rw-rw-r--  1 219      1002     375451 Nov 10 19:14 stabs.ps
-rw-rw-r--  1 219      1002     146611 Nov 10 18:48 stabs.texinfo
-rw-rw-r--  1 219      1002     135997 Nov 10 18:49 stabs.txt
-rw-rw-r--  1 219      1002       7062 Nov 10 18:50 stabs_toc.html
226 Transfer complete.
811 bytes received in 1.21 seconds (0.67 Kbytes/sec)
ftp>
```

This is a UNIX-style `ls -l` listing. Notice that some of the longer filenames have wrapped (beta-5, beta-7, beta-8, and latest). There's some other material at the end of the filenames. These four files are not actually files as we know them on Windows NT and Windows 95, but are symbolic links to files in another directory. This is very common on Internet ftp sites, since many of them use UNIX as their operating system. The first column in the directory listing is a list of permissions, the second is the number of hard links to that directory, the third is the id of the user who created the files, and the fourth is the group id of the user who created the files (you don't need to remember all that). These are followed by the file size, the file creation or modification date, and the filename. If you want to retrieve the file README (probably not a bad idea), do as is shown in the following example. Note the use of the hash command. This tells the ftp client to spit out a # every time it reads 2,048 bytes of data; this can be useful if you want some sort of progress indicator. The get command is used to copy the file to your computer.

```
ftp> hash
Hash mark printing On (2048 bytes/hash mark).
ftp> get README
200 PORT command successful.
150 Opening ASCII mode data connection for README (2053 bytes).
#
226 Transfer complete.
2115 bytes received in 1.40 seconds (1.51 Kbytes/sec)
```

If you want to read the file that you just retrieved with the get command, you can type the following command:

```
ftp> !more < README
```

The ! tells the ftp client to issue a Windows NT command in a subshell. The README file goes through a program called more.com, which lets you view it one screenful at a time. When you are done, it returns you to the ftp> prompt. Don't spend too much time paging through files this way; the number of ftp connections are limited at many sites, and many sites will log you out if you sit idle for too long. Unless you are executing an ftp command, you appear to be sitting idle.

Reading the README file, you learned that the most recent version of the GNU C compiler is located in the directory called latest/, which, as observed previously, is a symbolic link to another directory. In order to get the file we want, you can cd to latest, and get a listing of the files in there. If you do that, you'll notice that there's another README file in there. It tells you a lot about the latest release, what the filename is, and so forth. Since the file you want is a compressed file, it needs to be transferred in binary mode. You can set ftp into binary mode by typing bin or binary at the ftp> prompt. Note that you should set it back to ASCII mode with the `asc` or `ascii` command if you want to transfer any more ASCII files, like README. Having the file transfer type set incorrectly is one of the biggest sources of frustration when downloading files, as binary files transferred in ASCII mode are generally unusable!

```
ftp> bin
200 Type set to I.
ftp> get i386-win32-X-i386-win32.tar.gz
200 PORT command successful.
150 Opening BINARY mode data connection for i386-win32-X-i386-win32.tar.gz
(4676772 bytes).
```

When you are done with your ftp session, you can type `quit` at the `ftp>` prompt. Note the funny file extension on the file you downloaded. This indicates the type of compression used. The file has been "tarred" and "gzipped." This is another common UNIXism which is becoming more prevalent on Windows NT. The `gzip` (GNU zip) utility compresses a single file and adds the .gz suffix. The `tar` (tape archive) utility takes a directory tree and puts it into a single file, with no compression. This is what is responsible for the .tar suffix. It is called tape archive because it is traditionally used to dump a directory tree to a tape device, but can also dump to a file. You can also use `tar` to extract the directory structure. Before you decompress the file, it's a good idea to see what's in it. Using `gunzip` and `tar` (included in the \UTIL directory on the CD-ROM) can accomplish this.

```
gunzip -c i386-win32-X-i386-win32.tar.gz | tar tvf -
```

The `-c` switch tells gunzip to uncompress the file to the console, and the | symbol pipes this output to the `tar` command. The `t` switch tells tar to only print the filenames contained in the archive, the `v` switch tells it to be verbose, and the `f` switch tells tar to read its archive from a file (console input counts as a file). The naked - tells tar that the file is coming in from console input, which is where the | sends it from the `gunzip` command.

When you are ready to extract the files into the current directory, type

```
gunzip -c i386-win32-X-i386-win32.tar.gz | tar tvf -
```

Usenet

Usenet is made up of thousands of discussion groups, each concerned with a specific topic. When you enter Usenet, you can select which groups to view, read messages that others have posted, and post messages of your own. The software that you use to do this is called a *newsreader*. The number of available newsreaders varies from site to site; you can download various shareware and freeware newsreaders from anonymous ftp sites.

The discussion groups on Usenet, called newsgroups, are organized in a hierarchical manner. For example, many of the newsgroups pertaining to computer issues are organized under the *comp* hierarchy. That hierarchy is further refined into such areas as comp.databases (discussions related to database packages), comp.os (discussions related to specific operating systems), comp.binaries (uuencoded binaries), and so forth. Some of the names are quite long, such as comp.os.ms-windows.nt.software.compatibility or finet.freenet.oppimiskeskus.ammatilliset.sos+terv.oppisopimus.keskustelu. Some newsgroups do double duty as hierarchical groupings. For example, there is a newsgroup named comp.databases; several newsgroups are organized below it, such as comp.databases.sybase and comp.databases.xbase.fox.

Usenet is an invaluable resource for anybody who prefers not to work in a vacuum. There are a vast number of topics that are covered on Usenet; many have nothing to do with computers at all. Usenet can provide a planetary gathering of experts who often will take the time to answer well thought-out questions.

Before you post anything to Usenet, you should read the articles contained in news.announce.newusers. Usenet can be a lot like a foreign country; if certain customs are flouted, the natives may get upset. To avoid this type of situation, read the articles that are posted regularly for new users. Also, you should read the messages in a group for a while before posting. That way, you can get an idea of what the group is all about, as the name of the group may not always be a clear indication. Further, many groups have

FAQs (Frequently Asked Questions), which are posted regularly to the newsgroup and to news.answers. Also, most, if not all, FAQs can be obtained via anonymous ftp from ftp://rtfm.mit.edu/pub/usenet/.

The World Wide Web

Hopefully, you have some idea as to what the World Wide Web is about or you wouldn't have taken an interest in this book. But if you don't, congratulations on your initiative! Unless you bought every book in the store with the word WWW or Web on it, then you have zeroed in on what many agree is one of the newest frontiers. Next to executable content issues (such as Java or Python), connecting World Wide Web users up to database management systems is a hot issue.

The World Wide Web is a distributed collection of documents which are stored in a format known as HTML. Like Rich Text Format (RTF) and unlike many proprietary document formats, HTML is stored as ASCII text; all formatting codes use plain-text characters such as the greater than and less than signs (< and >). HTML is a rather simple document format that is recognized by special software known as a *Web browser*. The textual information in your HTML document is littered with formatting codes, known as HTML tags.

When you want to access an Internet resource from a Web browser, you must supply a Uniform Resource Locator or URL. The URL consists of three parts: a protocol specifier, a hostname, and a path to the resource. For example, to transfer the file used as an example in the ftp primer, you would specify the following URL

```
ftp://ftp.cygnus.com/pub/gnu-win32/latest/i386-win32-X-i386-win32.tar.gz
```

where

```
ftp:// is the protocol

ftp.cygnus.com is the hostname

and

/pub/gnu-win32/latest/i386-win32-X-i386-win32.tar.gz is the path to the resource.
```

The http protocol is used to fetch World Wide Web documents, and is specified as

```
http://
```

Here's an example of a URL which fetches one of my favorite home pages:

```
http://www.ids.net/~as220/home.html
```

These HTML documents are distributed on computers all over the world, connected via the Internet—hence, "World Wide." Since each of the documents can be linked to each other via hyperlinks, the vast number of documents are said to be connected to each other in a Web-like fashion.

HTML documents are transferred from Web servers to Web browsers over the Internet. A special transfer protocol called http (hypertext transfer protocol) is used when the files are transferred. Many Web browsers, such as Netscape, Mosaic, and Lynx understand other protocols. In addition to browsing the Web, you can use certain Web browsers to access an ftp site, using the ftp protocol.

HTML Documents: Tags, Elements, and Attributes The information that makes up an HTML document includes a variety of beasts known as elements, which control the way text and images are displayed in the user's browser. Elements are made up of tags and can also contain text. The tags are enclosed in the < (less than) and > (greater than) symbols. An element which is made up of a tag and some text looks like:

```
<tag_name> some text </tag_name>
```

An example of such an element is a header. There are six of them, `<h1>...</h1>` through `<h6> ... </h6>`. Header 1 (`<h1> ... </h1>`) is more emphasized (bigger and bolder) than the others; they decrease in emphasis down to header 6 (`<h6> ... </h6>`). Here's an example of a header element:

```
<h1>The Frodus Home Page</h1>
```

The tags `<h1>` and `</h1>` delimit the header element, which displays the text between the tags. A tag may optionally contain one or more attributes. Attributes allow you to control certain aspects of a tag. Attributes may be included in an element as shown.

```
<tag_name attribute = value [, attribute = value]>
```

One element which makes use of an attribute is the anchor element (`<a> ... </a>`), which can be used for several purposes. One such purpose is as a *hyperlink*, which is an active element of the HTML document. When users select a hyperlink (on graphical browsers, this is accomplished by clicking the mouse), it takes them somewhere else—it can be to another document or to another part of the same document. If the anchor is a hyperlink, it must contain the `href` attribute and a target:

```
<a href=target>
```

The target can be a location within the current document, another document, a location within another document, or a CGI script. Locations within documents are defined using the anchor element also, but the locations are defined with the `name` attribute, rather than an `href` attribute. Anchor locations are not displayed to the user and are similar to bookmarks used in word processing documents:

```
<a name="anchor_name"></a>
```

This can be very useful if you have one long HTML document, especially if the document has many subsections. You can then add an anchor location to each subsection and create a hyperlinked table of contents at the top of the document. Let's pretend that this chapter is an HTML document. If you added

```
<a name="what_is"></a>
```

to the first section in this chapter, then the hyperlink

```
<a href="#what_is">What is the Internet?</a>
```

would allow the user to jump to that section. The # symbol is required before the name of the anchor location. If you want to define a hyperlink which jumps to another document, you must include its URL as the target. The following hyperlink would give the user the option to jump to the AS220 home page:

```
<a href="http://www.ids.net/~as220/home.html">The AS220 Home Page</a>
```

You can also include hyperlinks to anchor locations within other web documents. The following hyperlink would jump to the "toc" anchor location (if there was one) on the AS220 home page:

```
<a href="http://www.ids.net/~as220/home.html#toc">The AS220 Home Page</a>
```

The `html` element is an element which makes up the whole HTML document. It, in turn, contains two other elements, which contain all of the other elements. The first element is the `head` element, and it usually contains the `title` element. The `title` element contains the text which is displayed as the document title. The next element contained in the `html` element is the `body` element; and it contains the meat of the HTML document.

Here's an example of a very simple HTML document; you can see what it will look like in a Web browser by looking at Figure 1.1.

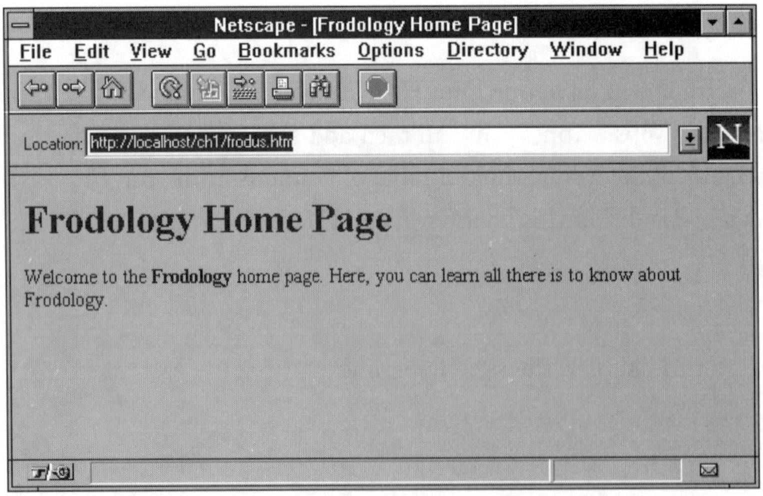

Figure 1.1 A simple HTML document in a Web browser.

```
<html>
    <head>
        <title>Frodology Home Page</title>
    </head>

    <body>
        <h1>Frodology Home Page</h1>

        Welcome to the <strong>Frodology</strong> home page. Here, you can
        learn all there is to know about Frodology.<p>

    </body>
</html>
```

Note that indentation has been added to make the `html`, `head`, and `body` elements stand out. In general, extra spaces are ignored when the document is shown in the browser, so this type of formatting is acceptable. The previous document demonstrates the use of the `h1` element, the `strong` element (this makes the text stand out a little more than the rest—it is generally rendered as bold), and the `p` element, which generates a paragraph break. For a very complete list of HTML elements, see

`http://kuhttp.cc.ukans.edu/lynx_help/HTML_quick.html`

which is an excellent HTML Quick Reference.

Here's an example of two documents linked together with hyperlinks (they are contained on the CD-ROM in \EG\CH1):

```
Example document 1 (http://localhost/ch1/frodus1.htm):
<html>
<head>
<title>Frodology Home Page</title>
</head>

<body>
```

```
<h1>Frodology Home Page</h1>

Welcome to the <strong>Frodology</strong> home page. Here, you can learn all
there is to know about Frodology.<p>

For some more information, see our

<a href="http://localhost/ch1/frodus2.htm">UK mirror</a>.<p>

</body>

</html>


Example document 2 (http://localhost/ch1/frodus2.htm):

<html>

<head>

<title>Frodology Home Page</title>

</head>


<body>

<h1>Frodology Home Page</h1>

Welcome to the <strong>Frodology</strong> home page.

Here, you can learn all there is to know about Frodology.<p>

For some more information, see our

<a href="http://localhost/ch1/frodus1.htm">US mirror</a>.<p>

</body>

</html>
```

Note that the hyperlink is defined by an anchor element. The anchor element is enclosed in the <a>...</a> tags. One of the key attributes that makes a particular anchor a hyperlink is the HREF attribute. This is included within the <a> tag. Everything between the <a> tag and the </a> tag is the text of the hyperlink that appears to the user in Web browser. When millions of these documents are linked together in this fashion, it makes for interesting browsing. Where else can you start out looking for information on TeX implementations for Win32 and end up downloading an Atari 800 emulator?

Windows NT and the Web

Windows NT and Windows 95 are excellent operating systems for running an Internet Web Server. They both can *preemptively multitask* applications, which means that, unlike Windows 3.1, the operating system is always in control of the applications you are running. You do not have to wait for something to finish before you can move on to another task. This feature is critical when running a Web server. A Web server can receive a large number of hits at once, and for every request that requires access to a database, one or more programs are run to accommodate that request. In circumstances such as this, it's really good to be running an operating system that can preemptively multitask.

While both Windows NT and Windows 95 are great operating systems for running an Internet Web server, Windows NT is clearly superior for a number of reasons. First, it is more robust, which means that it is less likely to become unstable if an application terminates abnormally or behaves in an unexpected manner. Secondly, the Windows NT service model supplies a great deal of flexibility and security, as you'll see in the following section.

Services

There is a slight difference in the way in which you will run your Web server, depending upon whether you are using Windows NT or Windows 95. On Windows NT, the operating system accommodates server software such as a Web server. Such programs are run as services, under the control of the service control manager. They can be started, stopped, and configured to log in as a certain user.

The ability to specify which user a service logs in as provides a significant advantage over Windows 95. Every time a request is made to the Web server to run a script (this occurs when a database is accessed, as will be seen as you work through the book), the Web server executes a program. While a properly configured Web site should preclude the possibility of harmful programs being run, configuring your Web server to log in as a user with limited rights is a bonus; if that user doesn't have the rights to delete every file in the \WINDOWS directory or format your hard drive, there's no way a security hole which exposes those parts of your system can be exploited. While security breaches of this type are somewhat rare, it is best to put up a strong defense against them before something happens.

One of the other advantages of the Windows NT service model is the ability to specify startup preferences for the service. You can set the service to be started manually or you can let Windows NT start it when it boots up. This enables you to have a Web server running without having to be logged in.

On Windows 95, your Web server will be started up just like any other application and will run on your desktop. For this reason, you must be logged in when your Web server is running.

Installing a Web Server on Windows NT

A Web server is included on the CD-ROM, under the directory \HTTPS. There are four versions of it included in this directory:

Filename	Description
hsALPHA.zip	HTTPS for Windows NT on DEC ALPHA Architecture
hsi386.zip	HTTPS for Windows NT on Intel Architecture
hsmips.zip	HTTPS for Windows NT on MIPS Architecture
hsPPC.zip	HTTPS for Windows NT on Power PC Architecture

It is version 0.99 beta of the EMWAC HTTP Server which is maintained and distributed by the European Microsoft Windows NT Academic Centre (http://emwac.ed.ac.uk). The https server only runs on Windows NT. The installation of https is simple and straightforward. After you have unzipped the distribution, you must move the following files to your %SystemRoot% \SYSTEM32 directory:

```
HTTPS.CPL

HTTPS.HLP

HTTPS.EXE
```

By the way, `%SystemRoot%` is an environment variable on Windows NT. It is quite often your C:\WINDOWS or C:\WINNT35 directory. You can determine it by typing the following at the command prompt:

```
C:\> echo %SystemRoot%
```

Once you have moved these three files to the %SystemRoot%\SYSTEM32 directory, they will be in your search path. To install the software, you can type:

```
C:\> https -install
```

You should have administrative privileges to perform this function. Having copied the files over and installed https, you can now access HTTPS.CPL through the Control Panel by double-clicking on the HTTP Server icon. This allows you to specify, among other things, the *data directory* for https. As you work through the examples in this book, it will be a good idea to copy the \eg subdirectory from the CD-ROM. (I would copy it somewhere like C:\EG, but that's only because I'm unimaginative.) Make sure you copy all the subdirectories, as well. This will become your https data directory.

Once you have copied the files from the CD-ROM, you can specify that directory as the data directory. Don't specify this directory as a logical drive (a drive created with SUBST or a network drive) when you set up the https data directory. When you type in the path, it will be verified to check that is a valid path. If you connect drive X: to C:\EG, and type in `X:\` as the data directory, https will not complain. But, remember that under Windows NT, services generally log in as another user, such as the default system account. That user may not have drive X: attached to C:\EG, and can't find the data directory. It's best to specify the physical path (C:\EG) wherever possible. See Figure 1.2 for a look at the https configuration screen.

If you want to configure the Web server to log in as a specific user or if you want to set it to start up when the system boots, you can enter the Services applet in the Control Panel and set these options. See Figure 1.3 for a look at this screen. Chapter 8 goes into this process in excruciating detail.

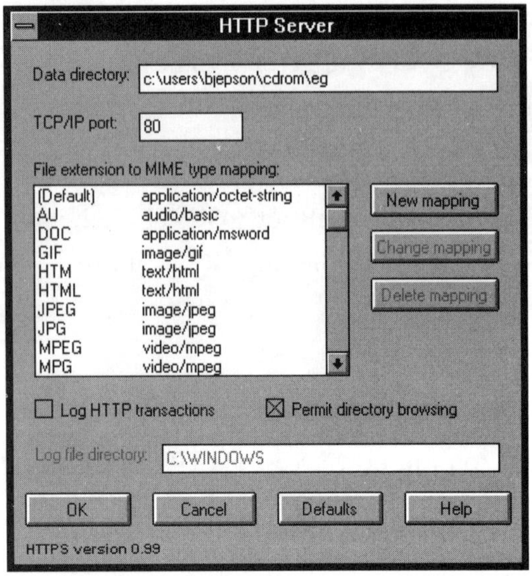

Figure 1.2 The https configuration screen.

The Services applet lists a lot of services. Scroll down until you find EMWAC HTTP Server, and highlight it. Then, you may click on the Startup... button to bring up its properties. If you set its Startup Type to Automatic, https will be started the next time the system boots. Any error messages will be displayed at startup, and you can enter the Event Log to

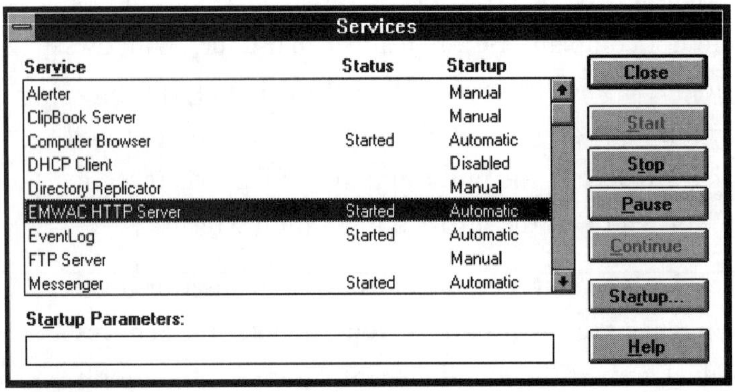

Figure 1.3 The Services applet.

view them. You can also specify that the service will log on as a specific user, under the "Log On As" section. By default, it is set to the system account, but you can change it to "This Account," and specify a username and a password. Figure 1.4 shows this screen. This is only suggested for those of you who have been using Windows NT for some time and are very familiar with the operating system.

Having configured https, you can start it from the command prompt by typing:

```
C:\> net start https
```

Installing the Examples

In order to use the examples included on the CD-ROM, you must install them under the HTTP server's data directory. It is highly recommended that you copy everything under the \EG directory (including subdirectories) to the HTTP server's data directory. The file default.htm contains links to each chapter's examples; you should be able to test them from your Web browser, once the http service is started.

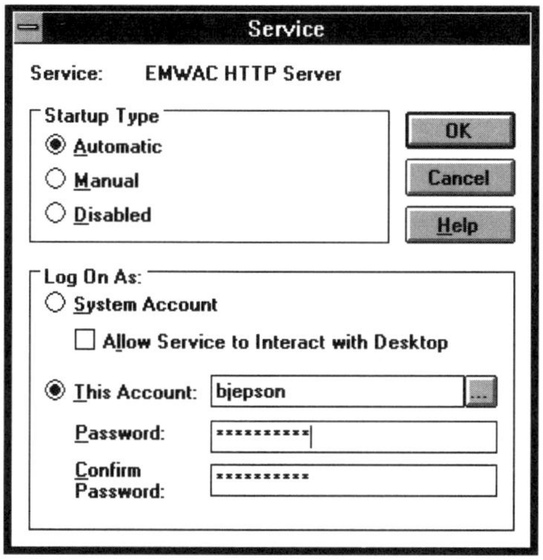

Figure 1.4 Changing the Service to "This Account."

In order to test them from your Web browser, you can specify either localhost or 127.0.0.1 as the hostname. This is a special IP address that always points back to the host computer you are working on. It's called the loopback adapter and allows you to use TCP/IP, even if you don't have a network card. It should be installed by default when you install TCP/IP on your Windows NT or Windows 95 computer.

Testing the Installation

Once you have installed the examples and have started the Web server (it can be started by issuing the command **net start https** from the command prompt), you can text-out the Web pages. Try issuing the following URL from your Web browser:

```
http://localhost/ch1/frodus.htm
```

You should see the first HTML example shown in this chapter.

Other Web Servers

Although the EMWAC HTTP server is an excellent Web server, you may want to use the examples in this book with other Web servers. Many of the commercial Web servers will allow you to execute Perl scripts in the same fashion as the EMWAC HTTP server, so no modification should be necessary. However, I will keep you posted on any issues that come up via the World Wide Web Database Programming for Windows NT FAQ, which is available on:

```
http://www.ids.net/~bjepson/www-database/FAQ.html
```

CHAPTER

2

AN OVERVIEW OF PERL

Although the primary occupation of an http server is to send HTML documents to clients, it does not always accomplish this task merely by reading a file from disk. Many such documents are generated on-the-fly. For the most part, it is those documents that this book really focuses on. These documents are generated by a special program known as a CGI (Common Gateway Interface) script. The CGI script executes on the server and has access to a lot of the machine's resources. A humble little programming language called Perl will be used to perform this task.

What Is Perl?

Perl stands for Practical Extraction and Reporting Language. It was written by Larry Wall and has grown due to his and others' efforts. In its current incarnation, which is version 5.002, it is an object-oriented development tool which combines many features of C, sed, awk, and UNIX shell scripts. Being one of the best tools on the block dealing with vast amounts of text, it happens to be one of the languages of choice for WWW development. Although it is not a compiled language, it is very fast.

Conventions and Terms

As with any other programming language (well, almost any other), the programs that Perl runs are saved in ASCII text files. There are two types of programs that Perl deals with: modules and scripts. Perl modules (with a file extension of .pm) contain class definitions and library routines. Perl scripts (generally with a file extension or .pl or .cgi) contain programs which make use of the libraries and classes contained within Perl modules.

A Hands-on Perl Primer

It has been said that Perl comes very easy to those with UNIX and/or C background. That may be true, but it's one of those generalizations that is more likely to scare people away. I know because I use it all the time. When someone asks me something like "Brian, do you think you could teach me how to use Windows?" I usually respond, "Well, I would, but you really should have some C experience." That usually makes them go away.

To prove that just about anyone can learn Perl, you're going to learn how to write a quick and dirty Perl program that can be run under your Web server as a script. The file will be called xyzzy.pl, and it is located on the CD-ROM under \EG\CH2\xyzzy.pl. You should have copied this along with the rest of the examples to a directory tree under your https data directory (see Appendix C for information on installing the examples).

Installing Perl

The CD-ROM includes a recent version of Perl for Win32. It is contained in the directory \NTPERL on the CD-ROM. Follow the instructions included in the file INSTALL.TXT. After installing, you may need to reboot your computer in order for https, the Web server, to recognize the location of the executable.

The Sample Script

The example script will read in a text file, called chekbook.dat. The file is located on the CD-ROM under \EG\chekbook.dat. This example script is a poor man's personal finance program (why would a poor man need a personal finance program, you might ask?). This file will contain one record on each line, with four comma-delimited fields: the date, purpose (or payee), D for debit or C for credit, and amount. Here's the copy I'm using:

```
checkbook.dat:
10-01-1995,  Opening Balance,          C,  1000.00
10-01-1995,  Grue Cleaners,            D,    30.00
10-01-1995,  Plugh Realty Corp.,       D,   550.00
10-06-1995,  Payday!,                  C,  7000.00
10-07-1995,  Taxes,                    D,  6500.00
```

Using Perl to Generate HTML Documents (CGI Scripting)

When you create a Perl CGI script that is going to generate HTML output, there are certain minimum requirements that must be met in order for the Web browser to understand what is being sent to it. The first piece of information the script must send over is the MIME type of the document, which is a very common method of identifying file types. This is one line of text, usually followed by two newlines; it is:

```
Content-type: text/html
```

After that is printed, your script can begin speaking in HTML. The Content-type information is only required when the output comes from a CGI script. It is not needed at the header of an HTML file that you save on disk.

This might be getting a little confusing, so now is a good time to recap. There are two types of HTML documents. The first is called *static*, which means it never changes unless you physically modify it by editing it. You generally type these into an HTML editor or a heavy-duty text editor like EMACS. Then you save them to a file, usually with the extension .html. The second type of HTML document is called *dynamic*, which means a different document is generated every time someone accesses it. These are created by programs called CGI (Common Gateway Interface) scripts which run on the Web server. A CGI script needs only to print its output to the console, but the first line must state what type of document it is. If it is an HTML document, it must follow the same conventions as the ones you type in: There must be an `html` element, and a `head` and `body` element.

Perl provides a nice way to print a whole bunch of junk without a whole lot of `print()` statements. This feature is called a *here-doc*. A here-doc will print everything between two delimited regions. You tell Perl where the document starts with `<<MARKER;`, where MARKER can be any sequence of alphanumeric characters. It is used to tell Perl when to start reading the here document; the here document stops when the text MARKER appears again. `EOF` is a very popular choice for the MARKER, but it should not be confused with EOF (end-of-file) as used in other contexts. It simply is used to delimit the beginning and end of the here-doc. What follows is an example which prints out the first several lines of a fairly average HTML document. It's only a small part of the Perl script which is found on the CD-ROM under \EG\CH2\xyzzy.pl:

```
print <<EOF ;
Content-type: text/html


<html>
<head><title>Hello, World</title></head>
<body>
<h1>Hello, World</h1>
EOF
```

In this example, everything between `<<EOF ;` and `EOF` is printed. This is the first few lines of xyzzy.pl. Note that we did not finish this with a `</body>` or a `</html>` tag; this is because we still have more things to print out. We need to process them a little bit, first.

Opening a file

The next chore is to write some Perl code that will read this file line by line, parse the values into variables that Perl can manipulate, and format the information into nice tables with some summary information, even! The first thing you want to do is open up chekbook.dat. This is accomplished with

```
open (CHECKS, "chekbook.dat") || die "Couldn't open chekbook.dat"
```

The open function as shown will attempt to open the file in read mode (See the Perl 5 HTML documentation for other access modes). The double-pipe || represents the OR operator. Think of the two statements

```
open (CHECKS, "chekbook.dat")
die "Couldn't open chekbook.dat"
```

As the left- and right-hand side of a logical expression "this or that." For those of you who remember Schoolhouse Rock's "Conjunction Junction," this may not be so difficult. A logical expression A or B will evaluate to true if one of the values is true and one of the values is false. Further, if A is known to be true, we know for a fact that the expression A or B evaluates to true, regardless of the value of B. In the previous Perl code, the `open()` function can return a true (non-zero) or false (zero) value. If it returns a true value (this means that the file was opened okay), Perl never bothers to evaluate the right-hand portion of the expression. So, `die()` is never issued. And that's a good thing, because `die()` causes immediate termination of the Perl script, which you only want to happen if the file could not be opened.

If all of that made no sense, or even if it only made a little sense, you can think of the expression as saying:

"Please open the file chekbook.dat. If you don't, then drop dead."

Processing a File You Just Opened

Once you have opened a file, it's really easy to process it line by line. If you enclose the name of the file handle in less than or greater than signs (<HANDLE>), you get a magic source of lines. Don't confuse this with the use of < and > in HTML tags. Perl and HTML are very different things. You can assign values from this source until you run out of lines in your file. The `while()` construct is very handy for dealing with this magic value source. The following example (this is not included in xyzzy.pl, it's just an example) also shows the `print()` function:

```
while (<CHECKS>) {
    print;
}
```

For each line in <CHECKS>, the statement(s) within the block (delimited by `{}`) is executed. This will print out every line in the file to the console. Note that you didn't have to assign the value of <CHECKS> to anything. This is because the <CHECKS> implicitly assigns each line to a special variable called `$_`. "But wait", you say, "I see no mention of `$_` in the print statement. Are you messing with me?" Well, yes, I am messing with you. But here's another secret: The `print()` function, if it is called with no arguments, implies use of `$_`. (`$_` is our little invisible friend, doing our bidding.)

You're going to apply the previous skills to processing each of the records in the data file. But first, you need to set up a few things. You've already created some of the HTML needed to make a wonderful looking document. If you haven't guessed by now, you're basically creating a report here. You've already put a title on screen, so let's add a report header. In order to accomplish this, you'll use another here-doc:

```
print <<EOF ;
<pre>
<strong>
Date            Purpose                          Amount          Balance</strong>
EOF
```

Note the use of the <pre> and <strong> tags. The <pre> tag tells the browser to render what follows as preformatted text, preserving all the spacing as it is typed. Normally, HTML browsers render multiple adjacent whitespace (space, tab, newline) as a single space. For example

```
This is        a test
of my browser,              dude.
```

will appear as

```
This is a test of my browser, dude.
```

This can often be desirable behavior, but in the case of the report, everything must line up nicely or the report will look awful.

The <strong> tag tells it to do what it takes to make the text between it and the </strong> tag emphasized, which usually means bold. Note that while you have closed out the <strong> tag with </strong>, the <pre> tag continues to be in full effect. This is because you still have the meat of the report to generate, which also needs to be preformatted. As each line is read from the data file, Perl will maintain a running balance and print out the data from each line.

Here's xyzzy.pl so far:

```
#
# xyzzy.pl
#
# A simple program to learn Perl
#

print <<EOF ;
Content-type: text/html

<html>
<head><title>Hello, World</title></head>
<body>
```

```
<h1>Hello, World</h1>
EOF

print <<EOF ;
<pre>
<strong>
Date          Purpose                    Amount       Balance</strong>
EOF
```

Perl Data Structures

Perl supports three basic data structures: scalar values, arrays of scalar values, and hashes. A *scalar* value is a simple variable that represents a single value. Here's an example of assigning the value `'hello'` to `$x`:

```
$x = 'hello'
```

Arrays may be defined which contain multiple scalar values. An *array* is a sequence of values, which can be referenced with a numeric *index*. The index corresponds to each element contained in the array. They are indexed from zero to *n*, where *n* is the number of elements in the array minus one. A 10-element array, for example, is indexed from zero to nine. Here are three ways to assign 13 elements to an array:

```
Way one:
$fab[0] = "Three";
$fab[1] = "quarks";
$fab[2] = "for";
$fab[3] = "Muster";
$fab[4] = "Mark!";
$fab[5] = "Sure";
$fab[6] = "he";
$fab[7] = "hasn't";
$fab[8] = "got";
$fab[9] = "much";
$fab[10] = "of";
```

```
$fab[11] = "a";
$fab[12] = "bark";
```

```
Way two:
@fab = ("Three", "quarks", "for", "Muster", "Mark!", "Sure", "he", "hasn't",
"got", "much", "of", "a", "bark");
```

```
Way!
@fab = split(' ', "Three quarks for Muster Mark! Sure he hasn't got much of a
bark");
```

Method one is probably the most obnoxious and tedious. In it, you are assigning each element of the array one at a time. Note that a $ is used when referring to a single array element. As you have seen, a $ is a required prefix for a scalar variable. When you reference a single array element (like `$fab[1]`) you are talking about a scalar value, so the $ is appropriate.

Method two uses a list notation to assign a group of values to an array. In this case, `@fab` represents the entire array, so $fab would not be correct. Method three is by far the coolest. It employs the `split()` function, which takes a string of text, and returns a list value divided on the delimiter specified. In this case, you are specifying a `' '` (a space) as delimiter, so you get the same results as the first two methods.

Associative arrays (also known as hashes) also can contain scalar values. However, rather than being indexed by a number, they are indexed by a string value. Each index is called a *key*. For example, when you run Perl, a hash is automatically available containing all of your environment variables. It's called %ENV (entire hashes are identified with the % prefix) and individual elements can be accessed like so

```
print $ENV{'TEMP'};
```

which would print out the setting of the environment variable `TEMP`. Note the use of the $ again; while an entire hash is prefixed with the % character, scalar values returned from the hash are prefixed with $, like any other scalar value. Unlike the arrays of scalar values, the `[]` is not used to surround array indices. Rather, hashes require the use of `{}`.

The index to a hash may be a string value:

```
$x = 'TEMP';
print $ENV{$x};
```

The last item concerning Perl's handling of data, particularly strings, is *variable interpolation*. Perl allows two types of string literals: those delimited with single quotes and those delimited with double quotes. Strings delimited with double quotes may include variables directly in the string. These variables are *interpolated* when the string is evaluated. Thus,

```
$x = 'World';
print "Hello, $x";
```

would print

```
Hello, World
```

but

```
$x = 'World';
print 'Hello, $x';
```

would print

```
Hello, $x
```

which is probably not what you want, unless you are an extremely silly person.

For a more comprehensive discussion of Perl data types, see the perldata.htm file included with the Perl 5 distribution in the Docs\ subdirectory.

format() and write(): Reporting Made Easy

Perl makes it very easy to create simple formatted reports. Two functions are provided for this purpose: `format()` and `write()`. The `format()` function allows you to associate a template with a particular file handle and to specify the names of variables to use in the report.

When you issue a bare

```
print;
```

Perl makes the assumption that you want to print what is in the magic variable $_. Perl makes another assumption as to the name of the filehandle you want to print to. Among the arguments that `print()` can take is the filehandle you want to print to. Suppose you've opened a filehandle for writing; let's call it BARNEY. If you want to print to BARNEY, you can simply include the filehandle before any other arguments to `print()`:

```
print BARNEY "Uh, Clem";
```

(Note that there are no commas between the filehandle and the data that you want to print.)

When a print is issued without a filehandle, STDOUT (standard output, or the console) is assumed. The same is true of the `write()` function, which allows you to write out a formatted record. This is important to know, because when you define a format, you must also specify to which file it is associated. Here's a really basic example of a format statement. When each `write()` function is issued on the filehandle STDOUT, this format will print the value of $_, right-justified, followed by an equals (=) sign, and the value of `$ENV{$_}` left-justified (don't type this into xyzzy.pl; it's just an example)

```
format STDOUT =
@>>>>>>>>>>>>>>>>>>>>=@<<<<<<<<<<<<<<<<<<<<<<<<<<<<<<<<<
$_,                   $ENV{$_}
.
```

The `@` symbol tells the format that a variable will be substituted according to the format which follows. > signifies that the text is to be right-justified; each > reserves space for the value. The < signifies that the text is to be left-justified. The second line includes a comma-delimited list of values to substitute. The $_ is substituted for the first `@` item in the template, and the `$ENV{$_}` is substituted for the second item in the template. `%ENV` is a special hash (associative array) that contains the *values* all of your environment variables, indexed by the names of the variables. Finally, a period (.) on a line by itself signifies that the format is complete.

After the format is defined, the following code will `write()` out lines for each environment variable:

```
foreach (keys %ENV) {

    write();

}
```

There are two new things included in the previous example. Can you spot them? The first is the `keys` operator. It operates on any associative array and returns a list of all the keys. For example, if your environment only has the following variables

```
USERNAME=bjepson

PATH=c:\dos;c:\windows;c:\windows\system32;d:\holygram
```

then, the associative array `%ENV` will have the keys

```
USERNAME

PATH
```

and the expressions

```
$ENV{'USERNAME'} eq 'bjepson'

$ENV{'PATH'} eq 'c:\dos;c:\windows;c:\windows\system32;d:\holygram'
```

will be true.

Perl provides different equality operators for string and numeric data. The following comparisons are meaningful (and true) for numeric data:

`1 < 2`	One is less than two
`2 > 1`	Two is greater than one
`1 <= 2`	One is less than or equal to two
`2 >= 1`	Two is greater than or equal to one
`2 == 2`	Two is equal to two (notice that this uses two equals signs!)
`2 != 1`	Two is not equal to one

The `keys` operator returns a list of these keys. Lists are suitable for assigning to arrays of scalars, but you can take a shortcut and feed its values to the `foreach` construct. The

```
foreach (@array) {
        do something;
}
```

construct will iterate over each value in the scalar array `@array`, putting the value of each array element in `$_` with each successive iteration. Since the `keys` operator returns what is to all intents and purpose an array, the following also works:

```
foreach (keys %hash) {
        do something;
}
```

Remember, the list returned by the `keys` operator is a list of all the keys in `%ENV`. Therefore, for any value of `$_` as the `foreach` construct iterates over the output of `(keys %ENV)`, the expression

```
$_
```

The following apply to string data:

`'foo' ne 'bar'`	'foo' is not equal to 'bar'
`'baz' eq 'baz'`	'baz' is equal to 'baz'

These are interesting, as they compare magnitudes of strings:

`'xyzza' cmp 'xyzzy'`	Equal to –1, because 'xyzza' is less than 'xyzzy'
`'xyzzy' cmp 'xyzzy'`	Equal to 0, because the two strings are equal
`'xyzzz' cmp 'xyzza'`	Equal to 1, because the value of 'xyzzy' is greater than that of 'xyzza'

will be the name of one of your environment variables and the expression

```
$ENV{$_}
```

will be its value. If you type the following Perl script into a file (call it baz.pl):

```
format STDOUT =
@>>>>>>>>>>>>>>>>>>>>=@<<<<<<<<<<<<<<<<<<<<<<<<<<<<<<<<<<
$_,                   $ENV{$_}
.

foreach (keys %ENV) {
    write();
}
```

and then run it with:

```
perl baz.pl
```

then, there's a good chance you will get output similar to:

```
             USERNAME =bjepson
         LIBRARY_PATH =e:\usr\local\lib
               PROMPT =$P$G
PROCESSOR_ARCHITECTUR =x86
                   OS =Windows_NT
            HOMEDRIVE =C:
            CLASSPATH =.;e:\win32app\java\classes
           SystemRoot =C:\WINDOWS
                SOUND =C:\SB16
                mouse =C:\windows\Mouse
                 HOME =C:\USERS\%USERNAME%
              ComSpec =C:\WINDOWS\system32\cmd.exe
               windir =C:\WINDOWS
                 Path =.;E:\win32app\perl\bin;C:\WINDOWS\
              BLASTER =A220 I5 D1 H5 P330 T6
                   TZ =EST5EDT
```

```
          GNUROOT =e:\usr\local
     COMPUTERNAME =OSCAR
          MSINPUT =C:\WINDOWS\MSINPUT
              tmp =C:\temp
   C_INCLUDE_PATH=e:\usr\local\include
C_PLUS_INCLUDE_PATH =e:\usr\local\include;e:\usr\local\
            FPDEV =ON
             TEMP =C:\temp
 CPLUS_INCLUDE_PATH =e:\usr\local\include;e:\usr\local\
         HOMEPATH =\users\default
       USERDOMAIN =OSCAR
  PROCESSOR_LEVEL =4
       Os2LibPath =C:\WINDOWS\system32\os2\dll;
             USER =%USERNAME%
      SystemDrive =C:
```

Note that, due to the width constraints of the format, some of the values are truncated.

Back to xyzzy.pl

Let's add the following format to xyzzy.pl. Although it contains variables not yet defined, it's okay because they will be defined very soon. Later, we will issue `write()` statements which utilize this format. Note how the columns correspond to the columns set up in the HTML earlier in the document.

```
format STDOUT =
@<<<<<<<<<<<< @<<<<<<<<<<<<<<<<<<< @>>>>>>>>>>>> @>>>>>>>>>>>>
$data[0] ,    $data[1],            $data[3],     $balance
.
```

Previously, you saw how to open a file with the `open()` function and how to iterate over it with the `while()` construct. Let's add the following `open()` statement to the xyzzy.pl program:

```
open(CHECKS, "chekbook.dat") || die "Couldn't open chekbook.dat.";
```

Also define a hash (associative array) here, called `%factor` that contains two keys: C for credit and D for Debit. The values that those keys reference are 1, and –1, respectively. The purpose of this is to aid in parsing the transactions. The data file, chekbook.dat, contains dates, descriptions, a debit/credit indicator, and the amount of the transaction. Assuming that you will parse each line of the data file and assign each column to an array element, you can isolate the value for the debit/credit column, and use that to retrieve either 1 or –1 from the `%factor` hash. Having done that, you can multiply the amount of the transaction by that value and use it in producing a total.

One way of assigning values to `%factor` would be:

```
$factor{'D'} = -1;
$factor{'C'} =  1;
```

But there is a niftier way. Perl provides a *constructor* (a constructor lets you construct something, such as an associative array) for associative arrays, which looks like this:

```
%factor = ('D' => -1,
           'C' => 1);
```

This is a little more visual. It allows you to assign to the entire array, by providing a list with key/value pairs. The key is on the left and the value it references is on the right. The => symbols provide a visual clue as to what is going on.

Also add a variable assignment for the running balance. Oddly enough, call the variable

```
$balance:
$balance = 0;
```

By now, xyzzy.pl should look like:

```
# xyzzy.pl
#
```

While it is not necessary to initialize a variable in Perl, it is polite to do so. The first time a variable is used, its original value is taken to be zero or "". So, an assignment like:

```
$x = $x + 5;
```

will result in `$x` being set to 5 if `$x` was previously undefined. By the way, this could also be written:

```
$x + =5
```

For string variables, the same is true. The following assignment:

```
$cat = $cat . 'meow';
```

will set `$cat` to meow if `$cat` is undefined. It could also be written:

```
$cat .= 'meow';
```

The `.` operator is the concatenation operator. As an example,

```
'meow' . 'bark'
```

produces a string whose value is meowbark.

```
# A simple program to learn Perl
#

print <<EOF ;
Content-type: text/html

<html>
<head><title>Hello, World</title></head>
<body>
<h1>Hello, World</h1>
```

```
EOF

print <<EOF ;
<pre>
<strong>
Date            Purpose                          Amount         Balance</strong>
EOF

format STDOUT =
@<<<<<<<<<<<<< @<<<<<<<<<<<<<<<<<<<< @>>>>>>>>>>> @>>>>>>>>>>>
$data[0] ,     $data[1],             $data[3],     $balance
.

open(CHECKS, "chekbook.dat") || die "Couldn't open chekbook.dat.";

%factor = ('D' => -1,
           'C' => 1);

$balance = 0;
```

Parsing Data in Perl

Here's where the fun begins. Now that you have set up much of your Perl program, you are ready to read in the data file. You have already opened it under the filehandle CHECKS. Earlier you saw how to iterate over a file line by line, using the `while()` construct. Use that construct here.

In order for the `write()` function to do anything useful, the values

```
$data[0], $data[1], $data[3], $balance
```

need to be defined, since they are explicitly referred to in the `format()`. You will recognize the first three as array elements and the last one as the variable initialized earlier. In a few moments, you'll meet a function called `split()`, which will take the line of text in `$_` (remember that the `<FILEHANDLE>` construct implicitly assigns a line of text to the `$_` variable) and return a list value, suitable for assigning to an array.

Before you split(), you need to perform a few transformations on the text. First of all, you want to remove any unnecessary space. (I'm defining "unnecessary space" as space between records.) You don't want that to be included in your data. Also, you want to remove any trailing spaces. In order to do this, you will rely on the s/// function, which performs substitutions on strings. As with many other functions and operators, s/// operates on $_ by default. This is very convenient, because that's where your data is. Here's the syntax for s///:

```
s/search argument/replacement argument/modifier
```

so:

```
s/a/z/;
```

will replace the first occurrence of a with z. If you want to perform these replacements on every occurrence, you can use the g modifier:

```
s/a/z/g;
```

The substitution function also employs a sophisticated set of pattern-matching tools, called *regular expressions*, to do its work. For example:

```
s/\s+/!/g;
```

will replace every instance of whitespace (space, tab, newline) with an exclamation point (!). For example

```
$_ = "hello, world. How are      you?"
s/\s+/!/g;
print;
```

will print out:

```
hello,!world.!How!are!you?
```

The \s will match any whitespace and the + which follows it makes it match any number of adjacent whitespaces. The substitution is performed on whatever is matched, so a group of seven spaces will be replaced with a single !.

You can modify how the replacements are to be done. If you wanted to change all occurrences of pre when they occur at the beginning of a word, you might try:

```
s/(^|\s)per\w/pre/g;
```

The first part of the search argument is grouped within parentheses, and the pipe symbol `|` works as an or; it tells Perl to match either `^` or `\s` in the first part of the string. `^` is a special symbol. It represents the beginning of the line, and it is included with `\s` (whitespace) as an alternate. After that grouped expression, the letters "per" appear and are followed by `\w`, which tells Perl to match any alphanumeric characters. This function will match portions of expressions such as:

```
'person'
'the person'
'perl is really cool'
'people who think Perl is really cool are deviated perverts'
```

Unfortunately, it also matches the space before, and the alphanumeric character after. So, if you ran this translation on the last item, you'd get some bogus results:

```
people who think Perl is really cool are deviatedpreerts
```

which is not what you want. Perl allows for backward references, which conveniently utilize the grouping operators, the parentheses. Each backward reference is numbered sequentially, starting with $1. For each set of grouping parentheses, another backward reference is created. When you include the $1 or $whatever in the replacement string, whatever matched the grouped expression is inserted. So, let's update your example to group like so:

```
/(^|\s)per(\w)
```

The expression which includes the start of line or whitespace is grouped as $1, and the expression which includes the words after per is grouped as $2. All you need to do is change your replacement expression to use these backwards references:

```
$1pre$2
```

and your `s///` statement looks like this:

```
s/(^|\s)per(\w)/$1pre$2/g;
```

Here's a little program to show this in action

```
$_ = 'people who think Perl is really cool are deviated perverts';
s/(^|\s)per(\w)/$1pre$2/g;
print;
```

which will produce the following output:

```
people who think Perl is really cool are deviated preverts
```

You're going to use a couple of substitutions as you read through the data file. For each line, you will perform a:

```
s/(\S)\s+$/$1/;
```

Within a regular expression, `$` refers to the end of the line. Note that the g modifier is not required; there is only one end to every line! This expression groups non-whitespace characters which are followed by one or more whitespace characters followed by an end of line. This includes the newline, so there is no need to remove it specially. Perl provides a special function just for chopping off newlines; it's called `chop()`, but you won't use it here.

Next, you want to eliminate any space between commas and the beginning of the next word. This should do the trick:

```
s/(,)\s+(\S)/$1$2/g;
```

Note that you want the g modifier here; there are many commas in each line. The first backwards reference preserves the comma, any repeating spaces are discarded, and the second backwards reference preserves the non-whitespace character which follows the whitespace.

Now that you've prepped the incoming data, assign each comma-delimited column to an array of scalars with:

```
@data = split(',');
```

This function, as was previously mentioned, produces a list as output. This list can be assigned to an array. The `split()` function takes two parameters; the first is the delimiter. In this case, a comma is used. The second parameter that `split()` takes is the value to split. As is so often the case, the default value is `$_`. Remember, you've passed `$_` through two substitutions, now you're `split()`ing it into pieces!

Having gotten this far, let's see what values are getting assigned to your array for the first line of the data file:

```
$data[0] = '10-01-1995';
$data[1] = 'Opening Balance';
$data[2] = 'C';
$data[3] = 1000.00;
```

Next, do a little magic with the `%factor` array:

```
$balance += $data[3] * $factor{$data[2]};
```

This increments $balance by the amount of the transaction ($data[3]). You will recall that the associative array `%factor` contains the value 1 indexed by C, and the value –1 indexed by D. The value of `$data[2]` gives you a way to retrieve 1 or –1. For your first line of data, this statement looks like:

```
$balance = 1000.00 * 1;
```

and as you know, 1,000 multiplied by 1 is still 1,000. However, line two of the datafile looks like

```
10-01-1995,  Grue Cleaners,          D,     30.00
```

and `$balance` will be updated like so:

```
$balance = 30.00 * -1;
```

Having updated the balance, you can now move on to displaying the values. Although you are more or less all set to call `write()` at this point, there is one problem: $data[3] (the transaction amount) is unsigned. Oh, sure, you could put a minus sign in front of it, maybe even multiply it by $factor{$data[2]}. That would be too easy. Let's wrap it in parentheses. Create an `if` construct for negative values:

```
if ($factor{$data[2]} == -1) {
        $data[3] = "($data[3])";
    }
```

An `if` construct evaluates everything within the curly braces (they define the boundaries of a block) only if the expression immediately following it evaluates to a non-zero value or true. The expression must be enclosed in parentheses.

To some of you, this may appear insane. This numeric value was previously used in the

```
$balance += $data[3] * $factor{$data[2]};
```

statement. But here, it is treated it as a string. What gives? Nothing, really. Perl is not as strongly typed as other languages and can evaluate values as strings or numbers based solely on context. This may drive some of you insane, but our therapeutic practices have gotten better over time, and you'll be back to work before you can say "disability claim."

In effect, the previous `if` construct is only true for negative values of $data[3]. But what's it doing to $data[3]? As previously mentioned, Perl provides a feature called variable interpolation. It only happens within double-quoted strings; single-quoted strings do not use it, so you can turn it off and on. What occurs here is that the value of $data[3] is interpolated into the string, so for your second line of data, $data[3] is reassigned as:

```
(30.00)
```

You're almost ready to print, but one problem remains: your numbers won't quite line up, because you have added a trailing parenthesis to some of them. For this, add an `else` to the `if` construct, which simply adds a space character to all values which are not negative. There's that treating numbers like strings again. Well, get used to it. This is Perl.

Here's what your completed `if/else` construct looks like:

```
if ($factor{$data[2]} == -1) {
      $data[3] = "($data[3])";
  } else {
      $data[3] .= ' ';
  }
```

Now, you are ready to issue a `write()`. Having done so, you can close off the block which the while loop owns and end your program with another here-doc

```
print <<EOF ;
</pre>
</body>
</html>
EOF
```

which ends the `pre` element, the `body` element, and the `html` element itself. Here, in all its glory, is the program you have just written:

```
#
# xyzzy.pl
#
# A simple program to learn Perl
#

print <<EOF ;
Content-type: text/html

<html>
<head><title>Hello, World</title></head>
<body>
<h1>Hello, World</h1>
EOF

print <<EOF ;
<pre>
<strong>
Date            Purpose                    Amount        Balance</strong>
EOF
```

```
format STDOUT =
@<<<<<<<<<<<< @<<<<<<<<<<<<<<<<<<< @>>>>>>>>>>>> @>>>>>>>>>>>
$data[0] ,    $data[1],             $data[3],    $balance
.

open(CHECKS, "chekbook.dat") || die "Couldn't open chekbook.dat.";

%factor = ('D' => -1,
           'C' =>  1);

$balance = 0;
while (<CHECKS>) {

    s/(\S)\s+$/$1/;
    s/(,)\s+(\S)/$1$2/g;
    @data = split(',');

    $balance += $data[3] * $factor{$data[2]};

    if ($factor{$data[2]} == -1) {
        $data[3] = "($data[3])";
    } else {
        $data[3] .= ' ';
    }

    write();
}

print <<EOF ;
</pre>
```

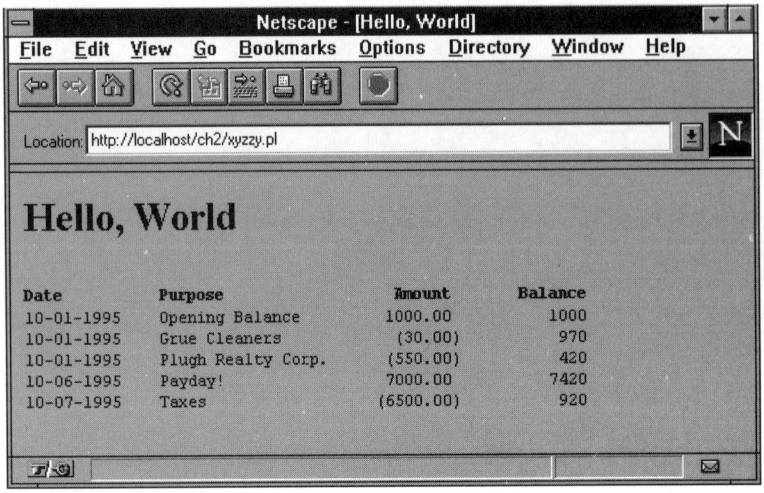

Figure 2.1 The 'xyzzy.pl' example.

```
</body>
</html>
EOF
```

If you have installed the examples according to the instructions in Appendix C, when you issue the URL

```
http://localhost/ch2/xyzzy.pl,
```

you should see something similar to Figure 2.1. If this does not work with localhost as the hostname, try your real hostname, your IP address, or the loopback address: 127.0.0.1.

Congratulations! You've just wandered through a maze of twisty little passages to arrive at a working Perl CGI program. This is the sort of thing that might be popular at cocktail parties, so keep a disk with you at all times!

Where to Go for More Information

Books

1. *Learning Perl* (Randal L. Schwartz; O'Reilly and Associates, 1993).
2. *Perl by Example* (Ellie Quigley; Prentice-Hall, 1995).

3. *Programming Perl* (Larry Wall and Randal L. Schwartz; O'Reilly and Associates, 1991).

4. *Software Engineering with Perl* (Carl Dichter and Mark Pease; Prentice-Hall, 1995).

5. *Teach Yourself Perl in 21 Days* (David Till; SAMS Publishing, 1995).

ftp Sites

The latest and greatest version of Perl for Win32 can be found on:

```
ftp://ntperl.hip.com/ntperl
```

The Comprehensive Perl Archive Network contains many useful Perl Modules and other things:

```
ftp://ftp.cis.ufl.edu/pub/perl/CPAN/
```

Web Sites

The Perl for Win32 home page:

```
http://info.hip.com/ntperl/
```

Tom Christiansens' Perl.COM Home Page:

```
http://www.perl.com/
```

Newsgroups

There are two main groups related to Perl on Usenet:

```
comp.lang.perl.misc
```

Discussion related to the Perl language.

```
comp.lang.perl.announce
```

Announcements related to the Perl language.

CHAPTER

3

AN INTRODUCTION TO ODBC AND DATABASE DESIGN

An Introduction to ODBC

ODBC is an abbreviation for Open Database Connectivity. It is an API (Application Programming Interface) put forth by Microsoft which has (strangely enough) flourished on Microsoft platforms such as Windows NT, Windows, and Windows 95. It has also become quite popular on UNIX platforms as well. The function of an API is, generally, to allow a program, such as Microsoft Excel or Borland Delphi, to ask the operating system or another program or service to perform certain tasks. The ODBC extensions to Perl for Win32 are a perfect example; when you open a connection to a data source, the ODBC API is employed to make this connection on Perl's behalf.

ODBC allows you to write programs that interact with a wide variety of database products. For each database product you want to access, you need to obtain a *driver*, which tells ODBC exactly how the data is to be physically accessed. ODBC is designed in such a way as to hide these gory details from the developer; you don't need to worry whether the database you are accessing is a flat text file on a floppy disk or a database server running on a mainframe. ODBC provides a database-neutral interface to a variety of supported database products. Although each data source may support a slightly different SQL syntax (for example, Oracle and SQL Server have different syntaxes), ODBC allows you to use a common syntax for accessing and updating data in different data sources. This feature is provided via special extensions to ODBC, which allow you to use a special ODBC syntax, which overrides the target database platform's native syntax.

Fortunately, a lot of programs have the ODBC API built right in as a regular feature of that program and you can utilize ODBC features without having to learn how to program to the ODBC API. Microsoft Excel is a perfectly good example of this. You can write VBA (Visual Basic for Applications) code in Excel to connect to ODBC data sources. Once you are connected, you can update or retrieve data from a data source. The same is true of Perl for Win32; ODBC is implemented as a dynamically loaded module and the ODBC extensions are available to the Perl programmer in an easy-to-use form. You simply need to open a connection to a data source, send a query, and fetch each row. What could be easier?

Configuring ODBC

When you set up an ODBC-enabled application or application suite (such as Microsoft Visual FoxPro or Microsoft Office), you are given the option to choose which ODBC drivers to install. If you do not have one of these products, you should contact Microsoft for the availability of ODBC driver kits. You must install a driver for each type of data source you want to access, since the driver does the actual work of carrying out the ODBC calls. You may add ODBC data sources through a tool called the ODBC Administrator which appears in your computer's control panel. This tool allows you to add, modify, or delete ODBC data sources. For example, suppose you have DBF (dBase, FoxPro, etc.) data in three directories on your system:

```
Sales Data       C:\USERS\SALES\*.DBF
Marketing Data  C:\USERS\MARKETING\\*.DBF
Doom High Scores Data   C:\DOOM\CONTEST\*.DBF
```

Since all of these data sources are of the same format, you will install the same driver (dBase or FoxPro) to access them. However, since you want to group them separately, you may install different data sources for them. Each data source is given a Data Source Name (DSN), which can then be used by programs such as Perl or Excel, or utilities such as IODBC. Whenever you work with an ODBC-aware program, you must, at the very least, supply a DSN. Data sources installed with certain drivers, such as Microsoft SQL Server, may require that you supply a user name and password when you access them.

Choosing a Data Source

If you're working with data that exists already, chances are good that you know what ODBC driver you want to use (i.e., you probably have no choice). If, for example, you've implemented a FoxPro system and want to hook that data up to a World Wide Web interface, it's not very likely that you'll use anything other than a FoxPro ODBC driver to access the data.

If you are building a database-driven Web server from the ground up, then the choice of ODBC drivers is your call. Although not absolutely necessary, it's a good idea to also have the database package if you want to use the ODBC driver. Microsoft has an ODBC driver pack which is available to registered users of Office 95, MSDN II, and development tools such as Visual FoxPro, Visual C++, and Visual Basic 4.0. Using this driver pack, you can create, update, and query data sources in FoxPro, dBase, Paradox, and Access (even Excel or Text files) without actually having to have any of these packages installed. This is because the data manipulation for these ODBC drivers is handled entirely by the ODBC driver DLL itself!

The same is not true of the SQL Server, Oracle, or other server-based drivers. These drivers require access to a server which is running one of these packages. If you can afford SQL Server or Oracle, or another database server product, then by all means procure it; these will provide the best performance on your Web site. Since the ODBC driver is not performing physical data access work, access times are much faster. SQL Server and Oracle are constantly running, waiting for clients to request data. When a request comes in, a special type of subprocess called a *thread* is spawned to handle the request. The ODBC driver on the client computer does not have to do the physical database access work. These sort of drivers are called *multiple-tier*. In contrast, drivers such as FoxPro, dBase, Paradox, Access, and others must "kick off" a separate process on the client machine which must open the table, read the data, and return the results. These are known as *single-tier* drivers, because the database file is processed by the driver. It is not efficient to run dozens of these processes on the same machine. If you can use a database server, then do so! If you can put the database server on a different machine than your Web server, you will get even better performance.

If a database server is not an option, then it is strongly suggested that you use the Microsoft Access data source. This data source provides some of the referential integrity and user access features of high-end database servers. However, it suffers from performance drawbacks like other single-tier drivers. It is also possible that, by the time you read these sentences, Microsoft will have released an ODBC driver for Visual FoxPro. This would also be a good choice, for it may provide some of the features included in the Access driver.

Certain drivers, such as the FoxPro and dBase drivers, allow you to specify a working directory when configuring a data source, which tells ODBC where to find the tables. This is almost always desirable; if you do not specify a working directory, ODBC will use the current working directory (whatever that is). This is not an issue when working with true client-server drivers like SQL Server. A particular server always knows where its data is. Microsoft Access, unlike FoxPro and dBase, stores all of its tables within a single database file. When you configure the Access driver, you will need to specify the database file.

Installing the Example Drivers

The CD-ROM includes some sample databases in Access and FoxPro. It is recommended that you copy these to a directory on a hard drive. You need only copy the database files for the ODBC driver which you will be using. For example, if you are going to use the FoxPro ODBC driver, you only need to copy the files in the \DATA\DBF directory. If you are going to use the Access ODBC driver, you only need to copy files from the \DATA\MSACCESS directory. Choose a location on your hard drive for the files (let's pretend that you chose C:\DATA\, and are installing the FoxPro files). You can copy them with the following command (assuming your CD-ROM is drive E:):

```
C:\USERS\DEFAULT\> XCOPY E:\DATA\DBF\*.* C:\DATA
```

If the directory does not exist, XCOPY will ask you the following (just answer "D" to the question):

```
Does c:\data specify a file name
or directory name on the target
(F = file, D = directory)? D
```

Once you have done this, you may install the data source using the ODBC Administrator which is found in the Control Panel. You should have installed the most recent version of ODBC. When you start the ODBC Administrator, a list of "User Data Sources" appears, which includes only the data sources installed for the user who is currently logged in. Starting with ODBC 2.5, the ODBC Administrator includes a push button for

"System DSN," which allows you to specify global data sources for all users. This is important, because the Web server does not log in under the same user as you and would not have access to the data sources you configured. Figure 3.1 shows the System DSN dialog box. When you press the add button, the Add Data Source dialog appears, which allows you to choose which driver to use for the new data source. If you do not have ODBC 2.5, then you should obtain it from Microsoft. It is suggested that you use the name "EXAMPLE" for your data source name, as that is the name used in the example scripts on the CD-ROM.

If no drivers appear in this list, then ODBC has not been installed correctly. If you installed ODBC from a product such as Microsoft Office or a development tool such as Visual FoxPro or Visual Basic, please check the installation notes for that product. Some systems may include icons for 32-bit and 16-bit ODBC; Perl requires that 32-bit ODBC be installed. Any 16-bit data sources will be invisible to Perl. Make sure that you use the 32-bit ODBC applet when configuring your data source. Figure 3.2 shows this icon.

Figure 3.3 shows the Add Data Source screen. When you have decided which driver to use, double-click on it in the list. This brings up the Setup dialog for that particular driver. The ODBC FoxPro Setup dialog is shown

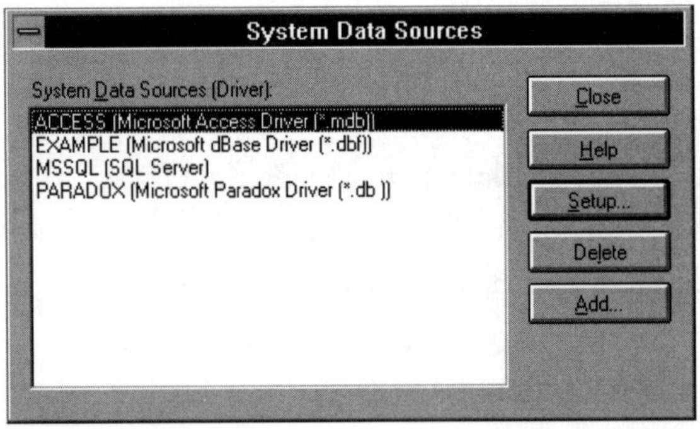

Figure 3.1 The System DSN dialog box.

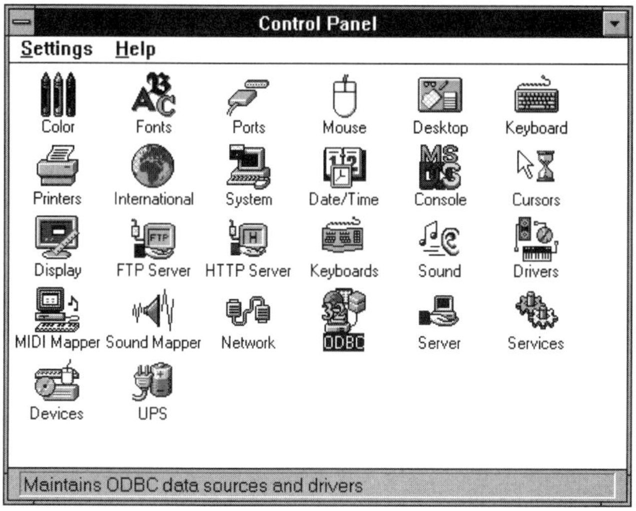

Figure 3.2 The 32-bit ODBC applet icon.

in Figure 3.4. You must provide a Data Source Name and select a directory. This directory will hold all of the tables that you create. Since the setup dialog defaults to version 2.0 of FoxPro, you may want to change it to the latest version supported by the ODBC driver, which is 2.6 as of this writing. Once you have done this, you may click on OK to add the data source. Depending upon which driver you choose to use, the procedure may differ slightly.

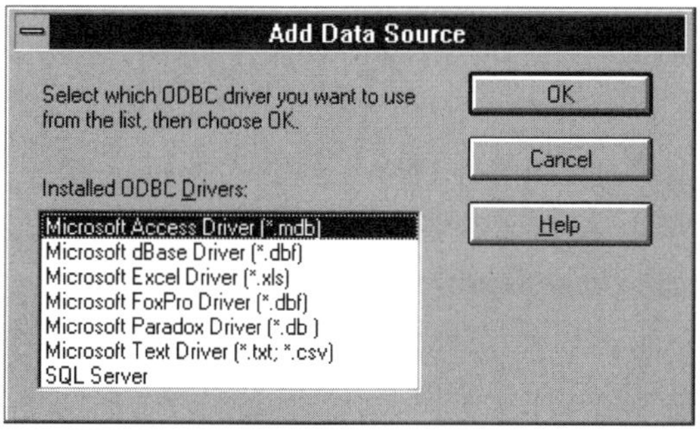

Figure 3.3 The Add Data Source screen.

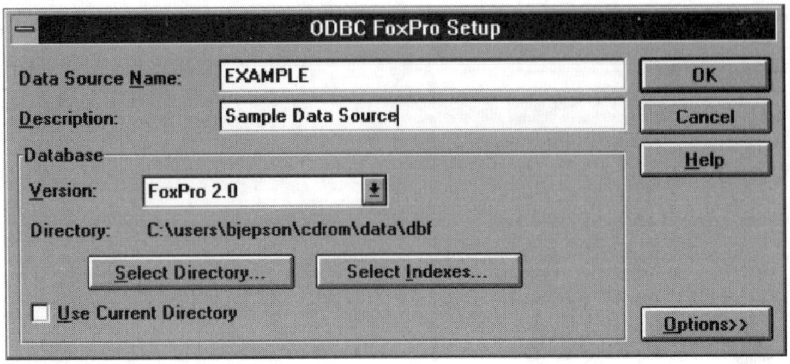

Figure 3.4 The Fox Pro Driver ODBC Setup dialog box.

If you are using a SQL Server data source, the directory \DATA\MSSQL on the CD-ROM contains the INSTALL.BAT and INSTALL.SQL files. If you execute INSTALL.BAT with the name of a user and that user's password, the example tables will be created and populated in that user's default database. If this happens to be the master database, you may want to change it. Before you can run this batch file, IODBC must be installed correctly. The installation procedure is shown later in this chapter.

Database Design and SQL Primer

Since this book draws on skills from two different disciplines (World Wide Web development and database development), it is entirely possible that a reader may come to this book with a high degree of expertise in World Wide Web development and none whatsoever in database development (or vice versa). With this in mind, prepare to embark upon a primer which will explain how to go about designing tables and how to work with IODBC (this is a command-line ODBC tool which allows you to interactively create and modify tables within a data source). Those readers who are very familiar with database design can skim over this section; they will probably only find useful those portions pertaining specifically to installing and using IODBC.

Table and Database Design

A table is a collection of rows. Each row is broken down into one or more columns. In many cases, database and table can be used interchangeably, but in this tome a collection of tables will be referred to as a database and a table as . . . well, a table. You can think of a table as a list. The rest of this chapter will be concerned with the database system belonging to a fictional collectors' club. Each member owns a vintage Atari home computer system and collects video game cartridges for that system. The club's list of members, systems, and games looks like this:

Collector	System	Defender	Miner 2049er	Missile Command	Pacman	Star Raiders
E. Wood	800	Yes	No	Yes	Yes	No
B. Jepson	1200XL	No	Yes	No	Yes	Yes
J. Lee	65XE	No	No	Yes	Yes	Yes
T. Johnson	800	No	Yes	Yes	No	No

Of course, there are probably a lot more games in each person's collection, but you get the idea. At first glance, this list looks pretty sane. However, experience shows that tables organized in this fashion are difficult to work with. If you were to design your table to look exactly like this list, you would start running into trouble when someone obtained a cartridge that wasn't already on the list.

The Relational Model and the First Normal Form

In 1970, a mathematician, Dr. E. F. Codd, established a theory for data modeling which forms the foundation for design methodology in relational database management systems (RDBMSs) such as SQL Server, Oracle, FoxPro, dBase, and Access. In a paper, "A Relational Model of Data for Large Shared Data Banks" (*Communications of the ACM* 13, No. 6, June 1970), which is available on the Web at http://www.acm.org/classics/nov95/, he established key guidelines of data normalization. *Data normalization* is a process which optimizes the way your data is represented in tables. Each step in normalization takes your data to what is called a normal form. Most people agree that there are three normal forms; some disagreement exists as to the validity of the fourth and fifth normal forms. I know this one fellow who hangs around the Providence, Rhode Island bus station; he claims there are 1000 normal forms. I like talking to him.

In order for the database design to adhere to the first normal form, it is necessary to *eliminate repeating columns*. In the previous list, there is a column for the person's name, the computer system he or she owns, and a column for each cartridge. That collection of cartridges is a perfect candidate for optimizing. It is a repeating group of columns. This is a remarkably inefficient way to store data. For one, storage space is wasted; for each person, there must be a column for each possible cartridge, whether that person has 0 or 10 cartridges. Also, if a new cartridge is added to the list, the database structure must be physically modified. This is a big no-no; if specifications have been adequately drawn up for a system, no modification to table structure should be necessary unless significant new requirements arise.

In order for this table to conform to the first normal form, it needs to be split into two tables. A new table will be created, called CARTRIDGE. This table will contain the name of the cartridge and two new columns. The first will be a cartridge id and the second will be a collector id. The original table, which will be referred to as COLLECTOR, will lose all of the cartridge columns, but gain a new one: collector id. The collector id will link the list of cartridges to the collector. Here's the "new look" for the COLLECTOR table.

Collector	System	Collector Id
E. Wood	800	1
B. Jepson	1200XL	2
J. Lee	65XE	3
T. Johnson	800	4

The CARTRIDGE table will look like this:

Cartridge Name	Cartridge Id	Collector Id
Defender	1	1
Missile Command	2	1
Pacman	3	1
Miner 2049er	4	2
Pacman	3	2
Star Raiders	5	2
Missile Command	2	3
Pacman	3	3
Star Raiders	5	3
Miner 2049er	4	4
Missile Command	2	4

Organizing the table in this fashion may make it harder for humans to read, but it really makes things easy for the computer. The new columns that were added reveal some of the method in normalized data design. Each table in a well-designed *schema* (a schema is a collection of tables which are connected to each other in some way) should have a column which acts as a *primary key*. A primary key is a unique identifier, which is a column or group of columns whose values are unique for each row in which it appears. The COLLECTOR table has the Collector Id as primary key; there must be no two rows which share the same Collector Id in that table. The primary key in the CARTRIDGE table consists of two columns: Collector Id + Cartridge Id. There can be no two rows which have the same Collector Id + Cartridge Id. I can see some of you raising your hands back there. What's that? "What if one collector has more than one of the same cartridge?" Hmmm. In that case, it's a matter of adding another column: quantity. Here's the revised CARTRIDGE table, to satisfy the nitpickers among this crowd (I can even let T. Johnson have two copies of Missile Command):

Cartridge Name	Cartridge Id	Collector Id	Quantity
Defender	1	1	1
Missile Command	2	1	1
Pacman	3	1	1
Miner 2049er	4	2	1
Pacman	3	2	1
Star Raiders	5	2	1
Missile Command	2	3	1
Pacman	3	3	1
Star Raiders	5	3	1
Miner 2049er	4	4	1
Missile Command	2	4	2

Hooray! The schema, which started out containing one horrible *denormalized* table, now consists of two tables, which are in the first normal form. Unfortunately, your work is far from done. It's traditional to take the tables in a schema at least to the third normal form before you try to write any programs which manipulate it.

Second Normal Form

The primary key for the CARTRIDGE table (Collector Id + Cartridge Id) satisfies the requirement of the definition of a primary key; the value of the two columns will be different for each row. You may have noticed that the Cartridge Name repeats; it is a dependent value. It is only dependent upon one of the components of the multi-valued primary key (the Cartridge Id). The application of the second normal form seeks to eliminate this type of relationship, and in doing so, it eliminates redundant data. Right now, the Cartridge Name appears wherever a cartridge is owned by a member. If one of the Cartridge Names is misspelled, it can cause reporting anomalies and you might not get the right count of cartridges. Even worse, if an error had been introduced into the system at an early date, such as the repeated misspelling of a cartridge name, it would require updating all of the records in the CARTRIDGE table, which is doing double duty as a cross-reference table.

In order to bring the tables in this schema up to snuff with the second normal form, it is necessary to create yet another table. This will the called the CARTRIDGE XREF table and will contain the Cartridge Id, Quantity, and Collector Id. The CARTRIDGE table will now only contain the Cartridge Name and Cartridge Id. Here's how the CARTRIDGE table will look:

Cartridge Name	Cartridge Id
Defender	1
Missile Command	2
Pacman	3
Miner 2049er	4
Star Raiders	5

Here is how the CARTRIDGE XREF table will look:

Cartridge Id	Collector Id	Quantity
1	1	1
2	1	1
3	1	1
4	2	1
3	2	1
5	2	1
2	3	1
3	3	1
5	3	1
4	4	1
2	4	2

Third Normal Form

The third normal form has some things in common with the second normal form, but it is a little pickier. It seeks to eliminate any columns which are not dependent upon the key. Looking back at the COLLECTOR table, note that there are three columns: Collector Name, System, and Collector Id. Of these, only Collector Name is dependent upon the Collector Id. The System name is independent of that. As proof, you can see that two collectors have the same system: Wood and Johnson both own 800s. Again, it is necessary to split tables. A new table will be created: SYSTEM. This will contain a System Name and a System Id. Also, another cross-reference table will be created: SYSTEM XREF. As a bonus of satisfying the conditions of the third normal form, Collectors may now own more than one system. Won't they be glad to hear that!

Here's the SYSTEM table:

System Name	System Id
800	1
1200XL	2
65XE	3

And here's the SYSTEM XREF table:

System Id	Collector Id
1	1
2	2
3	3
1	4

Finally, the COLLECTOR table can be modified as shown:

Collector	Collector Id
E. Wood	1
B. Jepson	2
J. Lee	3
T. Johnson	4

The Collection schema started out with one table. After taking it to the third normal form, it now consists of five tables: COLLECTOR, CARTRIDGE, CARTRIDGE XREF, SYSTEM, and SYSTEM XREF. After you learn how to install and run IODBC, you will learn how to define these tables within your data source and also how to add, update, delete, and query data.

Installing IODBC

Installing IODBC is quite simple. There is only one component, IODBC.EXE, and it must be placed in a directory which is in your search path. I'm the anal-retentive type; I don't like to put third-party utilities in my C:\DOS or C:\WINDOWS directory, so I create a directory called C:\LOCAL and add it to my system search path. I put all the important programs in there; tar, gunzip, zip, unzip, and so forth. Of course, you can install IODBC wherever you want. If you're using Windows NT , make sure that whatever path you choose is listed under System Environment Variables in the System applet under the Control Panel. If you are using Windows 95, you can include this path in your AUTOEXEC.BAT. IODBC.EXE is included on the CD-ROM in the \IODBC directory.

An SQL Primer

SQL is a specialized language for set-based data access. It's incredibly important that you understand SQL, because ODBC is an implementation of SQL. SQL, like BASIC, COBOL, FORTH, ADA, C, and JPL, is a programming language. Each implementation (for example, Visual Basic, GW/BASIC, Quick Basic) of a given language has different nuances. We programmers borrow a term from linguistics called dialect to state that the given language deviates somewhat from a standard version. There is an ANSI SQL standard with which ODBC unfortunately does not fully comply, but there is certainly enough functionality included in the ODBC dialect of SQL for you to do your work, and to do it well. In fact, if you are running ODBC to connect to an SQL data source like Microsoft or SYBASE SQL Server, you can ignore ODBC and write your programs and queries in SQL Server's dialect of SQL, which is a lot richer than ODBC and is known as Transact-SQL. ODBC will pass the Transact-SQL statements to the server and not try to process them itself.

Starting IODBC

IODBC can be started from the command line and requires a Data Source Name (DSN) as a parameter. If you are connecting to a data source that requires a user name and password, these must be entered on the command line as well. IODBC can be invoked as shown:

```
IODBC /S "Data Source Name" [/U "Username" [/P "Password"]]


examples:
IODBC /S "MSSQL" /U "bjepson" /P "maximegalon"
IODBC /S "EXAMPLE"
```

Once you are in IODBC, you may issue SQL commands, strike the enter key, and type the word GO followed by the enter key; the GO command tells IODBC to execute the SQL you typed in. The QUIT command terminates IODBC. Here's a sample session (what you type is shown in bold, output from IODBC is shown in regular type):

```
C:\>IODBC /S "MSSQL" /U "bjepson" /P "maximegalon"
iodbc  Ver. 0.11 (Beta 2)  Copyright 1995 FFE Software, Inc.
This is free software, and you are welcome to redistribute it under certain
conditions; type 'help ?' for details.
1> use pubs
2> go
1> select * from titleauthor
2> go
 au_id       title_id au_ord  royaltyper
 ----------- -------- ------  -----------
 172-32-1176 PS3333        1          100
 213-46-8915 BU1032        2           40
 213-46-8915 BU2075        1          100
 238-95-7766 PC1035        1          100
 267-41-2394 BU1111        2           40
 267-41-2394 TC7777        2           30
 274-80-9391 BU7832        1          100
```

```
409-56-7008 BU1032       1         60
427-17-2319 PC8888       1         50
472-27-2349 TC7777       3         30
486-29-1786 PC9999       1        100
486-29-1786 PS7777       1        100
648-92-1872 TC4203       1        100
672-71-3249 TC7777       1         40
712-45-1867 MC2222       1        100
722-51-5454 MC3021       1         75
724-80-9391 BU1111       1         60
724-80-9391 PS1372       2         25
756-30-7391 PS1372       1         75
807-91-6654 TC3218       1        100
846-92-7186 PC8888       2         50
899-46-2035 MC3021       2         25
899-46-2035 PS2091       2         50
998-72-3567 PS2091       1         50
998-72-3567 PS2106       1        100

(25 rows affected)
1> QUIT
```

IODBC can also be run in batch mode. A text file containing SQL commands can be run by using the redirection symbol (<) on the command line:

```
C:\>IODBC /S "MSSQL" /U "bjepson" /P "maximegalon" < SAMPLE.SQL
```

Using IODBC

When you start IODBC as previously shown, the first thing you see is the IODBC command prompt. This is the line number of the query you are typing. When you issue the GO command, the query is executed and the line number is reset to one.

A little note for SQL Server users: unless the data source has been configured to select a database when you connect, you will start out in whatever database the system administrator (sa) has assigned you. If the sa has not assigned you to a database, you will probably default to the master database. It's not a good idea to create objects in that database; in fact, for the purposes of exercises, it's probably a good idea to have a "playpen" set up, in which you can learn and make mistakes. A script is included on the CD-ROM, in the \EG\CH3 directory, called INSTWWW.SQL. If you run this through ISQL or IODBC as the system administrator (or get the sa to run it for you), a special database called www will be created and a user named wwwuser—who only has access to that database and has no password—will be created. Also, it will ensure that www is the database that that user defaults to on login.

Using SQL to Create Tables

One of the first SQL Statements you will find useful is the `CREATE TABLE` statement. It is used to create an empty table within your datasource. Once you have created a table, you can use the `INSERT` statement to add data to it. The `CREATE TABLE` syntax looks like this:

```
CREATE TABLE tablename
        (column_name column_type [(column_width[, column_precision])]
        [,column_name, column_type [(column_width[, column_precision])]]
        ...)
```

Each table must have a name; the names that will be used in this example will be no longer than eight characters. This will conform to the limitations of some ODBC drivers, such as FoxPro or dBase, and will not cause any problems with other ODBC drivers. Here's the first part of the definition for the COLLECTORS table (the table name will be shortened to COLLECT):

```
CREATE TABLE collect
```

This needs to be followed by one or more column definitions, which must include the column name and the data type of the column. The number of SQL Data Types supported by each ODBC driver varies, and you will have to consult the help file for each one (you can get help for a driver by clicking on the Help button while in the Setup screen for a data source under the ODBC Administrator). The two data types used in these examples include *int* and *char*. The size and precision of int varies from data source to data source, and the size of a char field is explicitly defined when you define the column. Here's the table definition for COLLECT:

```
CREATE TABLE collect
    (co_id int, co_name char(40))
```

Since the width of column names is limited to 10 in some drivers (FoxPro, dBase), these tables will be defined using names that are somewhat shorter than those seen earlier. Notice that each column in collect starts with the prefix co_ (short for collect). This can be useful when referencing columns from multiple tables. It allows you to determine from which table a column comes rather quickly. You may type the `CREATE TABLE` statement into IODBC. When you are done, you may type `GO` on a line by itself; if no error message appears, then the table was successfully created. If you made a mistake in the table definition, and it was created incorrectly, you may issue the command `DROP TABLE collect`. This will completely wipe out that table, so if you already have a table named collect, you will destroy it and lose all the data it contains. Remember, after you have typed in the SQL Statement, you must hit the enter key, type `GO`, and hit the enter key to execute the command.

Here's the rest of the `CREATE TABLE` statements that define the tables CART (corresponds to the CARTRIDGE table seen in the table design primer), CARTXREF (the CARTRIDGE XREF table), SYSTEM, and SYSXREF (the SYSTEM XREF table):

```
CREATE TABLE cart
    (ca_id int,
    ca_name char(20))
GO
CREATE TABLE cartxref
```

```
    (cx_ca_id_ int,
    cx_co_id_ int,
    cx_quant int)
GO
CREATE TABLE system
    (sy_id int,
    sy_name char(20))
GO
CREATE TABLE sysxref
    (sx_sy_id_ int,
    sx_co_id_ int)
GO
```

(This script is included on the CD-ROM in \EG\CH3\CREATE.SQL.)

One mark of the well-behaved database developer is the uncontrollable urge to document everything. With this in mind (and with the hopes of making everything clear), I am going to provide a poor man's data dictionary. This will list each table and field, and include the long name from the tables that were defined in the database design primer:

Table	Field	Description
collect	co_id	Collector Id
collect	co_name	Collector Name
cart	ca_id	Cartridge Id
cart	ca_name	Cartridge Name
cartxref	cx_ca_id_	Cartridge Id
cartxref	cx_co_id_	Collector Id
cartxref	cx_quant	Quantity
system	sy_id	System Id
system	sy_name	System Name
sysxref	sx_sy_id_	System Id
sysxref	sx_co_id_	Collector Id

Using SQL to Add Data to Tables

In order to add rows to a table, you must use the INSERT statement, which generally looks like this:

```
INSERT INTO table-name [(column-identifier [, column-identifier]...)]
     VALUES (insert-value [, insert-value] ...)
```

The INSERT statement requires the name of the table, a list of columns, and a list of values. The values must correspond to the columns in the list of columns. If you do not wish to specify the column list, you may omit it; in this case, all columns are assumed, and the list of values must correspond to the columns as they appeared in the CREATE TABLE statement. Therefore,

```
INSERT INTO collect (co_name, co_id)
VALUES ('E. Wood', 1)
```

is equivalent to

```
INSERT INTO collect
VALUES ('E. Wood', 1)
```

However, it is suggested that the former be used, since the explicitly stated field names make your code more self-documenting. Here's a series of INSERT statements that will populate the COLLECT table:

```
INSERT INTO collect
    (co_name, co_id)
    VALUES ('E. Wood', 1)
GO

INSERT INTO collect
    (co_name, co_id)
    VALUES ('B. Jepson', 2)
GO

INSERT INTO collect
    (co_name, co_id)
```

```
    VALUES ('J. Lee', 3)
GO

INSERT INTO collect
    (co_name, co_id)
    VALUES ('T. Johnson', 4)
GO
```

The following SQL `INSERT` statements can be used to populate the SYSTEM table:

```
INSERT INTO system
    (sy_name, sy_id)
    VALUES ('800', 1)
GO

INSERT INTO system
    (sy_name, sy_id)
    VALUES ('1200XL', 2)
GO

INSERT INTO system
    (sy_name, sy_id)
    VALUES ('65XE', 3)
GO
```

The CART table is populated with the following script:

```
INSERT INTO cart
    (ca_name, ca_id)
    VALUES ('Defender', 1)
GO

INSERT INTO cart
    (ca_name, ca_id)
```

```
   VALUES ('Missile Command', 2)
GO

INSERT INTO cart
   (ca_name, ca_id)
   VALUES ('Pacman', 3)
GO

INSERT INTO cart
   (ca_name, ca_id)
   VALUES ('Miner 2049er', 4)
GO

INSERT INTO cart
   (ca_name, ca_id)
   VALUES ('Star Raiders', 5)
GO
```

Finally, the cross-reference tables can be populated with:

```
INSERT INTO cartxref
   (cx_ca_id_, cx_co_id_, cx_quant)
   VALUES (1, 1, 1)
GO

INSERT INTO cartxref
   (cx_ca_id_, cx_co_id_, cx_quant)
   VALUES (2, 1, 1)
GO

INSERT INTO cartxref
   (cx_ca_id_, cx_co_id_, cx_quant)
   VALUES (3, 1, 1)
GO
```

```
INSERT INTO cartxref
   (cx_ca_id_, cx_co_id_, cx_quant)
   VALUES (4, 2, 1)
GO

INSERT INTO cartxref
   (cx_ca_id_, cx_co_id_, cx_quant)
   VALUES (3, 2, 1)
GO

INSERT INTO cartxref
   (cx_ca_id_, cx_co_id_, cx_quant)
   VALUES (5, 2, 1)
GO

INSERT INTO cartxref
   (cx_ca_id_, cx_co_id_, cx_quant)
   VALUES (2, 3, 1)
GO

INSERT INTO cartxref
   (cx_ca_id_, cx_co_id_, cx_quant)
   VALUES (3, 3, 1)
GO

INSERT INTO cartxref
   (cx_ca_id_, cx_co_id_, cx_quant)
   VALUES (5, 3, 1)
GO

INSERT INTO cartxref
   (cx_ca_id_, cx_co_id_, cx_quant)
   VALUES (2, 4, 1)
```

```
GO

INSERT INTO cartxref
   (cx_ca_id_, cx_co_id_, cx_quant)
   VALUES (4, 4, 2)
GO

INSERT INTO sysxref
   (sx_sy_id_, sx_co_id_)
   VALUES (1, 1)
GO

INSERT INTO sysxref
   (sx_sy_id_, sx_co_id_)
   VALUES (2, 2)
GO

INSERT INTO sysxref
   (sx_sy_id_, sx_co_id_)
   VALUES (3, 3)
GO

INSERT INTO sysxref
   (sx_sy_id_, sx_co_id_)
   VALUES (1, 4)
GO
```

(All of these examples are combined into one wonderful file on the CD-ROM under \EG\CH3\INSERT.SQL.)

Using SQL to Query Tables

Now that you've got some data in the tables, it wouldn't be fair if I didn't tell you how to query that data. The next SQL statement that will be visited is the `SELECT` statement. This is the belly of the beast as far as SQL is concerned. Depending upon what software you are using, an SQL statement will do a variety of things. In many RDBMSs, it will give you the result set in a cursor, which lets you manipulate the data in a variety of fashions. In IODBC, the result set comes back as a tabulated list. In Perl, each row in the result set can be read until there are no more rows; you can use this process to store the information into some sort of data structure, such as an associative array.

The most basic SQL `SELECT` statement looks like this:

```
SELECT column-list FROM table-list
```

The column-list is a comma-separated list of columns. It can also be replaced by *, which selects all columns. The table-list is also separated by commas. Here's a simple example from the COLLECT table, with one column and one table:

```
SELECT co_name
   FROM collect
GO
```

This prints out all of the collector names:

```
co_name
---------------------------------------
E. Wood
B. Jepson
J. Lee
T. Johnson

(4 rows affected)
```

If you plan to include more than one table, you will need to get acquainted with the `WHERE` clause. This provides the capability to specify filter conditions. If you were to include the SYSTEM table and the SYSXREF table, you would need to specify that the SYSTEM table is connected to the

SYSXREF table, and that the SYSXREF table is connected to the COLLECT table. The `WHERE` clause uses expressions like the following:

```
sx_co_id_ = co_id
```

If you feel that it improves the readability of your code, you can include the name of each table in the expression. When you do this, you must put it in front of the field name and separate them with the '.' character (period, full stop):

```
sysxref.sx_co_id_ = collect.co_id
```

Here's an example of an SQL `SELECT` statement which combines the COLLECT, SYSTEM, and SYSXREF tables:

```
SELECT co_name, sy_name
   FROM collect, system, sysxref
   WHERE sysxref.sx_co_id_ = collect.co_id
   AND   sysxref.sx_sy_id_ = system.sy_id
GO
```

Note that each expression in the `WHERE` clause is separated by an `AND`. The `OR` operator may be used and expressions can also be grouped with parentheses to force precedence. Here are the results of the above query:

```
co_name                                   sy_name
----------------------------------------- ---------------
E. Wood                                   800
B. Jepson                                 1200XL
J. Lee                                    65XE
T. Johnson                                800

(4 rows affected)
```

If the `WHERE` clause does not specify a *join condition* for each table, strange things begin to happen. Each row in each table is matched with each row in each other table, producing what is known as a *Cartesian product*. For example, if you were to attempt to get a list of names and systems without the SYSXREF table and without any join expression (don't laugh, this sort of mistake is common, and a pretty good first guess for lots of people learning the ropes);

```
SELECT co_name, sy_name
   FROM collect, system
GO
```

you would get the following results:

```
co_name                                    sy_name
----------------------------------------   -------
E. Wood                                    800
B. Jepson                                  800
J. Lee                                     800
T. Johnson                                 800
E. Wood                                    1200XL
B. Jepson                                  1200XL
J. Lee                                     1200XL
T. Johnson                                 1200XL
E. Wood                                    65XE
B. Jepson                                  65XE
J. Lee                                     65XE
T. Johnson                                 65XE
(12 rows affected)
```

Note that there are three rows in the SYSTEM table and four rows in the COLLECT table. Multiply the two together, and you get 12. Notice how each name is matched to each system. These results are not very useful, are they? Without some sort of join condition, it's hard to get useful results.

Filters in the `WHERE` clause may also be used to restrict the set of values that are returned. Here's an example that retrieves only those users who have an Atari 800:

```
SELECT co_name
```

```
    FROM collect, system, sysxref
    WHERE sysxref.sx_co_id_ = collect.co_id
    AND   sysxref.sx_sy_id_ = system.sy_id
    AND   system.sy_name    = '800'
GO
```

Here are the results:

```
co_name
----------------------------------------
T. Johnson
E. Wood
```

The last great feature of the SQL SELECT statement that you will see involves the aggregate functions. The SELECT statement provides a GROUP BY clause, which causes all of the rows in the result set to be condensed into summary rows. The aggregate functions, such as MIN, MAX, SUM, and COUNT can be used to return special calculated columns based on the summary values. Before you see what can be done with GROUP BY and the aggregate functions (hmmm . . ., "Group By and the Aggregate Functions," what an awesome band name), you'll see yet another SELECT statement:

```
SELECT co_name, cx_quant
    FROM collect, cartxref
    WHERE cx_co_id_ = co_id
GO
```

This produces the following results:

```
co_name                                      cx_quant
-------------------------------------------- ----------------------
E. Wood                                                    1.000000
E. Wood                                                    1.000000
E. Wood                                                    1.000000
B. Jepson                                                  1.000000
B. Jepson                                                  1.000000
B. Jepson                                                  1.000000
J. Lee                                                     1.000000
```

```
J. Lee                                          1.000000
J. Lee                                          1.000000
T. Johnson                                      2.000000
T. Johnson                                      1.000000

(11 rows affected)
```

These results may not seem too useful at first glance. In fact, they are rather difficult to use in the form presented. These results consist of one row for each cartridge that the collector owns, which includes a quantity for each cartridge. If you wanted to get a list of each name, followed by the number of cartridges owned, you could use `GROUP BY` (on the column co_name) and the `SUM` aggregate function (on the column cx_quant).

```
SELECT co_name, {fn SUM(cx_quant)} AS total
   FROM collect, cartxref
   WHERE cx_co_id_ = co_id
   GROUP BY co_name
GO
```

The ODBC escape terminators (`{` and `}`) are used to enclose the aggregate function. If I told you that ODBC was 100 percent portable across data sources, I was lying. Many drivers supply the same functions, but some of them are implemented under different names. If you want to be sure that your program will work across a variety of data sources, you can make sure that the ODBC SQL dialect is used for the "sensitive" parts of your SQL statement. ODBC function calls enclosed in the escape terminators look like this:

```
{fn function-expression }
```

The `fn` is a signal to ODBC that what follows should be interpreted using the ODBC dialect of SQL, regardless of what data source you are using. For example, the SQL Server driver's syntax may vary slightly from that of the FoxPro driver. To equalize it, you can put your function calls within the escape terminators and keep all your code portable.

Here are the results of that query:

```
co_name                                      total
-------------------------------------------  ---------------------
B. Jepson                                                 3.000000
E. Wood                                                   3.000000
J. Lee                                                    3.000000
T. Johnson                                                3.000000

(4 rows affected)
```

This SELECT statement also introduces the column label, which is preceded by `AS`. This is used to label (or relabel) a column name. Column labels may be used with or without aggregate grouping. You can rename columns or expressions.

```
SELECT co_name, ca_name, cx_quant AS number
   FROM collect, cartxref, cart
   WHERE cx_co_id_ = co_id
   AND   cx_ca_id_ = ca_id
GO
(prints out names, cartridge names and cx_quant renamed to number)

SELECT co_name, ca_name, cx_quant * 2 AS times_two
   FROM collect, cartxref, cart
   WHERE cx_co_id_ = co_id
   AND   cx_ca_id_ = ca_id
GO
(prints out names, cartridge names and quantity owned times two)

SELECT {fn UCASE(co_name)} AS uppercase
   FROM collect
GO
(prints out names, uppercased. Note the use of the ODBC scalar function extension)
```

There's a lot more to the SQL SELECT statement, a lot more power under the hood. You've seen enough to get you through many of the examples in this book. Appendix D is an ODBC reference which you might find helpful.

Using SQL to Update Data in Tables

You may find from time to time that you need to change the data in one or more rows. The `UPDATE` statement allows you to do this with ease. It can be used to update a single row or multiple rows. In each case, you will need to employ a `WHERE` clause, which is very similar to the one found in the `SELECT` statement. The `UPDATE` statement takes the form:

```
UPDATE table-name
SET column-identifier = expression
     [, column-identifier = expression]
     [WHERE search-condition]
```

The search condition is optional; if you do not specify one, the entire table is updated. Here's an example which updates the CARTXREF to double the number of each cartridge owned by each collector.

```
UPDATE cartxref
    SET cx_quant = cx_quant * 2
GO
```

You can also specify a filter condition in the `WHERE` clause. Here's an SQL `UPDATE` statement which only doubles the quantity of cartridges if the collector owns more than one of that particular cartridge:

```
UPDATE cartxref
    SET cx_quant = cx_quant * 2
    WHERE cx_quant > 1
GO
```

Some of the ODBC drivers support a *subquery* in the search-condition. This is a `SELECT` statement embedded in the `UPDATE` statement and bound to a column in the update table with the `IN` clause. This can be pretty useful, especially when you want to include criteria from another table. How would you update the collector's table (COLLECT) based on whether the collector had more than one of a particular cartridge? Here's an example which uppercases the name of every collector who has more than one of the same cartridge (those losers!).

```
update collect
 set co_name = {fn UCASE(co_name)}
 WHERE co_id IN (SELECT cx_co_id_ FROM cartxref WHERE cx_quant > 1)
GO
```

Subqueries can be quite useful in many contexts. They may also be used in a `SELECT` statement's `WHERE` clause:

```
SELECT *
   FROM collect
   WHERE co_id IN (SELECT cx_co_id_ FROM cartxref WHERE cx_quant > 1)
```

Note that this is equivalent to:

```
SELECT *
   FROM collect, cartxref
   WHERE co_id = cx_co_id_
   AND cx_quant > 1
```

Using SQL to Delete Rows from Tables

At some point in time, you may wish to delete rows from your tables. The `DELETE` statement looks like:

```
DELETE FROM table-name
   [WHERE search-condition]
```

Any of the search conditions shown for the `UPDATE` statement will work with the `DELETE` statement. Here's an example which will delete every collector who has more than one of the same cartridge (club rules, you know).

```
DELETE FROM collect
   WHERE co_id IN (SELECT cx_co_id_ FROM cartxref WHERE cx_quant > 1)
GO
```

You've seen a useful, if not comprehensive, explanation of some of the more common SQL statements and their features. The next chapter will allow you to put some of these to use. For further study, however, see Appendix D, an ODBC Reference.

CHAPTER

4

SIMPLE DYNAMIC DOCUMENTS

The preceding chapters gave you a quick start on databases, Perl, and the World Wide Web. This chapter will take you through implementing your first web page with links to an ODBC data source. Although Perl figures in heavily behind the scenes here, you won't have to write any Perl in this chapter.

The simplest kind of interactive database system is one which allows users to specify filter criteria for predefined queries. In many cases, a developer will create a customized screen which prompts the user for values. These values are compared with records in the database; each record which matches the values is returned in a report or in an on-screen form. This chapter will take you through the steps of building such an interface, starting with some really elementary features and spicing it up as you wend your way to the end of the chapter and to higher planes of consciousness.

Using Query Templates

Applications of this sort will require little or no Perl programming. The CD-ROM includes a Perl script (\EG\CH4\template.pl) which provides the Webmaster with SQL templates; these allow the developer to define an SQL query, identify which columns are significant, what form variables (if any) can be included in the query, and what the finished document should look like. These templates require only two pieces of information: the SQL Statement which captures records from the data source and the HTML document template.

After the query has been executed, the template generates detail information for each record in the result set. Each column in the result set is available within the templates as variables having the same name as the columns. The template.pl script takes care of converting them into Perl variables, and automatically inserting them into key places in the resultant HTML document. Because of this, columns can be included in the HTML template much in the same way as they might be included in a report writer tool. For each record in the result set, the variables are inserted as appropriate within the generated HTML document.

The templates can be created using any editor which can save in text-only format, such as GNU EMACS, Notepad, or WordPad. Once you have created the template, you must open it from your Web browser, either by typing in a URL or including a link to it from an HTML document.

ODBC Extensions to Perl

In order to connect Perl to an ODBC data source, a few files will have to be installed under Perl's lib\ directory. These are Dan Demaggio's ODBC extensions to Perl. The home page for these is:

```
http://www-personal.umich.edu/~dmag/Fun_With_Perl.html
```

If you have installed the Perl distribution under C:\WIN32APP\PERL5\, there will be a directory named C:\WIN32APP\PERL5\lib\. There are two files on the CD-ROM: \ODBC\ODBC.pll, and \ODBC\ODBC.pm. ODBC.pll must be installed in the directory lib\Auto\NT\ODBC under the Perl installation (the directory ODBC might not exist; you must create it if this is the case). ODBC.pm must be installed in the directory lib\NT\ under the Perl installation. Once you have done this, you can use the examples shown in this chapter.

Specifying a URL to a CGI Script

You've already seen URLs which can be used to fetch a document. A URL such as http://bjepson.org/info/cgi.html contains the name of the protocol (http://), the name of the server (bjepson.org), and the path to the document (/info/cgi.html). URLs that refer to a CGI script have one more optional component: a list of variables which are passed in to the scripts. These immediately follow a ? (question mark) and have a couple of quirks: Spaces must be replaced with the + (plus) sign and any non-alphanumeric (or _) characters must be replaced with a special notation. When you fill out an HTML form and submit it to a CGI script, this is all taken care of for you. But, if you are going to embed the URL within a document, or type it directly into the browser, you may need to take these considerations into account. To see exactly how this works, an HTML document and a script have been included in \eg\ch4 (cgi.htm and cgi.pl, respectively). If you have copied everything in the \eg directory and below (see Chapter 1 for more detailed instructions) into your HTTP data directory, you can issue the following URL

```
http://localhost/ch4/cgi.htm
```

and the form shown in Figure 4.1 will appear. Figure 4.2 shows the results of clicking on the OK button, which should give you an idea as to how the conversions are handled. Characters other than '_' and non-alphanumeric

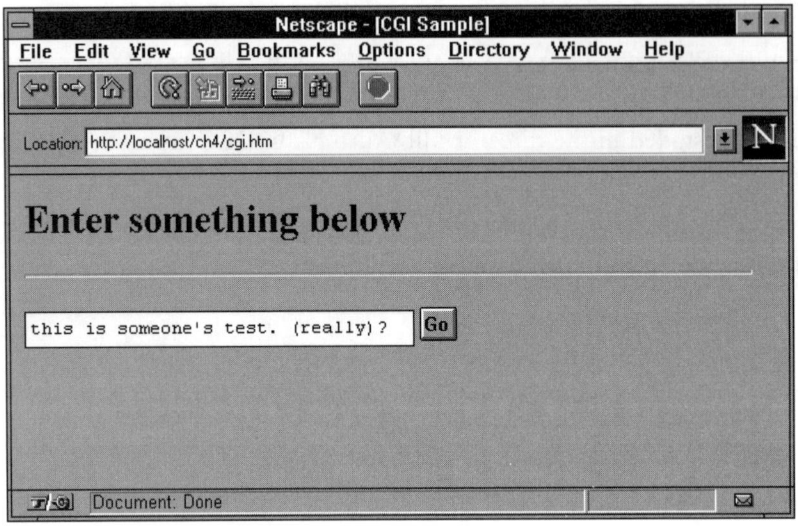

Figure 4.1 An HTML form, which runs a sample CGI script.

characters are encoded in the following way: They are prefixed with a percent sign (%); this is followed by their hexadecimal ASCII code. Fortunately, the Perl module CGI_Lite (\eg\CGI_Lite.pm), written by Shishir Gundavaram (shishir@bu.edu) will decode this gibberish into something you can use in a Perl script or module!

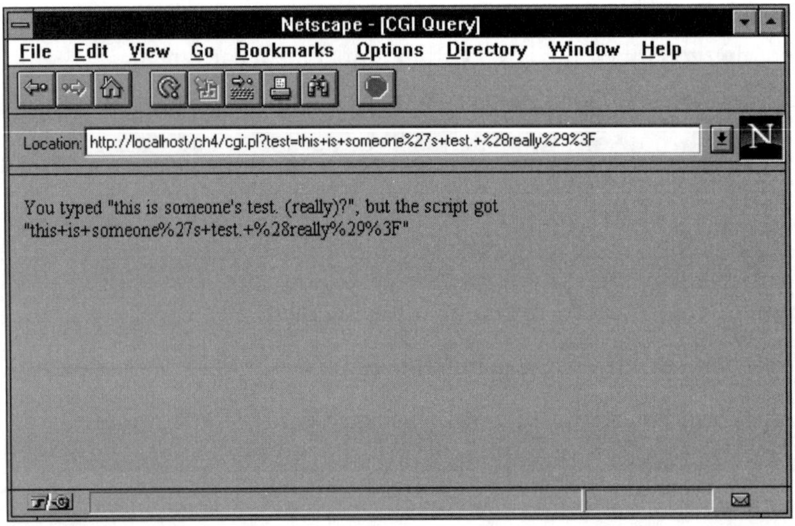

Figure 4.2 The results of the sample CGI script.

Specifying a URL to TEMPLATE.PL

The URL which references template.pl needs to include some of these variables. You will only need to worry about converting spaces to + signs if your data source name contains spaces. It's not very likely that your data source name includes any of the oddball characters that require hexadecimal conversion. So, as well as specifying the location of template.pl, the URL you will use to load a template contains the following information:

The Data Source Name (CGI variable DSN).

A user name (USERNAME), if necessary.

A password (PASSWORD), if necessary.

The path to the template file, which is specified relative to the server root (TEMPLATE).

Here's an example of such a URL:

```
http://localhost/template.pl?TEMPLATE=ch4/sample1.tpl&DSN=EXAMPLE
```

Within a URL, the / after the hostname signifies the root of the data directory. However, when you are specifying the location of the template file, it is expecting the actual location of the file on your hard drive. Since HTTPS executes the script from within the server data directory, the path to the template file can be specified relative to that directory. In the previous example, the data directory (as specified in the HTTPS control panel applet) could be something like C:\USERS\BJEPSON\CDROM\EG. The template directory is in C:\USERS\BJEPSON\CDROM\EG\TEMPLATE, but since the script executes in C:\USERS\BJEPSON\CDROM\EG, all you need is template/sample1.tpl to specify the name of the template file. If you are having problems, or using a different Web server which executes scripts from another directory, you can try specifying the full path to the template, as in:

```
http://127.0.0.1/ch5/template.pl?DSN=EXAMPLE&TEMPLATE=c:/users/bjepson/cdrom/eg/
ch5/cast.tpl&py_id=2
```

Note the required conversion of \ to /, to maintain compatibility with UNIX pathname conventions. Perl for Win32 understands both path separators, but it is generally safest (and more portable) to use /.

Server-based Data Sources

If the EXAMPLE data source is a server-based data source, such as Oracle or SQL Server, it will be necessary to supply a URL which includes a user name and password, such as:

```
http://localhost/template.pl?TEMPLATE=template/sample1.tpl&DSN=EXAMPLE&USER-
NAME=bjepson&PASSWORD=mysecurepassword
```

If you are designing a web site which provides access to all users, you may wish to set aside a database within your server for this purpose. You also will want to create a guest account with no password and give them limited access. You can further ensure security by restricting them in such a way as to only allow queries and use stored procedures to handle inserts.

Example Tables

Like the examples in the other chapters, the tables that are used in this chapter are contained in one of the subdirectories on the CD-ROM. The directory \DATA contains three subdirectories: DBF\, ACCESS\, and MSSQL\. The DBF directory contains FoxPro tables, the ACCESS directory contains a Microsoft Access database file, and MSSQL contains a batch file, INSTALL.BAT, which installs the files on your server. See Chapter 2 for more information on installing these files under an ODBC data source.

The example tables that will be used in this chapter and the next three describe the fictionalized repertoire of a real dinner theater in Pawtucket, Rhode Island: City Nights Dinner Theatre. This chapter will involve creating a *fictional* interactive Web system for browsing information about the theater and the plays that will be performed there. Here's a list of the tables and their structures that will be used for these examples.

PLAYS: A list of all plays to be performed at the theater.

Field	Type	Size	Description
py_id	int	n/a	Primary key (unique identifier)
py_name	char	35	Name of the play
py_au_id_	int	n/a	Primary key in authors table
py_desc	char	254	Description of the play

PLAYERS: A list of all actors and actresses.

Field	Type	Size	Description
pl_id	int	n/a	Primary key (unique identifier)
pl_fname	char	15	Player's first name
pl_lname	char	15	Player's last name
pl_bio	char	254	Player's biography

AUTHORS: A list of the authors of plays.

Field	Type	Size	Description
au_id	int	n/a	Primary key (unique identifier)
au_fname	char	15	Author's first name
au_lname	char	15	Author's last name

PYPLXR: A cross-reference to assign players to a play.

Field	Type	Size	Description
pp_py_id_	int	n/a	Play Id
pp_pl_id_	int	n/a	Player Id
pp_name	char	25	The name of the character they play

Template Internals

The script template.pl is responsible for reading in and making some sense out of the template files. When it parses out the SQL SELECT statement, it uses another Perl module to send the query to an ODBC data source. When the results come back from the query, template.pl produces an HTML document according to the template file used, and the column values in the SQL result set are *interpolated* into the HTML document which is defined in the template.

Each template is composed of four portions, separated by a semicolon. The first portion is the SQL Statement, the remaining three make up the HTML document.

Template File Element	Contains
SQL STATEMENT	*SQL Statement*;
Header portion of HTML Template	<html> <head> [*HTML Header Elements*] </head> <body> [*Other HTML Elements*];
Detail portion of HTML Template	[*Detail Elements*];
Footer portion of HTML Template	[*Footer Elements*] </body> </html>

The SQL statement may contain Perl variables, which must begin with a $. Each and every parameter passed into the script on the URL line is created as a variable. For example, if the URL looks like

```
http://localhost/template.pl?TEMPLATE=template/sample1.tpl&DSN=EXAMPLE&py_id=1
```

a variable is created at runtime, called `$py_id`, with the value of 1. This variable corresponds to the py_id column in the plays table. That column suffices to uniquely identify each row in the table (it is the table's *primary key*). This variable can be included as a filter condition in the SELECT statement. The value of py_id for the record which refers to the play "MacBird" is 255. The SQL statement that follows will retrieve the name of the play, the full name of each actor in the play, the character that each is portraying, and a biographic summary for each one.

```
SELECT  py_name,
        pl_fname,
        pl_lname,
        pp_name,
        pl_bio
FROM players, plays, pyplxr
WHERE pp_pl_id_ = pl_id
AND   pp_py_id_ = py_id
AND   py_id = $py_id
```

Note the inclusion of the variable `$py_id` (the $ tells Perl that it is a variable). Remember that the URL contains an encoded value for py_id. The template.pl script defines Perl variables corresponding to each variable it finds in the URL; these are available within the SQL statement. Since the value of py_id was 255, the SQL statement previously shown will be sent to the ODBC data source as:

```
SELECT  py_name,
        pl_fname,
        pl_lname,
        pp_name,
        pl_bio
FROM players, plays, pyplxr
WHERE pp_pl_id_ = pl_id
AND   pp_py_id_ = py_id
AND   py_id = 255
```

Note that you are responsible for including the correct delimiters within the SQL statement. ODBC requires delimiters for certain data types; character data must be delimited within single quotation marks. Since this example compares numeric values, no delimiters are necessary. It's important to include the delimiters if required, since Perl doesn't recognize as many data types as ODBC and cannot make these decisions for you. Perl only recognizes two datatypes, numeric and character, and uses context to determine their interpretation. That is to say, if

```
$x = 1;
$y = '00001';
```

then,

```
$x == $y;
```

is a true expression! Because of this ambiguity, TEMPLATE.PL leaves it up to you to put the delimiters in the SQL statement.

The *header portion* of the template file is a set of HTML tags only printed once per query. It must contain the tag used to begin the `html` element and must contain the `head` element in its entirety. It can contain all the elements usually found in the `head` element, such as `title` or `isindex`, but the header portion must also contain the `<body>` tag which marks the beginning of the `body` element. This can be followed by any HTML tags you want to print only once. You can think of the header portion of the template document as analogous to the header portion of a report writer.

The *detail portion* is printed once for every record. This can contain any sort of *markup* (HTML elements) which is normally found within the `body` element. Like the header portion, the *footer portion* is also printed only once (at the very end of the document). It must contain the `</body>` and `</html>` tags that terminate the `body` and `html` elements, respectively.

Here's a sample template that can be used to query the players and plays tables, given a value for the py_id within the URL that calls it. It's called cast.tpl, and is contained in the \eg\ch4 directory:

```
SELECT  py_name,
        pl_fname,
```

```
        pl_lname,
        pp_name,
        pl_bio
    FROM players, plays, pyplxr
    WHERE pp_pl_id_ = pl_id
    AND   pp_py_id_ = py_id
    AND   py_id = $py_id;
<html>
<head>
<title>List of Players</title>
</head>
<body>
<h1>List of Players</h1>;
<h2>$pl_fname $pl_lname</h2>
<address>as $pp_name</address><br>
$pl_bio<p>;

<hr>
</body>
</html>
```

Figure 4.3 shows the results of passing the following URL to a Web browser:

```
http://localhost/ch4/template.pl?DSN=EXAMPLE&TEMPLATE=ch4/cast.tpl&py_id=255
```

Linking a Template to Another Template

It might be nice to give the users a list of all the plays ever performed and let them choose which plays they want to see the cast for. This is a little better than forcing them to look at play number 255, whichever that is.

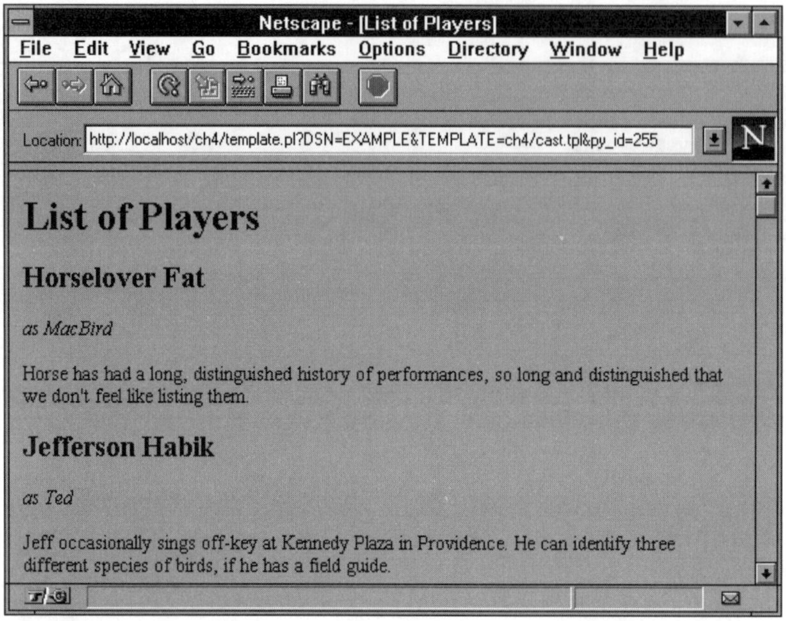

Figure 4.3 Results of the cast.tpl template.

We will walk through the steps necessary to create a template that will bring up a list of all plays which have been performed at the theater. The document which is generated will contain links to cast.tpl, so that the user can select a link and see the cast information associated with each play.

The first step is to construct a `SELECT` statement that will retrieve the name of each play, along with the play's description and its id. Since this information is available within the detail portion of the template, we can build links within the detail portion which call template.pl to bring up the cast template, passing the py_id to the cast.tpl template. Here's the `SELECT` statement as it appears in the template, \eg\ch4\plays1.tpl:

```
SELECT py_name, py_id
    FROM plays;
```

Since this template will select all the plays in the system, there is no need to include any variables in the `SELECT` statement or the URL that you use to call the template.

The header portion will put a title and a heading on the HTML document.

```
<html>
<head>
<title>List of all Plays</title>
</head>
<body>
<h1>List of all Plays</h1>;
```

The detail portion of the document contains the name of the play, followed by a URL. This URL is used to call the cast.tpl template that you saw earlier.

```
<h2>$py_name</h2>
<a href=template.pl?$persist&TEMPLATE=ch4/cast.tpl&py_id=$py_id>
The Cast of $py_name</a>;
```

When the template is generated, a number of variables are interpolated into the string. For each performance in the plays table, this detail is generated, and the value of $py_id is substituted with the play's py_id. Similarly, $py_name is replaced with the name of the play (column: py_name).

The variable `$persist` is a special variable which is created to make your life easier. It causes the DSN, USER, and PASSWORD variables to be populated with the values they had when TEMPLATE.PL was called. This allows you to make sure these values persist between each template from which you generate an HTML document. When the document is actually generated, the HTML may look something like this:

```
<h2>MacBird</h2>
<a
href=template.pl?DSN=EXAMPLE&USER=&PASSWORD=&TEMPLATE=ch4/cast.tpl&py_id=255>
The Cast of MacBird</a>
```

Here's the template in its entirety (plays1.tpl):

```
SELECT py_name, py_id
   FROM plays;
<html>
```

```
<head>
<title>List of all Plays</title>
</head>
<body>
<h1>List of all Plays</h1>;

<h2>$py_name</h2>
<a href=template.pl?$persist&TEMPLATE=ch4/cast.tpl&py_id=$py_id>
The Cast of $py_name</a>;

<hr>
</body>
</html>
```

This document can be accessed with the URL:

```
http://localhost/ch4/template.pl?DSN=EXAMPLE&TEMPLATE=ch4/plays1.tpl
```

and Figure 4.4 shows how it will appear in the Netscape Navigator browser.

Jazzing It Up

Because the template allows you to define repeating elements within a detail section, it is extremely simple to design a template which produces really snazzy output in an HTML table format. You need to be aware that some browsers, especially the text-based *Lynx*, do not support tables and some tables may appear strange on some users' screens. Regardless, many Web developers use HTML tables quite effectively. Judicious use of the tables can produce some very nice effects.

HTML tables fit rather nicely into the template files you have been using so far. All that's required of you is that you place the `<table>` and any `<th>` (table header) tags within the template header. The table rows (<tr>) and

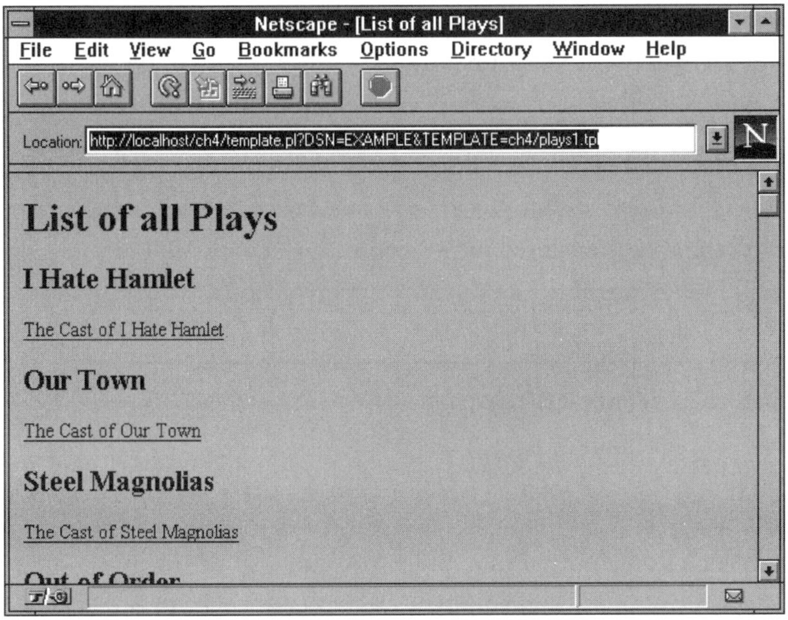

Figure 4.4 Results of a template showing all plays.

table columns (<td>) appear in the detail section of the template, and the `</table>` tag must appear in the footer.

If you haven't seen an HTML table before, here's an example of some HTML which will produce a nice little table.

```
<table border>
        <th>Header 1</th><th>Header 2</th>
        <tr>
                <td>Column 1, Row 1</td><td>Column 2, Row 1</td>
        </tr>
        <tr>
                <td>Column 1, Row 2</td><td>Column 2, Row 2</td>
        </tr>
</table>
```

The entire table element is enclosed within the <table>...</table> tags. Any number of headers may be defined before the table rows with the <th>...</th> tags. When you put columns in the rows, they are automatically lined up under the headers.

A row in the table is enclosed within <tr>...</tr> tags. In turn, each cell (or column) within the row is enclosed in the <td>...</td> tags. The previous example will look something like this in your browser:

Header 1	Header 2
Column 1, Row 1	Column 2, Row 1
Column 1, Row 2	Column 2, Row 2

In order to polish up the look of the document which gets produced from plays.tpl, you will enclose the output in a table. You can also throw in a background image (this is an attribute added to the <body> tag). In order to add some more interesting information to the header, grab the first performance date from the shows table, by using a join to that table and a GROUP BY on the py_id and py_name:

```
SELECT py_name, py_id, min(sh_date) AS start
   FROM plays, shows
   WHERE sh_py_id_ = py_id
   GROUP BY py_id, py_name;
<html>
<head>
</head>
<body background=/images/bgmask.gif>
<title>City Nights Dinner Theatre Repertoire</title>
<h1>City Nights Dinner Theatre Repertoire</h1>
<table border><th>Name</th><th>Performance Date</th><br>;

<tr>
<td>$py_name</td>
```

```
<td>$start</td>
<td>
<a href=template.pl?$persist&TEMPLATE=ch4/cast.tpl&py_id=$py_id>
See Cast</a>
</td>
</tr><br>;

</table>
<hr>
</body>
</html>
```

This document is on the CD-ROM under \EG\CH4\plays2.tpl. If you installed the examples correctly under your Web server, it can be loaded via the URL.

```
http://localhost/ch4/template.pl?DSN=EXAMPLE&TEMPLATE=ch4/plays2.tpl
```

Figure 4.5 shows this really beautiful document as it appears in the Netscape browser.

Creating an HTML Page to Link to a Template

Now, it would be foolish of you to expect the visitors to your Web pages to type in something like

```
http://localhost/ch4/template.pl?DSN=EXAMPLE&TEMPLATE=ch4/plays2.tpl
```

just to see a list of plays. It's very simple to integrate that URL into an HTML document. While you're at it, you can even extend the power of the template to allow the users to specify a parameter which will filter the query. Perhaps the users would like to be able to specify a string value and only get a list of plays whose title contains that value. This is a job for the

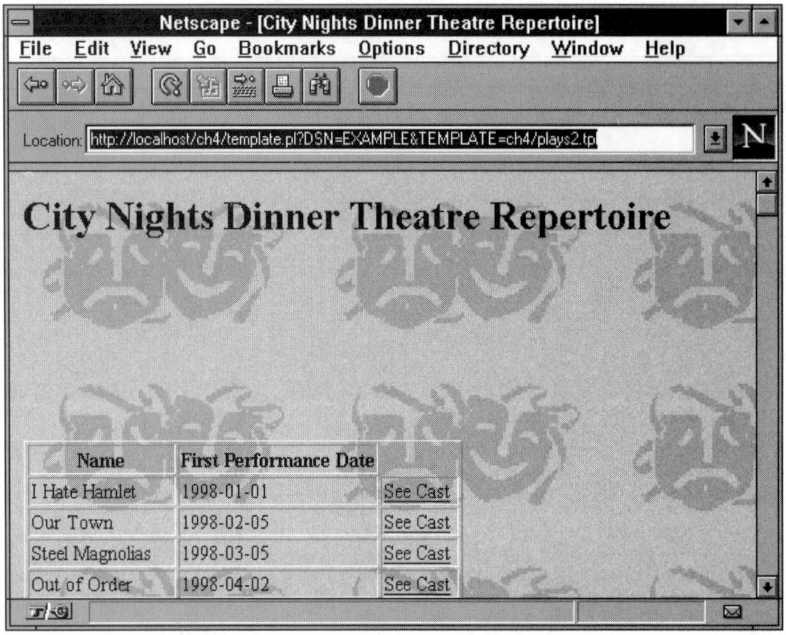

Figure 4.5 A much fancier rendition of the plays template.

LIKE predicate, which is a powerful feature of the SQL `SELECT` statement. It can be used in a `WHERE` clause in the following fashion:

```
SELECT *
    FROM plays
    WHERE pl_name LIKE 'Who%'
```

This will return a list of all plays which start with the word "Who." In the LIKE predicate, the % character functions a lot like the * wildcard character in UNIX and MS-DOS shells, and the _ (underscore) character corresponds to the ? wildcard character. The % character will match any sequence of characters, including no characters whatsoever, and _ will match any single character. For example:

```
Be_tles
```

will match

```
Beetles or Beatles
```

```
Be%
```

will match

```
Be
Bet
Bed
Beetles
Beatles
```

You can use the construct %*string*% to find values which contain the value of *string* anywhere within that value. In order to take advantage of this feature, you can modify the SQL statement within plays.tpl to read:

```
SELECT py_name, py_id, py_date
    FROM plays
    WHERE py_name LIKE '%$likeval%';
```

A value for $likeval will be supplied by the user, who can type it into a form on an HTML document. This document is called plays.htm, and can be found on the CD-ROM in \EG\CH4\plays.htm. This HTML document includes two forms which specify template.pl as their action attribute. As was previously shown in cgi.htm, a form allows the user to specify certain values and include them as parameters to a CGI script. As well as a query string for the name of the play, you can also embed the DSN and TEMPLATE variables within the form, using hidden form elements, which are not visible from the Web browser. However, if the users' browsers allow them to view the HTML source, they can see the hidden elements within the code (nothing is secret!).

Two forms are included in this HTML document. One is customized for an SQL Server (or other data source requiring a username and password), where the username and password are also provided as input fields. Notice that the password field is specified as an input type of password, which causes the Web browser to display asterisks as the user types. The data source name is MSSQL. The other specifies a data source named EXAMPLE, which requires no username or password. Of course, you can modify it to have another data source name altogether. Here's plays.htm:

```
<html>
<head>
<title>City Nights Dinner Theatre</title>
</head>

<body>
Welcome to the City Nights Dinner Theatre home pages. We've
just started to put some of our information on line,
starting with a searchable index of performances:<p>

<hr>

Use this form for a SQL Server Data Source named MSSQL:
<form action=template.pl method=post>

   <input type=hidden   name=DSN      value=MSSQL>
   <input type=hidden   name=TEMPLATE value=ch4/plays.tpl>

   Username: <input type=text     name=USER><br>
   Password: <input type=password name=PASSWORD><br>

   Search for plays containing:<input type=text   name=likeval><br>
   <input type=submit>

</form>

<hr>

Use this form for a single-tier data source named EXAMPLE:
<form action=template.pl method=post>

   <input type=hidden   name=DSN      value=EXAMPLE>
   <input type=hidden   name=TEMPLATE value=ch4/plays.tpl>
```

```
    Search for plays containing:<input type=text   name=likeval><br>
    <input type=submit>

  </form>
```

Two hidden form elements, DSN and TEMPLATE, contain the information needed to attach to the data source and find the template. You can substitute the value of the DSN field to correspond to whatever data source you are using.

It is especially important that you use the *post method* for the form when you are passing a password. While it does not supply any encryption, when you use a *get method*, all the parameters are passed in a URL, which are immediately visible on-screen if there is a location bar on your Web browser. This is not true of forms designed using the post method; the parameters are not shown on-screen. There's not much sense in using a password field (which shows only asterisks as you type), if it's going to show up in the location bar at the top of the screen! Chapter 5 will go into HTML forms in much greater detail. This HTML document can be loaded via the URL:

```
http://localhost/ch4/plays.htm
```

and Figure 4.6 shows it as it would appear in the Netscape Navigator Web browser.

You may have noticed by now that the HTML form contains a text input field for a variable called *likeval*. Remember, if the SQL `SELECT` statement in the template contains a reference to a Perl variable, it is interpolated before the SQL statement is issued. Also, the variable is available to the rest of the template, so you can modify the title and header to contain the search value and remind the users what they searched for. Here's the modified template, where `$likeval` is used within an SQL `LIKE` clause. Note that the quote character is prefixed with a \, as in \". This prevents any confusion within Perl, when each line of text is evaluated to perform variable interpolation. If you want to include the double quote character within your template, be sure to prefix it with the \ character, or you may get bizarre results.

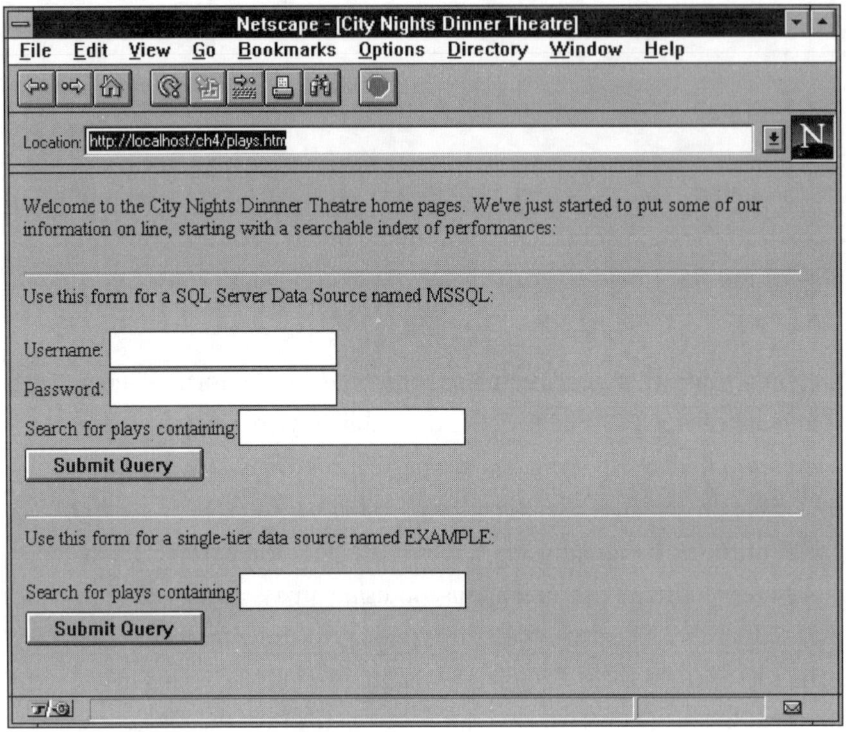

Figure 4.6 HTML document as it appears in Netscape Navigator Web browser.

```
SELECT py_name, py_id, min(sh_date) AS start
   FROM plays, shows
   WHERE py_name LIKE '%$likeval%'
   AND   sh_py_id_ = py_id
   GROUP BY py_id, py_name;
<html>
<head>
<title>Results of Search for \"$likeval\"</title>
</head>
<body background=/images/bgmask.gif>
<h1>Results of Search for \"$likeval\"</h1>
```

```
<table border><th>Name</th><th>First Performance Date</th><br>;


<tr>
<td>$py_name</td>
<td>$start</td>
<td>
<a href=template.pl?$persist&TEMPLATE=ch4/cast.tpl&py_id=$py_id>
See Cast</a>
</td>
</tr><br>;


</table>
<hr>
</body>
</html>
```

Figure 4.7 shows an example of the output of this template, when you search for the word "Bird."

Figure 4.7 Template output when searching for the word "Bird."

Well, so much for simplicity. What started out as a fairly simple template file is now two templates and one HTML document! But, it looks pretty sharp and actually provides some pretty nice functionality without a whole lot of work. Using the template approach, it's possible to get a data-driven Web site up and running pretty quickly. However, there's a lot more that can be done. If you are willing to get your hands a little messy doing some real programming, then roll up your sleeves (unless you, like Captain Kirk in many Star Trek episodes, are not wearing a shirt) and dive into the next chapter.

CHAPTER

5

DATA ENTRY ON THE WEB

In our fictional alternate universe, having established a presence on the Web, City Nights Dinner Theatre found that a lot of their existing customers found their way to the Web site. Fortunately, they had established their Web presence in the midst of an enormous explosion of new Internet users. Further, they found that many new customers came to the theater after stumbling across the Web site.

Many customers asked, "Can I make reservations over the Web?" Tired of answering "no" to these questions, City Nights set about looking for a way to make this happen. Somehow, they had to tie their current reservations system, a legacy system implemented in PNP (pen 'n paper), to the Web. In this chapter, we will introduce you to some more features of Perl, including the object-oriented features, as we develop part of the system needed to accomplish this task. In Chapter 6, we'll use what we learned here to develop an interactive system that customers can use to make reservations on-line.

Developing Specifications

Concerned about security, City Nights decided not to implement any Web-based credit card features, but chose to employ a simple verification cycle. Customers will be required to sign up for this service and, in doing so, provide City Nights with a name and telephone number. In turn, City Nights provides a password. The customers would use this password when making reservations and City Nights will confirm the reservations a few days before the show, by calling the number provided. Finally, they decided that only one-third of each show's available seats would be available for reservation on the Web and that each customer could reserve no more than four seats per show via the Web. That will keep pranksters from doing too much harm, should someone's password fall into the wrong hands.

The folks at City Nights also thought it would be appropriate if a Web-based data entry system for customer profiles is developed. This will allow them to manage their information using Web-based forms. This will be the chunk that we take a bite of in this chapter; the rest of the system will follow in the next chapter.

In keeping with what many developers consider *best practices*, the development of this system will be an iterative process; one component will be put together, tested, and deployed. This type of development methodology is critical in situations where the technology base or the business requirements are rapidly changing. Gone are the days when systems analysts would ponder the design of a system for months. In the space of a week, the entire technological aesthetic of the computer industry can be turned on its head! It's best to shoot first and ask questions later.

Table Design

Before doing any real programming, we'll identify some of the data. There are two parts that City Nights is trying to glue together here: customers and seats. Since this chapter is involved with a data entry system for new customers, we won't focus on seats just yet. We will, however, nail down those data elements that are specific to the customer. This is what we came up with:

First Name

Last Name

Address

City

State

Zip Code

Beyond that, the system will need some means of identifying the customer: A customer id will be needed. Also, the customer will need some way of authenticating users to the system, so we'll add a password to the table's structure. Here's the script that we'll run through IODBC:

```
CREATE TABLE cust
(cu_fname char(25),
cu_lname  char(25),
cu_id     int,
cu_passwd char(12),
cu_addr1  char(25),
cu_addr2  char(25),
cu_city   char(30),
cu_state  char(2),
cu_zip    char(10))
GO
```

This script is located on the CD-ROM in \EG\CH5\INIT5.SQL. If your Data Source Name is EXAMPLE and you copied everything under \EG to C:\BOOK\EG, you could run it through IODBC with the following command:

```
IODBC /S "EXAMPLE" < C:\BOOK\EG\CH5\INIT5.SQL
```

The tables in this example are installed in the various directories under \DATA on the CD-ROM; DBF\ contains FoxPro/dBase files; ACCESS\ contains an Access database file; and MSSQL\ contains an installation script for SQL Server. See Chapter 4 for instructions on installing the tables.

Diving Right In

Having created the tables, it might be a good idea to put some data in them. The most enjoyable way to do this would be to write a user interface to accomplish this task. In addition, you will need to implement some Perl scripts which will run on the back end.

There's a couple of challenges that will need to be dealt with. One, you need a good way of generating a unique, sequential id for the customers. For some reason, people are rather fond of sequential ids (I'll explain this later). Also, you need some method of generating reasonably unique passwords. In order to facilitate this, I have provided two perl programs: NTNextID.pm, and unqpass.pl. I'm not going to go into the internals of these scripts, but I will tell you what you need to know to use them.

Generating Sequential Keys

The Perl module NTNextId.pm will generate a sequential key for a given key. A *sequential key* is a numeric value that is incremented when you want to obtain a new value for it. Every time you call the nextid method (don't worry about methods; these will be explained in painful detail shortly) in NTNextID, the value associated with that key is incremented and returned to the program which called it. For example, if the last record that you added to the database had a key value of 137, the next key value would be 138. Why would you want to do such a thing? Well, when designing a database, it's important to identify a key value which uniquely identifies each record. These key values are used when linking records from one table to another; they must be values which are assigned to the record when it is created and *never change*. First name plus last name will not suffice; people change their names for various reasons; if you spelled it wrong, you will have to change it. Imagine if you had one thousand historic reservation records for customer John Jones, and he called up to tell you that he was really from Mars and that his name was J'onn J'onz. You'd have to go into the table with the historic records and change each reference to John Jones with his real name! It would be a lot simpler to associate a system-generated number with each of the historic records; then, when you need to change his name, you only need to do so in one place.

I prefer to use a sequential value for this purpose, which has nothing to do with the other data elements. However, some designers may choose to use something else, like a Social Security number, although some people are hesitant to divulge that information, particularly those with something to hide. Also, it's very easy to design the system so no one ever has to use the numeric code. A perfect example of this is shown in Chapter 6, when we provide a user interface on the Web for making reservations. The users are allowed to type in their name rather than their user id and the system automagically finds their records.

Many systems, such as SYBASE System 10 and Microsoft Access, make it easy to do this sort of thing. They allow you to define a *counter* data type for your columns; each time you add a record to the table, this number is incremented and stored. Including a field such as this in the table eliminates the need to use NTNextId.pm.

Here's an example of records from a sample database, showing the columns cu_fname, cu_lname, and cu_id:

cu_fname	cu_lname	cu_id
Leonard	Schneider	1
Abiezer	Coppe	2

There are two schools of thought for generating these id values; one side says that they should be numeric and the other says they should be character. I usually don't give a fiery flying roll either way, but I am going to stick with a numeric (int) value.

NTNextID() takes care of safely retrieving these numbers in a multi-user environment. Here's an example of a Perl script which will call NTNextID() many times in a row and print out the value (it's in the file testcnt.pl under \eg\ch5 on the CD-ROM):

```
#
# testcnt.pl
#
use File::NTNextId;
$id = new File::NTNextId("C:/TEMP/SOME_UNIQUE_VALUE");
for (1..10) {
  $temp = nextid $id(10);
  print "$temp\n";
}
```

You can execute this script by first making sure that your current directory is the copy you made of the CD-ROM's \EG directory (you should have copied all of the \EG directory and its subdirectories by now) and typing:

```
perl ch5\testcnt.pl
```

What exactly does NTNextId do that's so special? A lot of folks may wonder why we can't just issue an SQL statement like this:

```
SELECT MAX(cu_id) + 1
FROM cust
```

in order to get the next available id. Unfortunately, it is not quite so simple. Since the world of World Wide Web development is very multi-user, it is quite possible (and very likely) that two processes can get the same answer and they would end up inserting duplicate key values into the database. This is a very Bad Thing. Many database engines provide facilities to prevent this;

for example, in SQL Server, if a unique index is generated on a key, any INSERT statement which attempts to insert duplicate data will be rejected with an error!

How does NTNextId get past this limitation? It's quite simple. The subroutine locks a system resource, increments the number, and unlocks it. A lock prevents other processes from doing the same thing.

Since NTNextId is not allowed to increment the value unless it has a lock, concurrent processes will fail if a lock is not achieved. If the lock failed, NTNextId returns a -1. If it was successful, the value of the next key is returned.

Developing an HTML Form

HTML provides a forms interface, which lets you define a form right on the HTML document. This form contains various interface elements, such as input fields, select fields, and text areas. While other HTML elements may define text or images for the user to look at, forms allow the user to enter information and submit it to a CGI script. The `form` element can be inserted anywhere within the `body` element. You can put other elements within the form element, such as images or text. Where necessary, you may want to add paragraph breaks (the `<p>` tag) or line breaks (the `<br>` tag) to separate form elements.

There are several types of form interface elements. The most common is the `input` field, which allows you to define anything from text input fields to push buttons, but the list also includes `select` fields and text `areas`.

Input Fields

The input field can be used to define a text or password field, checkbox, radio button, submit button (submits the form to a CGI script), reset button (returns all form elements to their default value), or a hidden field (which is not shown to the user; it is generally used to maintain persistence between different forms on different Web pages).

The input element is defined solely with the `<input>` tag (there is no `</input>`). It may contain the `type`, `name`, `value`, `checked`, `size`, and `maxlength` attributes.

The type Attribute

The type attribute may be text, checkbox, radio, submit, hidden, or password. Examples are:

```
<form>
    Please enter your name: <input type="text"><p>
    <input type="submit"><p>
</form>
```

Figure 5.1 shows how this will look in a browser.

The name Attribute

The `name` attribute is any name you care to give to the field. This is the name that is used when the results of the form are sent to a CGI script. Examples are:

```
<form>
    Enter your name: <input type="text" name="my_field"><p>
```

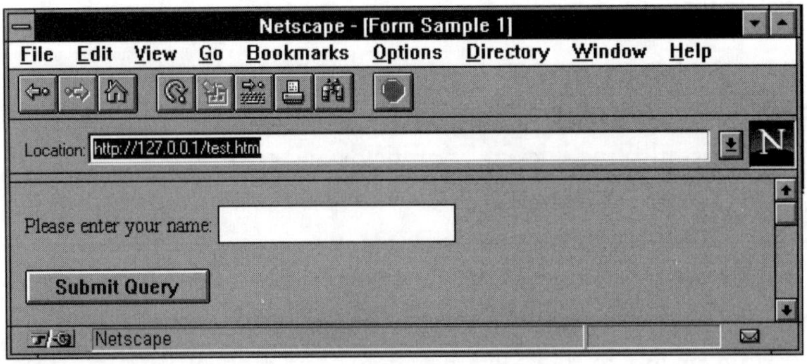

Figure 5.1 A simple form example.

```
    Enter your password: <input type="password" name="your_password"><p>
</form>
```

The `value` Attribute

The value attribute is used as a default value for type of text or password. For type of reset or submit, the value attribute is the title of the button that appears. By default, they are reset and submit, respectively. For type of checkbox or radio button, the value attribute is the value that gets sent to the CGI script if that particular object was selected by the user. An example (you can see how this will look in Figure 5.2):

```
<form>
<input type="checkbox" name="checkbox1"><br>
<input type="radio" name="radio1" value="radio1">Option 1<br>
<input type="radio" name="radio1" value="radio2">Option 2<br>
<input type="radio" name="radio1" value="radio3">Option 3<br>
<input type=submit value="Hit Me!">
<input type=reset  value="Back to Square One">
</form>
```

The `checked` Attribute

You can include the `checked` attribute with type of radio or `checkbox`. It will make the input field checked or selected by default. An example is:

```
<form>
<input type="checkbox" name="checkbox1" checked><br>
<input type="radio" name="radio1" value="radio1" checked>Option 1<br>
<input type="radio" name="radio1" value="radio2">Option 2<br>
<input type="radio" name="radio1" value="radio3">Option 3<br>
<input type=submit value="Hit Me!">
<input type=reset  value="Back to Square One">
</form>
```

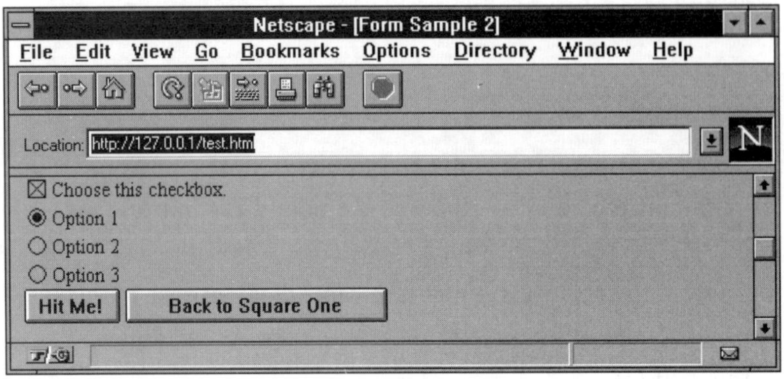

Figure 5.2 A form sample showing various elements.

The `size` *Attribute*

The `size` attribute can be used to control the width of a text or password input type. Here's an example; you can see what it looks like in Figure 5.3:

```
<form>
   Enter your name:
    <input type="text"     name="name"     size="30"><p>
   Enter your password:
   <input type="password" name="password" size="12"><p>
</form>
```

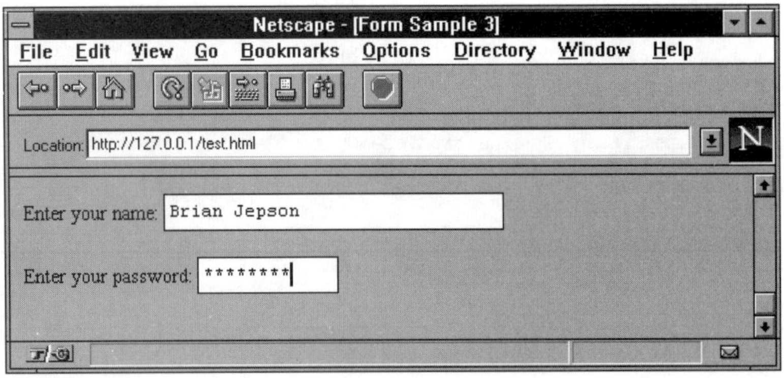

Figure 5.3 Using the size attribute.

The `maxlength` Attribute

This attribute is used to restrict the number of characters that the user can type into the field. The `size` attribute, in contrast, only controls the width of the field displayed, but does not limit the number of characters a user may type. An example is:

```
<form>
Enter your name:
<input type="text"     name="name"     maxlength="40"><p>
Enter your password:
<input type="password" name="password" maxlength="15"><p>
</form>
```

Textareas

A textarea is a lot like an input type of text, but it allows the user to enter multiple lines of text. It supports the optional attributes `name` (this performs the same function as the name attribute in the input fields), `rows`, and `cols`. The `rows` attributes determine the number of rows that the textarea will occupy on the Web page and the `cols` attribute controls the number of columns. You can see what the following example looks like in Figure 5.4:

```
<form>
Enter your name:
<input type="text"     name="name"     maxlength="40"><p>
Enter your password:
<input type="password" name="password" maxlength="15"><p>
Enter a comment:
<textarea name="comment" rows=5 cols=30></textarea>
</form>
```

You may include some default text for the object between the `<textarea>` and the `</textarea>` tags.

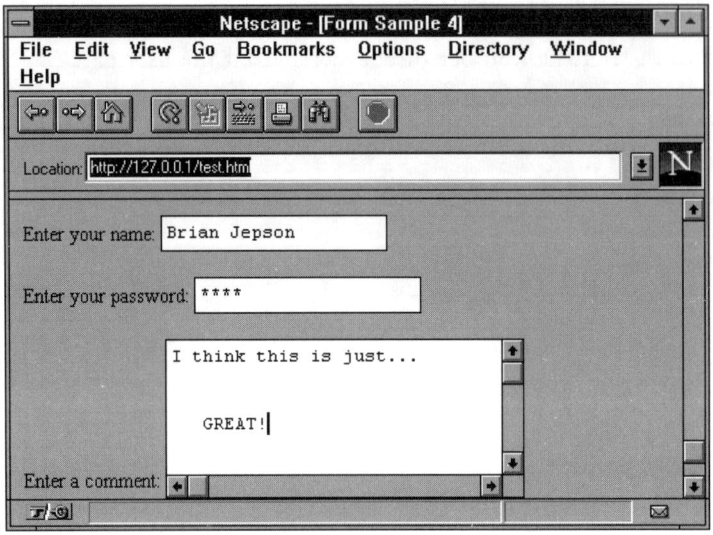

Figure 5.4 A form that includes the textarea element.

Select Fields

A select field allows users to make a choice from a list. Two types are supported: single-selection and multiple-selection lists. Like the other fields, the select field supports the `name` attribute. You may also specify a size, which controls the number of options that are displayed in the list. If you want to create a select field which allows multiple items to be selected, you may include the `multiple` attribute.

In order for a select field to be of much use to you, you will need to add some *option items*. Each option item adds an item to the list from which the user chooses. The option element is composed of an `<option>` tag and the text of the option. There is no `</option>` tag. Here's an example of both single and multiple select elements:

```
<form>
Select field with a single choice:<p>
<select name=games>
```

```
<option>Dig Dug
<option>Pac Man
<option>Defender
</select><p>

Select field with multiple choices:<p>
<select name=computers multiple>
<option>Atari 400
<option>Commodore 64
<option>Apple II
</select>
</form>
```

Figure 5.5 shows what this would look like in a browser.

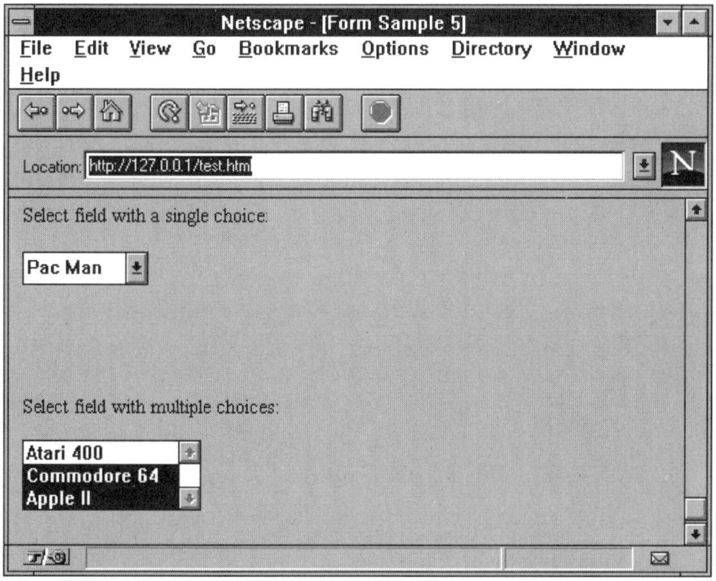

Figure 5.5 Two different select fields.

Life After Submission

The big question is what happens when the user hits the Submit button? This is where the `name` attribute comes in handy. The `<form>` tag allows you to specify an `action` attribute. This is usually the name of a CGI program, which will take the values of each form field and use the values in calculations or store them in a database. When the script is executed, the variables are sent to the script in a manner specified by another attribute, the method attribute. For the most part, it doesn't matter which method you choose, but GET and POST are good choices. There is a Perl module called CGI_Lite.pm which takes care of determining which method was used to send the form field data to the CGI script, and it makes these values available in your Perl script.

Having gone over the components of a form in rather excruciating detail, you are probably ready to start putting the pieces together. The following HTML document is included on the CD-ROM in the \EG\CH5 subdirectory and includes a form which uses the POST method to send data to a script called adduser.pl:

```
adduser.htm:
<html>
<head>
<title>Add New Customer</title>
</head>

<body>
<h1>Add New Customer</h1>
<hr>

<form action=adduser.pl method=post>
            <input type="hidden" name="DSN"      value="MSSQL">
            <input type="hidden" name="USER"     value="wwwuser">
            <input type="hidden" name="PASSWORD" value="">
```

```
Name:       <input type="text" name="cu_fname" size="25">
             <input type="text" name="cu_lname" size="25"><p>
Address 1: <input type="text" name="cu_addr1" size="25"><p>
Address 2: <input type="text" name="cu_addr2" size="25"><p>
City:       <input type="text" name="cu_city"  size="30">
State:      <input type="text" name="cu_state" size="2"><p>
Zip Code:  <input type="text" name="cu_zip" size="10"><p>
<input type=submit value="Add User">
</form>
</body>
</html>
```

Figure 5.6 shows how this will look in the Web browser.

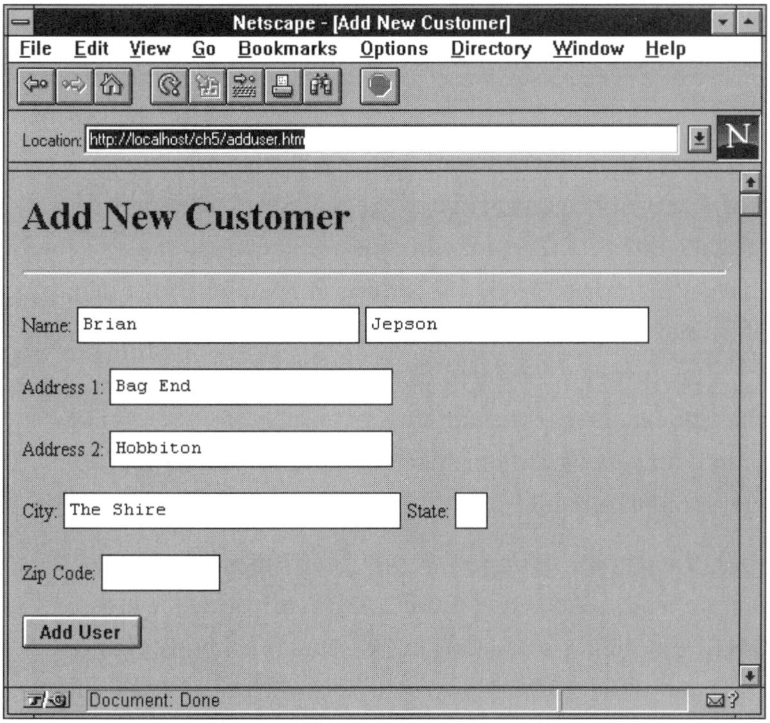

Figure 5.6 The customer data entry form.

This form will generate a POST method, which will be sent the Perl script adduser.pl. We'll be using the CGI_Lite.pm module, by Shishir Gundavaram, to parse whatever the form sends in. Here's a sample of how it is invoked:

```
use CGI_Lite;
$cgi      = new CGI_Lite ();
%results = $cgi->parse_form_data ();
```

Big Tangent: Perl Objects and References

This is quite possibly the first time that you are seeing any examples of Perl's object-oriented features. It looks quite innocent, really. You may have seen the `require` function, which is used to load in a library script. The `use` function is similar, in that it loads a Perl module. Perl modules contain class definitions for objects that you want to use.

In typical structured programming, you make use of *libraries*, which contain *subroutines*. In object-oriented programming, you create definitions for a special data type called *objects*. These definitions are known as *classes*. Each object can have a number of *properties*, which are data elements that belong to a specific object. When you create (instantiate) a new object from a class definition, its properties are isolated from those of other objects, whether they be instantiated from the same class definition or another. The class definitions also define *methods*, which are special subroutines that perform operations specific to that object.

There are two types of methods: *static* and *virtual*. Static methods are used to work with the class itself; an example is the *constructor*, which is used to instantiate an object from the class description. A virtual method is used to work with objects; most of the methods you will see and write yourself will fall into this category.

In Perl, when you create (or instantiate) an object, you need to pass the class name to the constructor method, which is usually named new. Static methods such as constructors expect class names as their first argument. Each time you instantiate the object, you create a variable which contains a reference to an array which holds all of the information relevant to that object; this information is called the object's properties. You can maintain such information as "favorite color"; each instance of the object can have its own favorite color.

Here's an example of a simple class, called person (it is stored in a file called person.pm).

```
person.pm:
# person.pm
#
package person;
    sub new {
    my ($class, $color, $weight) = @_;
    my $self = {};
    $self->{'Favorite Color'} = $color;
    $self->{'Weight'} = $weight;
    bless $self;
    $self;
}

sub whats_your_favorite_color {
    my ($self) = @_;
    print "My favorite color is $self->{'Favorite Color'}.\n";
}
1;
```

You can create a new instance of person (and include his or her favorite color as a parameter) simply with the following line of code:

```
$me = new person('blue', 150)
```

Of course, you must also include the line

```
use person;
```

somewhere at the top of your Perl script.

More than one class can be contained within a single file; they are defined with the `package` declaration. A method called `new` should be included, which takes care of creating a special variable, which is traditionally called `$self` when referenced within the object's methods. `$self` is a scalar variable which contains a reference to a hash (associative array). It is this array which contains all the properties of the object, such as favorite color. The `bless()` function is used to bless a reference into becoming a class, and then it's important to return the reference to whoever called the `new()` method in the first place. Perl packages are mechanisms which allow the developer to separate portions of code, arrays, filehandles, and variables into distinct namespaces. Objects are simply references that "know" to which package they belong. The perlmod.htm file in the Docs\ directory under the Perl installation explains everything you could want to know about modules and packages.

You can also pass in any number of arguments to the new() method, but the first one is always the class that the object belongs to. The `my` function is used to make sure that the variables you are defining are local to the method invoked. Let's go step-by-step through what happens when the line of code

```
$me = new person('blue', 150)
```

is executed.

```
my ($class, $color, $weight) = @_;
```

Is a special notation used to assign the parameter list to a series of variables. The `my` function makes sure that the variables are local to this particular invocation of the subroutine. This is particularly important, since when you are doing object-oriented programming, you often will use the same class to define many instances of objects and you don't want them trouncing each others' variables.

The special variable `@_` contains the parameters that were passed to the method. Method invocations may look a little strange ($me = new person('blue', 150)). You've got the name of the method, that's clear enough, but you have three different arguments. One of them (person) kind of dangles after the method name, but the other two (color and weight) are in parentheses. This is perfectly fine. This is the way that the method syntax is invoked. Another way that it can be invoked is:

```
$you = person->new("red", 108);
```

The first parameter is always the name of a class/package or instantiated object, followed by other arguments. This parameter enters the methods via the @_ variable, which is a list of all the parameters. Once you have issued the line

```
$me = new person('blue', 150)
```

the new method is invoked; after the first line, the following values are assigned:

variable	value
$class	person
$color	blue
$weight	150

The next line of code that is executed,

```
my $self = {};
```

causes the scalar value $self to contain a reference to what is called an anonymous hash. An important point, and one which will help illustrate what a reference is: we are not creating a hash called %self, but rather a single scalar variable. This variable is a reference to a hash, and has its own special notation. Here's how you assign the color and weight to the hash:

```
$self->{'Favorite Color'} = $color;
$self->{'Weight'} = $weight;
```

If we were (and we're not) assigning to a hash named %self, it would look like this:

```
$self{'Favorite Color'} = $color;
$self{'Weight'} = $weight;
```

The advantage of this is that each time `new()` is invoked, a new anonymous hash is created and assigned to a variable called `$self`. Since we are using the `my` function as we create the variable, that anonymous hash is created and assigned to a unique, local variable each time. Note that we've used two different syntaxes when using `my`:

```
my ($class, $color, $weight) = @_;
my $self = {};
```

When assigning to a series of values from the `@_` variable, the parentheses are very important. They ensure that `@_` is interpreted in an array context (which yields each element in the array) rather than in a scalar context (which yields the number of elements in the array). If we omitted the parentheses:

```
my $class, $color, $weight = @_;
```

then `@_` would be evaluated in a scalar context, and neither $color nor $weight would get a value; actually, $class would get the number of elements in `@_`, which is not what we want at all! Further, when the my function is invoked on more than one value, parentheses are required. Parentheses: Don't leave home without them.

When we issue:

```
bless $self;
```

`$self` magically becomes a special type of reference; it is now a reference that knows to which package it belongs. Finally, so the calling program doesn't lose the value of $self and everything it points to, $self can be put on a line by itself

```
$self;
```

which causes the `new()` method to return the value of $self. And it is $self that gets assigned to the variable `$me`, when everything returns back to the statement:

```
$me = new person('blue', 150)
```

Accessing Methods

The person object contains a method called person::whats_your_favorite_color(). When that method is invoked, the person will respond with:

```
My favorite color is x.
```

(x will contain the name of his or her favorite color). The method is invoked in a similar fashion to the way the `person::new()` method was invoked. However, when we invoked the `person::new()` method, we gave it the name of a class. And that's perfect, because naturally, we had not yet instantiated an object, and were, in fact, asking `person::new()` to return a reference to the object. But once we have instantiated an object, we have a reference to it and can access the methods that the object inherits from the class definition. In order to ask the object $me to tell its favorite color, simply issue the statement:

```
whats_your_favorite_color $me;
```

or

```
$me-> whats_your_favorite_color;
```

and it will respond with:

```
My favorite color is blue.
```

Here's a Perl script (located on the CD-ROM in \eg\ch5\person.pl) which instantiates two different objects of the class person, with different weights and colors:

```
person.pl:
use person;
$me  = new person("blue", 150);
$you = person->new("red", 108);

whats_your_favorite_color $me;
$you->whats_your_favorite_color;
```

Note that both ways of invoking methods are shown here. Here's what it prints when it is run with the command `perl person.pl`:

```
My favorite color is blue.
My favorite color is red.
```

Back on Track

While every class that you instantiate into an object will do slightly different things, what you have just seen demonstrates some of the more common things that are performed upon object instantiation. Our adduser program starts out with:

```
use NT::ODBC;
use NTNextId;
require "unqpass.pl";
use CGI_Lite;
$cgi     = new CGI_Lite ();
%results = $cgi->parse_form_data ();
```

Here, we're using the same techniques discussed in our little digression. Notice something different about the way that ODBC is used? There's this little matter of the NT:: which is prepended to it. Well, all of the standard

Perl modules as well as groups of modules included in the CPAN archive are organized in a hierarchical fashion. If you take a look in the Lib/ subdirectory below the Perl installation, you'll notice many subdirectories. One of these is NT/; all of the Perl modules which are related to Windows NT belong there. This sort of grouping requires that the subdirectory name prefix the module name and also keeps Perl developers organized. Along with the other two modules, we're using the CGI_Lite module; this gives us access to any classes in that module. This module provides a number of services for dealing with CGI input which is the parameters that the Web browser sends to the gateway program, in this case, a Perl script called adduser.pl. If you take a look at adduser.htm, you'll see that the following form variables are defined:

```
cu_fname
cu_addr1
cu_addr2
cu_city
cu_state
cu_zip
```

There are a couple of ways that the browser sends this data to the script, but CGI_Lite knows how to deal with them. This is important, and demonstrates one feature of object-oriented programming called *encapsulation*. Encapsulation hides all of the underlying complexity of a class from people like us, who are implementing the class. We don't have to make any decisions about where the CGI query data comes from:

```
$cgi      = new CGI_Lite ();
```

instantiates a new object which "knows" how to handle CGI query data, and

```
%results = $cgi->parse_form_data ();
```

invokes the method, CGI_Lite::parse_form_data(), which handles parsing the query. The %results hash contains all of the variables and values in the query.

Moving Right Along

Now that we've used CGI_Lite to capture the results of whatever query data comes from the form, we can set about manipulating it. First, let's get a head start on the HTML output to the client. Add the following lines of code:

```
print <<EOF;
Content-type: text/html

<html>
<head>
<title>Request Submitted</title>
</head>
<body>
<h1>Request Submitted</h1>
<hr>
EOF
```

We're using the here-doc syntax to let the client know that we got their query. However, we still need to do something with the query; once we've done that, we'll be able to tell the client what the disposition of it was.

Remember our friend the sequential id? Well, now's a good time to try to get one. If we don't get it, we can tell the user that there was a problem with it, and they can complain to the website administrator. Let's take a look back at the `use()` statements that we had at the top of our program:

```
use NT::ODBC;
use NTNextId;
require "unqpass.pl";
use CGI_Lite;
```

Since this Perl script has used the NTNextId module, it's quite simple to obtain the next sequential id. The following two lines of code instantiate an instance of the NTNextId object and invoke its `nextid()` method. The parameter that is sent to the `new` method is the location of the counter file. Make sure that the directory shown exists! It is really important that this file not be moved or deleted after the first time you create it, since it is created if it is not found. The parameter passed to the `NTNextId::nextid()` method is the number of tries to lock the semaphore, which is a way that processes tell each other that they are performing a privileged activity. If another process tries to increment the same counter, it is prevented from doing so until this one has finished its work. Note that the code is assigning directly to the %results hash. This is because the SQL INSERT statement that will be executed is generated from the values and keys contained within the hash. Since the form did not contain fields for cu_id and cu_passwd, it follows that they must be generated, if they are to be populated with something other than a null!

```
$id = new NTNextId("C:/COUNTERS/CUSTID.CNT");
$results{'cu_id'} = nextid $id(10);
```

If there was a problem incrementing the counter, then $results{'cu_id'} will contain a value less than zero. For this reason, the next part of the program looks like this:

```
if ($results{'cu_id'} < 0) {
print <<EOF;
The server is unable to process your request at this time.<br>
You may try to submit it again by reloading this page...
EOF
} else {
...
(the rest of the code that I don't want you to worry about now!!!)
...


}
print "</BODY></HTML>";
```

This causes an unnerving error to appear in place of a comforting affirmative response.

Since the block under the else is what makes up the body of this program, it's a good time to dissect that part. There's actually quite a bit going on here. The next step that occurs involves adding another value into the %results array. As was previously mentioned, this is the array that will be used to generate the SQL `SELECT` statement, which in turn, inserts the new values into the CUST table. There are two columns that were not included in the form: the user id and the password. The earlier code retrieves the value of the id; the next lines of code will retrieve a semi-random password.

```
$results{'cu_passwd'} = &unqpass();
```

Back at the top of this program, we included the line:

```
require "unqpass.pl";
```

The `require()` function is somewhat similar to `use()`, except that it is used to load a script in, making any subroutines which are in that script available to the program that is `require()`ing it. In this case, a subroutine called `unqpass()` is included, and does some twiddling of times and process ids to come up with a semi-random password. It's good enough for this example, but in real life, the user should be allowed to choose his or her passwords and the robust programs like the password-checking Perl script in the Camel book should be used. You have been warned.

Dynamically Generating SQL Statements

Following this, there are some really strange gymnastics going on:

```
$noDelim{'cu_id'} = 1;
foreach (keys %results) {
      if (/^cu_/) {
            $fields[$#fields + 1] = $_;
```

```
            if ($noDelim{$_}) {
                  $val = "$results{$_}";
            } else {
                  $val = "'$results{$_}'";
            }
            $values[$#values + 1] = $val;
      }
}
```

For those of you not fully initiated into the Perl cabal (raise your hands), this may seem arcane. Well, that's because it is. But don't worry, all will be made clear.

First, set up an associative array (a.k.a. hash) of all the fields which need no delimiter. When the ODBC interface to Perl matures a bit, it should be very easy to ask ODBC to tell you what the data type is. Then, you can distinguish between numeric, character, date, and all the other great data types. This is important, because numeric data shouldn't have delimiters, but character should. The delimiter for character data is a single quote. Note that later on in this code sample, the %noDelim hash is examined. If the current column (as held in $_) has a non-zero entry in the hash, then the script uses the $results{$_} expression for the value. Otherwise, if it is not in the hash, then that column requires a delimiter and '$results{$_}' is used.

The next thing that goes on here involves setting up a loop

```
foreach (keys %results) {
```

will iterate over each of the keys in %results, storing each key in $_ for each iteration. The foreach construct extracts all of the elements of the array. If this construct read

```
foreach (%results) {
```

then, the key and value would alternatingly appear in the loop, something like that shown in the following table (assuming sample values for each form field).

Iteration	Value of $_
1	cu_city
2	Providence
3	cu_addr1
4	3000 Messer Street
etc...	

This is not what is desired. In order to process this data in the most useful manner, it's better to obtain one iteration for each hash element. Using the following construct:

```
foreach (keys %results) {
```

Here's what the iterative values of $_ (and $results{$_}, since $_ can be used to index into the hash) would look like:

Iteration	Value of $_	Value of $results{$_}
1	cu_city	Providence
2	cu_addr1	3000 Messer Street
etc...		

Having set up a loop correctly, here's the first line of code which is executed within the loop:

```
if (/^cu_/) {
```

What's this? Earlier chapters included some examples of operators and functions that work on the $_ variable by default. You have also visited with the `s///` function, which performs a substitution on a string. The `m//` operator (the m is optional, and I exercised my option not to use it previously) attempts to match a pattern within a string and returns a true or false. The ^ is regexp notation for "beginning of line," and cu_ is, cu_. If you look at the structure of the CUST table, you'll see that each field begins with cu_. Hmm . . . could this be a coincidence?

As has been previously mentioned, this program will generate an SQL statement for each column referenced in the %results hash. You were familiarized with the concept of normalizing data; here, you are normalizing your program. It's entirely possible to replace the effort being made here with something like

```
$sql = "INSERT INTO cust (cu_name, cu_addr1, ...) VALUES
($results{'cu_name'}, $results{'cu_addr1'}, ...)"
```

but this is unnecessary and somewhat problematic; if the structure of the table changes, then the programmer must change not only the form, but also the script. On the other hand, if the programmer relies on 1) the fact that the incoming CGI query data will contain all of the fields needed (except cu_passwd and cu_id, which are exceptions) and 2) the fact that each field starts with the same three characters, then the adduser.pl script can be made smart enough to generate the SQL `SELECT` statement itself.

This brings us back to

```
if (/^cu_/) {
```

Sitting pretty in the middle of the `foreach{}` loop, this little fellow will only execute the code within the `if {}` construct when processing an element of the %results hash which is a field name in CUST. This causes form fields such as:

```
<input type=hidden name=DSN value="EXAMPLE">
```

to be ignored when constructing the SQL `INSERT` statement.

The code that is contained within the if construct takes care of creating two arrays. One is @fields, which contains all of the fields that match the /^cu_/ expression, and the other is @values, which contains all of the corresponding values. You can see the usage of the %noDelim hash, as was previously discussed. Note the funny values $#fields and $#values. These are magic variables that contain the index of the last element in each array. This value is –1 if the array is undefined. Since Perl arrays start at zero, the expression $#fields + 1 will equal zero the first time this line is executed, and the value of $results{$_} will be assigned (correctly) to element zero, which is the first element. The next time the line is executed, the value of $results{$_} is assigned to element one, and so on.

```
if (/^cu_/) {
      $fields[$#fields + 1] = $_;
      if ($noDelim{$_}) {
            $val = "$results{$_}";
      } else {
            $val = "'$results{$_}'";
      }
      $values[$#values + 1] = $val;
}
```

When the loop is finished, the `join()` function is called in to create a comma-delimited list of fields and values, perfect for including in an SQL statement:

```
$fields = join(', ', @fields);
$values = join(', ', @values);
```

After these lines are executed, the value in $fields might look like

```
"cu_city, cu_addr1, cu_id, cu_addr2, cu_lname, cu_state, cu_passwd, cu_zip,
cu_fname"
```

and the value in $values might look like:

```
"'Suffragette City', '462 Eighth Street', '8', 'Apartment 107', 'Jepson',
'RI','NMLUMA', '02800', 'Brian'"
```

Note that the order appears somewhat random. This is due to the way that the hash %results is optimized. Since the arrays @fields and @values are defined side-by-side, the values correspond correctly when the `join()` function is called. Once these two values are defined, the following command can be issued to create a valid SQL `INSERT` statement:

```
$sql = "INSERT INTO cust ($fields) VALUES ($values)";
```

$fields and $values are interpolated into the string, producing something that might look like:

```
INSERT INTO cust
      (cu_city, cu_addr1, cu_id, cu_addr2, cu_lname,
       cu_state, cu_passwd, cu_zip, cu_fname)
      VALUES ('Suffragette City', '462 Eighth Street', '8',
              'Apartment 107', 'Jepson', 'RI', 'NMLMLOUMA', '02800',
              'Brian')
```

None of this will make a whole lot of sense unless you realize that $fields is a scalar variable, and @fields is an array of scalar values. They are not the same variable at all. In order to refer to a scalar value from @fields, something like $fields[1] would be correct.

We've almost reached the end here. Before we can print out whether the `INSERT` succeeded, it must be executed. Going back to the object-oriented toolkit, let's instantiate an `NT::ODBC` object, called $query. It needs the DSN, the USER, and PASSWORD fields from the CGI query. These are interpolated into the connection string that is passed to the `new` method of the `NT::ODBC` class:

```
$dsn      = $results{'DSN'};
$user     = $results{'USER'};
$password = $results{'PASSWORD'};
$query    = new NT::ODBC("DSN=$dsn;UID=$user;PWD=$password;");
```

The `sql ()` method is used to execute the SQL INSERT statement:

```
if ($query->sql($sql)) {
      $error = $query->error;
}
```

And that's all there is to executing the query. Since the `INSERT` statement doesn't return any data, there is no need to get involved with processing the result set from the query. However, we are interested in any errors that might occur. If the `sql()` call returns a non-zero value, it indicates failure and an error has occurred processing the query. If that is the case, we can obtain detailed information about the error by retrieving the results of the `NT::ODBC::error()` method. If there was an error, we can print that out. Otherwise, it might be a good idea to print out some comforting message, as follows.

```
if ($error) {
      print $error;
} else {
      print "Your request has been submitted successfully.<P>";
      print "The new user's password is: $results{'cu_passwd'}.";
}
```

All that now remains is to add the

```
print "</body></html>";
```

to close out the HTML document, and our work is done here. In all its resplendent glory, here is adduser.pl:

```
# -*- Perl -*-
#
#

use NT::ODBC;
use NTNextId;
require "unqpass.pl";

use CGI_Lite;
$cgi     = new CGI_Lite ();
%results = $cgi->parse_form_data ();

print <<EOF;
Content-type: text/html

<html>
```

```
<head>
<title>Request Submitted</title>
</head>
<body>
<h1>Request Submitted</h1>
<hr>
EOF

$id = new NTNextId("C:/TEMP/CUSTID.CNT");
if ($results{'cu_id'} < 0) {
   print <<EOF;
   The server is unable to process your request at this time.<br>
   You may try to submit it again by reloading this page...
EOF
} else {
     $noDelim{'cu_id'} = 1;
     $results{'cu_id'} = nextid $id(10);
     $results{'cu_passwd'} = &unqpass();
     foreach (keys %results) {
       if (/^cu_/) {
            $fields[$#fields + 1] = $_;
            if ($noDelim{$_}) {
              $val = "$results{$_}";
            } else {
              $val = "'$results{$_}'";
            }
            $values[$#values + 1] = $val;
       }
     }

    $fields = join(', ', @fields);
    $values = join(', ', @values);
```

```
        $sql = "INSERT INTO cust ($fields) VALUES ($values)";
        $dsn      = $results{'DSN'};
        $user     = $results{'USER'};
        $password = $results{'PASSWORD'};
        $query    = new NT::ODBC("DSN=$dsn;UID=$user;PWD=$password;");
        if ($query->sql($sql)) {
          $error = $query->error;
        }

        if ($error) {
          print $error;
        } else {
          print "Your request has been submitted successfully.<P>";
          print "The new user's password is: $results{'cu_passwd'}.";
        }
    }
    print "</body></html>";
```

Variations for SQL Server and Microsoft Access Users

If you're using SQL Server or a similar product, this code can be simplified quite a bit. Microsoft SQL Server 6.0 provides a new property called *identity*. Columns having the following datatypes may be assigned this property: int, smallint, tinyint, decimal, and numeric. In order to take advantage of this feature, you need to modify the CREATE TABLE statement found in init5.SQL to read:

```
CREATE TABLE cust
    (cu_fname  char(25),
    cu_lname  char(25),
    cu_id     int identity,
    cu_passwd char(12),
```

```
    cu_addr1  char(25),
    cu_addr2  char(25),
    cu_city   char(30),
    cu_state  char(2),
    cu_zip    char(10))
GO
```

If you're using Microsoft Access, you can specify that the cu_id column have the COUNTER datatype, which accomplishes the same thing.

```
CREATE TABLE cust
    (cu_fname char(25),
    cu_lname  char(25),
    cu_id     counter,
    cu_passwd char(12),
    cu_addr1  char(25),
    cu_addr2  char(25),
    cu_city   char(30),
    cu_state  char(2),
    cu_zip    char(10))
GO
```

Now, every time a new record is INSERTed into the CUST table, the cu_id column is automatically assigned the next sequential id.

When working in a server-based environment, it is critical to let the server take care of assigning the sequential ids. If you wanted to build a Microsoft Access front-end to the dinner theater's database, you couldn't very well have it call the Perl module for generating sequential ids now, could you? And it would be complete chaos to have one Access program for getting the ids, and one Perl program to do the same, and who knows how many others for each front-end you would want to use.

Indeed, it's a lot easier, if you're using a server-based data source, to let this happen on the server! If you use this approach, you can throw out the parts of adduser.pl that assign the value to cu_id. For these data sources, the script should look like:

```
# -*- Perl -*-
#
#

use NT::ODBC;
require "unqpass.pl";

use CGI_Lite;
$cgi     = new CGI_Lite ();
%results = $cgi->parse_form_data ();

print <<EOF;
Content-type: text/html

<HTML>
<HEAD>
<TITLE>Request Submitted</TITLE>
</HEAD>
<BODY>
<H1>Request Submitted</H1>
<HR>
EOF

$results{'cu_passwd'} = &unqpass();
foreach (keys %results) {
    if (/^cu_/) {
      $fields[$#fields + 1] = $_;
      $val = "'$results{$_}'";
      $values[$#values + 1] = $val;
    }
```

```
}

$fields = join(', ', @fields);
$values = join(', ', @values);

$sql = "INSERT INTO cust ($fields) VALUES ($values)";
$dsn      = $results{'DSN'};
$user     = $results{'USER'};
$password = $results{'PASSWORD'};
$query    = new NT::ODBC("DSN=$dsn;UID=$user;PWD=$password;");
if ($query->sql($sql)) {
    $error = $query->error;
}

if ($error) {
    print $error;
} else {
    print "Your request has been submitted successfully.<P>";
    print "The new user's password is: $results{'cu_passwd'}.";
}

print "</BODY></HTML>";
```

Other datasources, such as SYBASE System 10, provide similar capabilities. You will need to modify the init5.sql script to take advantage of these features.

CHAPTER

6

COMPLEX DATA ENTRY

Actually, the title of this chapter is a bit of a lie. The data entry itself is not complex. Rather, the nature of the problem is a little complex. Data entry, and user interfaces in general, should never have to be complex.

In the previous chapter, you learned how to put together a simple HTML form which adds names to the CUST table. Now, you'll work out a way for customers to make reservations. In order to make their life simpler, this task will be accomplished using the friendly *wizard* interface. Anyone who has installed Windows 95 or used some of the Microsoft Office tools will recognize a wizard. You can hardly click on anything in Windows 95 without bringing up a wizard (is this good or bad?). For those of you who have never seen a wizard before, now's a good time to become familiar with it.

The Wizard Interface

A wizard is a simple series of screens which presents the users with a sequence of simple steps. In most cases, the users are not going through these steps without a purpose. They are usually trying to accomplish something. At each step, the users are asked a few painless questions. When they are finished, they have performed data entry which might have been a little intimidating, had they done it the "Usual Way." The "Usual Way" involves a monolithic (I promised a friend of mine I would use that word in the book) screen with hundreds of buttons and fields, and can scare off novice users. Wizards are a painless approach to data entry tasks. Figures 6.1 and 6.2 show examples of screens from the Microsoft Word Resume Wizard.

Since you are implementing a data entry system on the Web, this approach is quite useful. Many of the options available in the screens will be dependent upon selections made by the user. For example, you are providing a picklist of available show dates. You would like this list to be filtered based upon which play the user has selected or whether he or she has reserved up to his or her limit for that day, and so forth. Unfortunately, HTML and CGI scripts do not allow for this sort of dynamic interplay between screen

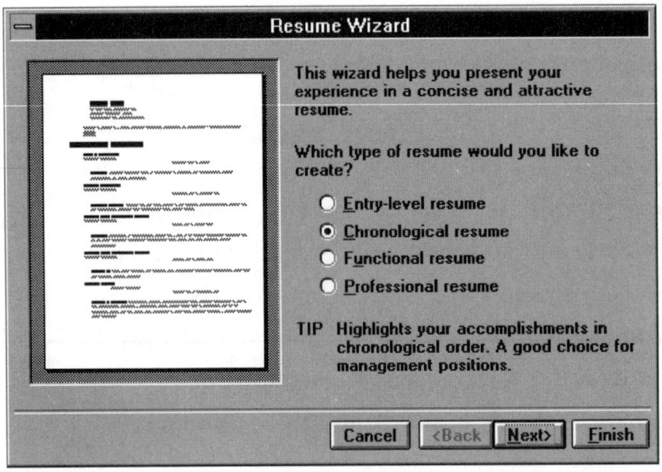

Figure 6.1 Screen from Microsoft Word Resume Wizard.

elements; the play listbox cannot tell the dates listbox that the currently selected play only runs in September. Since you cannot dynamically update a list of available seats based on user input, the results of each form must be processed, and a new form must be presented with the correct options available. Fortunately, this more or less describes how the typical wizard works.

There are certain things we need to get from the users. Their names might be a good place to start. Rather than present the users with a picklist of names, you can let them type their name in. If more than one name is matched, the user can choose from the list. The Reservation Wizard, as we will call it, should also capture the name of the play that the customer would like to attend. Also, the performance date and number of people in their party would be helpful, followed by (naturally) a seat selection.

Figure 6.3 shows how you might implement the data entry screen in a Windows-based programming environment. When the user chooses the name of a play, the combo box (or pull-down) with the list of dates is updated to show which dates are available for that play. As was previously mentioned, this is not possible with an HTML form; a restricted list of these choices must be made available on a subsequent page.

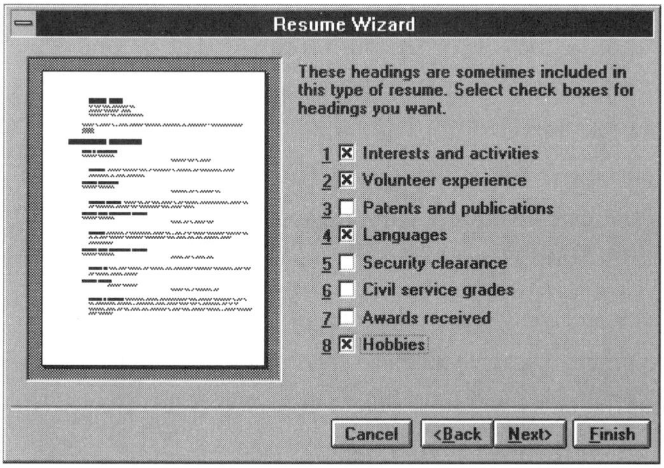

Figure 6.2 Screen from Microsoft Word Resume Wizard.

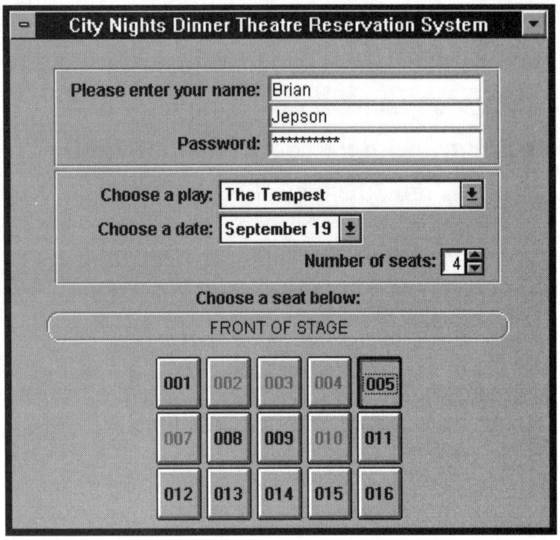

Figure 6.3 Implementing the data entry screen in a Windows-based environment.

Since each Web page is dependent upon the previous, certain tidbits of information must be preserved between pages. These will be passed through CGI variables and a neat feature called a *shopping cart.* As each of the pages is developed, you'll see how easy it is to maintain "state" between forms.

The first web page will include a form which prompts the user for his or her first name, last name, and the play he or she wishes to see. The second page will present the user with a list of names which most closely matches the user's name. This minimizes the possibility of data entry errors. The user can click on the name to move to the next page. The third page provides a form which allows the user to choose from a list of performance dates and select the number of people in the party.

The fourth page gives the user a crudely drawn diagram of the theater, which shows each table and the number of seats available. Only tables which have sufficient seats for the size of the party will have links to the next page. The user merely selects the desired table, and it's on to the next page.

The fifth page summarizes the reservation preferences and prompts the user for his or her password. When the user clicks on the form button, he or she is told whether the reservation was accepted by the server.

We'll be adding a couple of new tables at this point. In the previous chapter, the CUST table was introduced. Its primary key is cu_id; some of the tables defined in this chapter will refer to it. Here are some of the tables that we've worked with already:

PLAYS

Field	Type	Size	Description
py_id	int	n/a	Primary key (unique identifier)
py_name	char	35	Name of the play
py_au_id_	int	n/a	Primary key in authors table
py_desc	char	254	Description of the play

CUST

Field	Type	Size	Description
cu_fname	char	25	First name
cu_lname	char	25	Last name
cu_id	int	n/a	Primary key (unique identifier)
cu_passwd	char	12	Password
cu_addr1	char	25	Address
cu_addr2	char	25	Address
cu_city	char	30	City
cu_state	char	2	State
cu_zip	char	10	Zip code

Here are the new tables that are introduced in this chapter.

SHOWS

Field	Type	Size	Description
sh_py_id_	int	n/a	Play id
sh_date	date	n/a	Performance date

RESERVE

Field	Type	Size	Description
re_cu_id_	int	n/a	Customer id
re_py_id	int	n/a	Play id
re_sh_date	date	n/a	Performance date
re_table	char	4	Table id
re_seats	int	n/a	Number of seats to reserve

SHOWS contains a reference to the PLAYS table. Each record in SHOWS corresponds to a performance date of the play referenced by SH_PY_ID_. For the purposes of this book, we are only allowing one performance of each play per day.

RESERVE contains a cross-reference between CUST, PLAYS, and SHOWS. A record in this table tells us which customer has reserved how many seats at which table for a given performance of a given play.

Building a Wizard

The Wizard will be implemented using six Web pages. Each page will contain either a form or a series of hyperlinks. As you have seen, an HTML form can have multiple input fields, which may be of varying types. Most of them will perform roughly the same activities; the first will involve parsing out the WWW form data, whether it is encoded within a URL or sent via a POST method. The next step may involve performing one or more database queries. The results of these queries are used in the next step, which is to generate an HTML form using the result set.

Persistence

What happens to the information that the user enters on each page of the Wizard? Each page of the Wizard is dynamically generated from a Perl script. Each page offers some sort of choice to the user, which then must be passed on to the next form. There are two possibilities for how this can be handled. One way is to dynamically generate a Web page which is composed solely of hyperlinks; the user can then select an option from the hyperlink, which is linked to a script. Steps two and four will use this approach. The second way is to use an HTML form; whatever the user selects is posted to the script. The two approaches do not differ too much.

One of the problems with either approach is that each consecutive session accumulates a lot of information which must be maintained until the last page. It is possible to embed the information in each URL that gets passed on, but that means the URL keeps getting bigger and bigger; wouldn't it be nice if there was an elegant way?

Shopping Carts

Well, there is an easier way. A *shopping cart* is a kind of virtual depository for information between Web pages. When you create a shopping cart, your Perl script gets a unique identifier, which lets you find the shopping cart in subsequent CGI scripts. All you have to do with each page is make sure that the cart id makes it into the URL of any hyperlinks or into a hidden field in the form that you use. Once you have the shopping cart, it is good for an hour (it gets deleted after that point) and you can put values in it and take them out until you are finished. So, in step two, you can put the id of the play that was selected in step one and take it out again when you need it in step three. What could be simpler?

Reservation Wizard: Step One

The object of step one is to supply the user with a screen from which he or she can choose a play and type in his or her first and last name. The only values that must be sent to this script are the data source name, the user name (if required), and the password (if required). Here's an example of a URL which can be used to call up this page of the wizard using a SQL Server data source which has been configured as MSSQL:

```
http://localhost/ch6/reswiz01.pl?DSN=MSSQL&USER=wwwuser
```

The first thing that this script needs to do is use three Perl modules. CGI_Lite.pm is used to parse out the CGI query variables (DSN, USER, PASSWORD), NT::ODBC.pm manages the ODBC connection and queries, and Cart.pm is used to maintain the shopping cart.

```
# -*- Perl -*-
#
# Reservation Wizard: Page 1
#

use CGI_Lite;
use NT::ODBC;
use Cart;
```

As shown in previous chapters, the CGI_Lite object is instantiated, the `CGI_Lite::parse_form_data()` method is called, and its return value is assigned to an associative array called %results.

```
######################################
#
# parse the results of the CGI query
```

```
#
####################################
$cgi = new CGI_Lite;
%results = $cgi->parse_form_data ();
```

Once the results of the CGI variables are stored in %results, they can be moved into Perl variables for more convenient handling.

```
$dsn    = $results{'DSN'};
$user   = $results{'USER'};
$passwd = $results{'PASSWORD'};
```

In order to set up a shopping cart, the script must call the Cart::new method. Once a new Cart is instantiated, then the Cart::getitem method can be called to retrieve that cart's id:

```
####################################
#
# set up a new shopping cart
#
####################################
$cart = new Cart;
$cartid = $cart->getitem('id');
```

The three ODBC variables ($dsn, $user, $password) will be very nice to have in subsequent steps of the wizard. Now is a good time to "drop" them into the shopping cart and write out the cart to disk.

```
####################################
#
# Add the ODBC connection info to
# the shopping cart
#
####################################
$cart->additem("DSN", $dsn);
$cart->additem("USER", $user);
```

```
$cart->additem("PASSWORD", $passwd);
$cart->writeitems;
```

The next bit of Perl causes a generic HTML document header to come up. This includes the title, a header, and a horizontal rule to make things look pretty. The advantage of placing the HTML header here is that if any errors come up, they can be printed, the script can terminate, and the user will be able to see the message. If an error message is printed without so much as a content-type string, the best the user can hope for is "404 Not Found," which is not terribly helpful.

```
######################################
#
# here-doc syntax to print out the
# top part of the HTML document
#
######################################
print <<EOF;
Content-type: text/html

<html>
<head>
<title>The Reservation Wizard</title>
</head>

<body>

<h1>The Reservation Wizard</h1>
<hr>
EOF
```

A Little More SQL

A little bit further down, you will see this script create a couple of lists. One is a `select` element, which provides a list of all plays. The second is an HTML table, which provides a list of plays and performances for handy reference. To make this possible, an SQL SELECT statement is now issued, which retrieves play names and other information:

```
####################################
#
# issue an SQL SELECT statement to
# get a list of all plays, along
# with their start and end dates
#
####################################
$query = NT::ODBC->new("DSN=$dsn;UID=$user;PWD=$passwd");
if ($query->sql("SELECT py_name,
                         MIN(sh_date) AS dtstart,
                         MAX(sh_date) AS dtend
                      FROM plays, shows
                      WHERE sh_py_id_ = py_id
                      GROUP BY py_name
                      ORDER BY 2")) {

   print $query->error;
   print "</body></html>";
   exit;
}
```

Notice that the SHOWS table is joined to the PLAYS table with py_id = sh_py_id_. This `SELECT` statement makes use of the `GROUP BY` clause, and causes the result set to group on the name of the play. The `GROUP BY` clause works in conjunction with the aggregate functions `MIN()` and `MAX()` to produce summary values for each column in the `GROUP BY` clause. If, for example, the play “Antigone” has four performance dates—12/01/97, 12/08/97, 12/15/97, and 12/22/97—and the play “Frankenstein” has four performance dates—01/01/98, 01/08/98, 01/15/98, and 01/22/98—then the results from this SELECT statement would look like:

py_name	dtstart	dtend
Antigone	12/01/97	12/22/97
Frankenstein	01/01/98	01/22/98

This SQL `SELECT` statement also includes an `ORDER BY` clause. This clause can take a list of columns as an argument, each of which may be optionally followed by the ASC or DESC modifier, which causes that particular column to sort ascending or descending, respectively. If neither modifier is included, ASC is assumed. The `ORDER BY` clause can also take the column's numeric position. In this case, the results of the `SELECT` statement are `ORDER`ed `BY` column 2, which happens to be the first (`MIN`) starting date for each play. If an error occurred in the SQL statement, the error message is printed out and the script terminates.

If an error was not encountered, the script continues normally. Since all is going well, the data entry form can be displayed. This form will offer fields for first name and last name, and also provide a list of plays. The cart id is included as a hidden field. This isn't a security precaution; it hides the complexity from the user by keeping the field hidden. Even though a user cannot see a hidden field, the hidden field and its value become part of the CGI query just like all the other fields when the form is submitted. The first two text fields allow the user to type in first and last name; before the here-doc is terminated, a `<select>` tag appears. But, no options have been assigned to the select field. These are added with the `<option>` tag and will come directly from the results of the SQL query.

```
######################################
#
# here-doc syntax to print out a
# form that the users can put their
# name in; they can also choose the
```

```
# play here.
#
######################################
print <<EOF;
Step 1: Please enter in your user name and the play you wish to reserve for.
<br>
(A list of plays and run dates appear below)
<form action="reswiz02.pl" method=get>
                  <input type="hidden" name="cartid" value="$cartid">
      First Name: <input type="text" name="cu_fname"><p>
       Last Name: <input type="text" name="cu_lname"><p>
   Choose a play: <select name="py_name">
EOF
```

Using NT::ODBC::fetchrow, each row in the result set is retrieved. For each of these rows, an `<option>` tag is displayed, followed by the name of the play. While this loop iterates over the results of the query, a variable named $summary is also being populated, to be used later on, after the form is done. It is going to contain the "meat" of an HTML table which consists of a list of plays and their start and end dates. At the end of this HTML document, this variable will be interpolated into a here-doc which includes a `table` element. This is a reference table which enables the users to see which dates are available for each play.

```
#####################################
#
# add each play to the popup in the
# form. As we go, we'll also create
# the summary entries in the variable
# $summary.
#
#####################################
while ($query->fetchrow) {
```

```
    $py_name = $query->data('py_name');
    $start   = $query->data('dtstart');
    $end     = $query->data('dtend');
    print "<option>$py_name";
    $summary .= "<tr><td>$py_name</td><td>$start</td><td>$end</td></tr>";
  }
```

When the `while()` loop is finished, another here-doc is employed to print the `</select>` tag, which terminates the `select` element. The final object added to the form is a submit button, which causes the values in the form to be sent to the form's action target: reswiz02.pl.

When the `form` element is terminated with the `</form>`, a table is displayed with headers for Play, Start Date, and End Date. Then, the variable $summary is interpolated; this produces the meat of the table. Finally, the `table` element is terminated with `</table>`, and so is the HTML body and document, with `</body></html>`. Figure 6.4 shows what the finished form looks like in the Netscape browser.

```
####################################
#
# Close the form and put up a table
# for the list of plays, with the
# $summary variable embedded.
# Then the HTML document can be
# closed.
#
####################################
print <<EOF;
   </select><P>
   <input type="submit" value="Next">
</form>

<table border>
```

```
<th>Play</th><th>From</th><th>To</th>

$summary

</table>
</body>
</html>
EOF
```

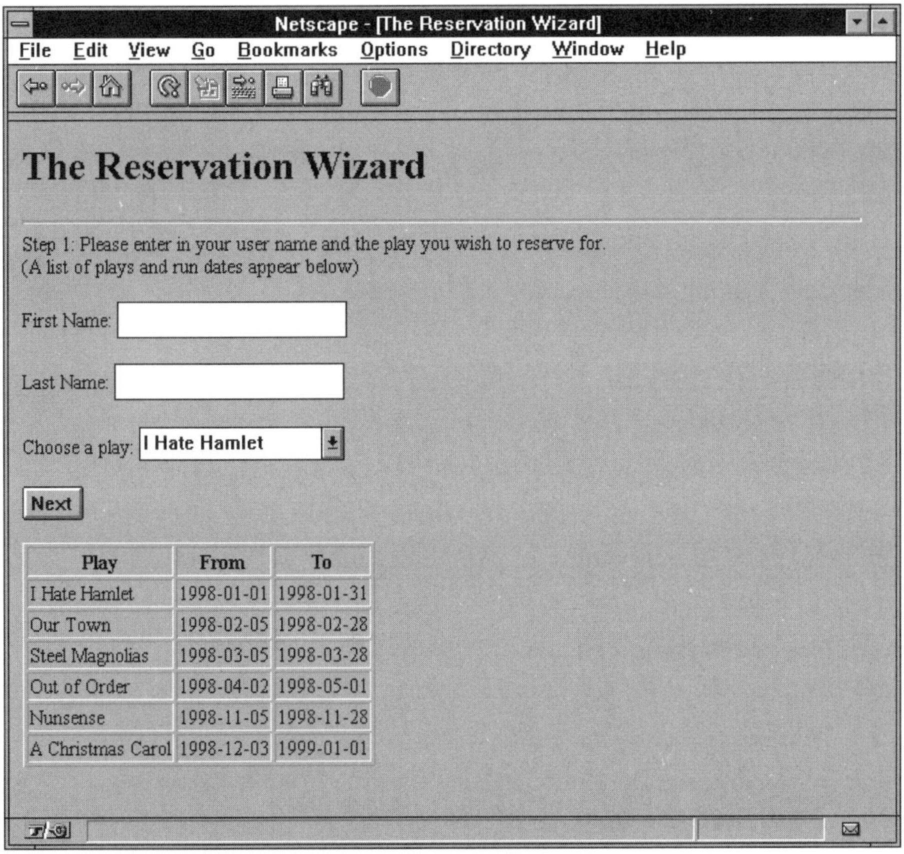

Figure 6.4 The first Reservation Wizard form.

Reservation Wizard: Step Two

The next step in the Reservation Wizard allows the user to select his or her name from a list of possible matches. In order to do this, the name entered in step one must be compared against the CUST table.

After step two, there are four more steps. Throughout all of these, it is essential to *remember* certain things that the user selected along the way. One of these is the name of the play. Well, it's not exactly the name. It's a lot more efficient to pass the id of the play from step-to-step; you can always get the name using the id. However, at step two, all you have is the name. Another SQL query will need to be made during step two: finding out the play id based on the name the user selected.

Like all of the other steps in the Wizard, step two must use NT::ODBC, CGI_Lite, and Cart:

```
# -*- Perl -*-
#
# Reservation Wizard: Page 2
#

use NT::ODBC;
use CGI_Lite;
use Cart;
```

The results of the CGI query must be parsed into the %results associative array:

```
####################################
#
# parse the results of the CGI query
#
####################################
$cgi = new CGI_Lite;
%results = $cgi->parse_form_data ();
```

In order to ease the manipulation of the CGI query values, the values in %results will be stored as Perl scalar variables. The first name and last name fields are going to be treated differently than other CGI query values you have seen so far. When they are compared against possible matches in the CUST table, they are used in a wildcard comparison; it would be helpful if they (and the value they were to be compared to) were in the same case. When the SQL `SELECT` statement is created, the `UCASE()` function will be used to uppercase the columns in the search expression, but when the Perl variables are created for the first and last name, they will be uppercased as follows:

```
####################################
#
# uppercase the first and last name
# that came in from the
# CGI query
#
####################################
$ucfname = "\U$results{'cu_fname'}";
$uclname = "\U$results{'cu_lname'}";
```

The \U modifier is shown within a double-quoted string. The \U tells Perl to uppercase until the end of the string or until Perl encounters a \E. Since interpolation occurs within double-quoted strings, whatever the user put in as his or her first and last name is uppercased and stored in the variables $ucfname and $uclname, respectively.

Another variable which is included in the CGI query is the py_name variable. It contains the name of the play that the user selected in step one:

```
####################################
#
# assign the play name to a variable
#
####################################
$py_name = $results{'py_name'};
```

Next, a here-doc is used to print out the HTML document header, and the body with a title and horizontal rule.

```
####################################
#
# print out a basic here-doc to put
# up required HTML stuff and some
# header info
#
####################################
print <<EOF;
Content-type: text/html

<html>
<head>
<title>The Reservation Wizard</title>
</head>
<body>
<h1>The Reservation Wizard</h1>
<hr>
EOF
```

The CGI query also included the unique id of this user's shopping cart. This is stored as $cartid, and is passed to the Cart::new method. This tells Cart to use the old cart when the object is instantiated. If the cart is still on the server (it resides as a file on disk), then the new Cart object created here picks up what is in the cart. The name of the method, `new`, might be a little confusing. It is used to create a new Cart object. However, one of the attributes of a Cart object is the id of the actual shopping cart. So, although you must instantiate a new Cart for each Perl script that uses a cart, it can be a cart left over from a previous script. And that is the heart of how persistence works here: a new script can pick up the cart that belonged to an old script; the id of the cart is passed between scripts via the CGI query variable cartid. If an error occurred instantiating or initializing the cart, the error is printed, and the script terminates. This can occur if the user has left the cart sitting around too long; they have a lifespan of 3,600 seconds (1 hour).

```
####################################
#
# set up the shopping cart
#
####################################
$cartid = $results{'cartid'};
$cart = new Cart($cartid);
if ($cart->{'error'}) {
  print $cart->{'error'};
  exit;
}
```

All of the ODBC connection data is sitting in the cart. If you are to perform any SQL statements in this script, you better pull this information out.

```
####################################
#
# take the ODBC connection info
# out of the cart.
#
####################################
$dsn    = $cart->getitem('DSN');
$user   = $cart->getitem('USER');
$passwd = $cart->getitem('PASSWORD');
```

Next, an NT::ODBC object ($query) is instantiated, which will be used to process the queries in this script. The next step is to use the $query object to issue an SQL SELECT statement; this SELECT will retrieve the list of all plays that have the same name as the one the user selected.

```
####################################
#
# issue an SQL Statement to get the
```

```
# id of the play which was
# selected in the previous form
#
####################################
$query = new NT::ODBC("DSN=$dsn;UID=$user;PWD=$passwd;");
if ($query->sql("SELECT py_id FROM plays
                      WHERE py_name = '$py_name'")) {
  print $query->error;
  print "</body></html>";
  exit;
}
```

If an error occurs in this select statement, it is printed out and the script terminates. As there should only be one play in this result set, it is only a matter of calling NT::ODBC::fetchrow() once. The NT::ODBC::fetchrow method grabs the row from the result set, making it available through the NT::ODBC::data method. You only need to pass the name of the column that you want and it is returned. Here, you can do a neat little trick with the assignment. If you parenthesize an assignment in Perl, as is done in the following example, you can use the =~ operator to bind the assignment to a substitution. After the value of $query->data(py_id) is assigned to $py_id, $py_id is modified by the substitution. The s/\s//g simply removes any blanks from the expression. Once this value is retrieved, it is dropped into the cart and the cart is written out to disk for use by later scripts.

```
####################################
#
# fetch the row from the result set
# (there should only be one), then
# grab the py_id column and strip
# any blanks and add it to the
# shopping cart.
#
####################################
```

```
$query->fetchrow;
($py_id = $query->data('py_id')) =~ s/\s//g;

$cart->additem("py_id", $py_id);
$cart->writeitems;
```

Another SQL `SELECT` is issued; it uses the LIKE predicate to find all names which match those entered by the user in step one. The variables $ucfname and $uclname are included in the matching expressions, surrounded by the % (wildcard) character. Further, these expressions are compared to the uppercased cu_fname and cu_lname using the LIKE predicate.

This SQL `SELECT` will return first names, last names, and ids of any names matching what the user typed. For example, if the user put in "B Jepson," the `SELECT` would retrieve any person whose first name started with a "B" and whose last name was Jepson. If the user just put in "Brian," then the SELECT would retrieve everyone named Brian. If an error occurred, it is printed and the script terminates.

```
####################################
#
# issue an SQL Statement to retrieve
# customer names which match what the
# user typed.
#
# Note the use of ODBC scalar function
# extensions in calling the UCASE()
# function.
#
####################################
if ($query->sql("SELECT cu_fname, cu_lname, cu_id
                       FROM cust
                       WHERE {fn UCASE(cu_fname)} LIKE '%$ucfname%'
                       AND   {fn UCASE(cu_lname)} LIKE '%$uclname%'")) {
```

```
    print $query->error;
    print "</body></html>";
    exit;
  }
```

Now that the SQL SELECT has been issued, it remains to do something meaningful with the results. The following section of code will iterate over each row in the result set, producing a series of hyperlinks to the next step of the Reservation Wizard. These links will be a URL which includes the customer id, with the first name and last name of the customer as the text of the link. The URL will also contain a field for the cart id, so the next script can take values out of the cart (and put some in). One link will be displayed for each name that is matched. Here's an example of what the URL might look like for the customer whose cu_id is equal to 1:

```
http://192.168.254.17/ch6/reswiz03.pl?cu_id=1&cartid=0008202753100147
```

In order to build this URL, the variables $cu_id, $cu_fname, and $cu_lname will be defined for each row in the result set. These are combined into the $namelist variable, which contains a running list of all the links. The links are simply appended to the end each time the loop iterates. This link makes use of the anchor (<a>) element, with the href attribute (a hyperlink), and includes a line break (<br>) after it, to keep the links from running into each other.

```
####################################
#
# create a series of links, each
# linked to the reswiz03.pl script, but
# containing a cust id corresponding
# to each name which was matched in
# the SQL SELECT just issued.
#
####################################
while ($query->fetchrow) {
```

```
    $cu_id    = $query->data('cu_id');
    $cu_fname = $query->data('cu_fname');
    $cu_lname = $query->data('cu_lname');

    $namelist .= "<a href=reswiz03.pl?cu_id=$cu_id&cartid=$cartid>" .
      "$cu_fname $cu_lname</a><br>\n";
  }
```

The variable $namelist is tested within the `if()` construct. Remember, in Perl, a non-zero value will evaluate to true. So, if there is anything in the $namelist, the user is prompted to choose his or her name and the list is printed. Otherwise, the user is told that no names matched the one typed in.

```
####################################
#
# If there are any names in the list,
# print the list out. Otherwise,
# print out an error message.
#
####################################
if ($namelist) {
  print "Step 2: Please choose your name from the list:<P>";
  print $namelist;
} else {
    print "There were no names matching your query.";
}
```

The next step is to print out the HTML tags needed to close the `body` and `html` elements:

```
# the final HTML tags:
#
print "</body></html>";
```

That wraps up step two of the reservation wizard. Figure 6.5 shows an example of what this web page might look like.

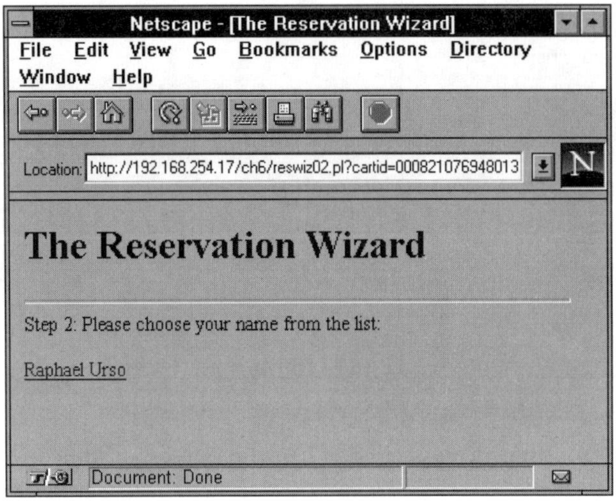

Figure 6.5 The second Reservation Wizard form.

Reservation Wizard: Step Three

The pace will pick up a little bit now; you've seen most of the techniques that will be used in building this wizard. Step three builds on these techniques. As with the other steps of the wizard, the modules NT::ODBC, CGI_Lite, and Cart are used here. A new CGI_Lite object is instantiated, and a customer id is pulled out of the %results associative array and stored in a Perl variable.

```
# -*- Perl -*-
#
# Reservation Wizard: Page 3
#

use NT::ODBC;
use CGI_Lite;
use Cart;

$maxparty = 4;
```

```
####################################
#
# parse the results of the CGI query
#
####################################
$cgi = new CGI_Lite;
%results = $cgi->parse_form_data ();
$cu_id  = $results{'cu_id'};
```

The variable $maxparty is defined; it is the maximum number of seats that may be reserved. This is later dropped into the cart and used in other modules where necessary. So, if you need to change it, you only need to change it in this script.

The HTML header and part of the body goes up next.

```
####################################
#
# print out a basic here-doc to put
# up required HTML stuff
#
####################################
print <<EOF;
Content-type: text/html


<html>
<head>
<title>The Reservation Wizard</title>
</head>
<body>
<h1>The Reservation Wizard</h1>
<hr>
EOF
```

The Cart is now instantiated, and the cu_id is put into the cart, while the data source name, user, password, and play id are taken out of the cart.

```
###################################
#
# set up the shopping cart
#
###################################
$cartid = $results{'cartid'};
$cart = new Cart($cartid);

if ($cart->{'error'}) {
  print $cart->{'error'};
  exit;
}

###################################
#
# Add customer id and maximum party
# size to the cart.
#
###################################
$cart->additem("cu_id", $cu_id);
$cart->additem("maxparty", $maxparty);
$cart->writeitems;

###################################
#
# take the ODBC connection info
# and play id out of the cart.
#
###################################
```

```
$dsn    = $cart->getitem('DSN');
$user   = $cart->getitem('USER');
$passwd = $cart->getitem('PASSWORD');
$py_id  = $cart->getitem('py_id');
```

The mission of this Web page is to have the user (1) choose the desired performance date and (2) pick the number of people in the party. Since all of the tables in the dinner theater schema are so well-designed (hah!), it's quite simple to obtain a list of performance dates for a given play. The SQL SELECT

```
SELECT sh_date FROM shows WHERE sh_py_id_ = $py_id
```

will do the trick. After instantiating a new NT::ODBC object, that object is used to process this query:

```
####################################
#
# issue a SELECT statement which
# will retrieve all available show
# dates for the selected play.
#
####################################
$query = new NT::ODBC ("DSN=$dsn;UID=$user;PWD=$passwd;");
if ($query->sql("select sh_date
                        from shows
                        where sh_py_id_ = $py_id
                        order by sh_date")) {
  print $query->error;
  print "</body></html>";
  exit;
}
```

As always, if an error occurred, the error message is printed and the script exits.

Another here-doc is included to prompt the user and display a form. The action target of this form is, naturally, the next step in the wizard (reswiz04.pl). It includes hidden fields for the cart id. Next, a plain-text prompt appears, "Choose Performance," and is followed by a select form field. As with the select form field in step one, this produces a pop-up list. The values in this list will come from the SQL SELECT statement issued earlier.

```
####################################
#
# print out a prompt and the first
# part of the form
#
####################################
print <<EOF;
Step 3. Please select the performance date and the number of people in your
party (no more than $maxparty).

<form action="reswiz04.pl" method=get>
 <input type="hidden" name="cartid" value="$cartid">
 Choose Performance: <select name="py_date">
EOF
```

The NT::ODBC::fetchrow method is called, along with the NT::ODBC::data method; this makes it simple to print out one `<option>` for each record in the result set. Each option corresponds to one bar on the pop-up.

```
####################################
#
# add each performance to the select
# form object
#
####################################
```

```
while ($query->fetchrow) {
    $sh_date = $query->data('sh_date');
    print "<option>$sh_date";
}
```

Another `<select>` form field is created, but this one allows the user to choose the number of people in his or her party.

```
####################################
#
# create a select form object for the
# number of people in the party.
#
####################################
print <<EOF;
   </select><p>
    Number in Party: <select name="count">
EOF
```

The `for()` construct is used to create one pop-up bar for each choice. The `for()` construct is similar to the `for()` construct found in C and the `for...next` loop found in BASIC and xBase. It generally looks like:

```
for ($value = start-value; $value operator comparison-value; increment-expression) {
   Perl code goes here...
}
```

Here's an example:

```
for ($x = 1; $x < 10; $x++) {
   print "$x\n";
}
```

The previous example initializes the variable \$x to 1 at the start of the loop (\$x = 1) and executes the loop while \$x continues to be less than 10 (\$x < 10). For each iteration of the loop, \$x++ is executed, which increments \$x by 1. There's a shorthand for this, which looks like:

```
for (start-value .. end-value) {
   Perl code goes here...
}
```

As is the case with many things in Perl, the value of the loop index goes into $_. This is the syntax that our script uses. It starts a loop at 1, and ends at the value of $maxparty. This is a convenient way of looping from 1 to whatever the value of $maxparty is; while in the loop, an <option> can be printed out, followed by whatever is in $_ (the current loop index).

```
for (1..$maxparty) {
     print "<option>$_";
}
```

Now, all that remains is to clean up a little. The select element needs to be terminated with the `</select>` tag, the submit form field needs to be displayed, and the form needs to be terminated with `</form>`. Also, the body and html element are terminated with `</body>` and `</html>`:

```
print <<EOF;
   </select><p>
   <input type="submit" value="Next">
</form>
</body>
</html>
EOF
```

Thus ends the third Web page which comprises the reservation wizard. Figure 6.6 shows what this will look like.

Reservation Wizard: Step Four

Step four of the reservation wizard performs some rather interesting, even amusing tricks with HTML. By now, you are used to seeing the following

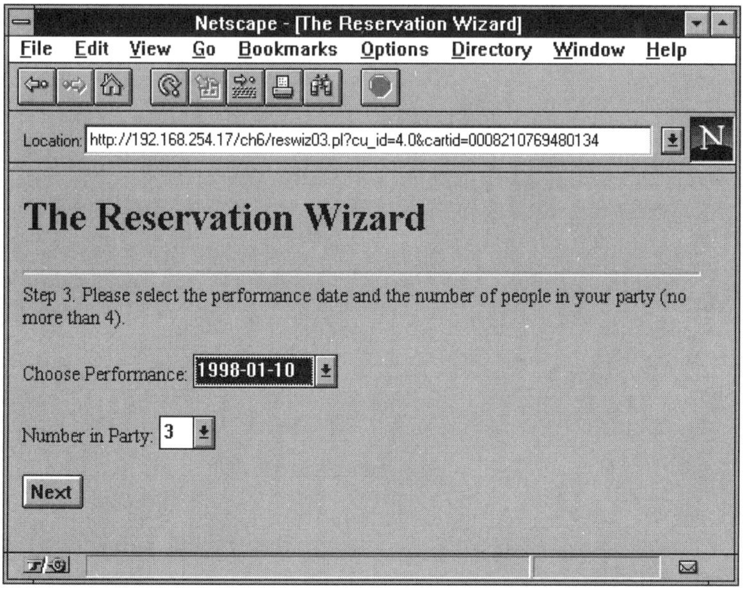

Figure 6.6 The third Reservation Wizard form.

items: use of NT::ODBC, CGI_Lite, and Cart; the parsing of the CGI query; the HTML document header and some of the body; the shopping cart getting set up, inserting any new items, and pulling out any old items. This all goes on in the following code. The new items retrieved from the CGI query (and then placed in the cart) are the number of people in the party and the play date.

```
# -*- Perl -*-
#
# Reservation Wizard: Page 4
#

use NT::ODBC;
use CGI_Lite;
use Cart;
```

```
####################################
#
# parse the results of the CGI query
#
####################################
$cgi = new CGI_Lite;
%results = $cgi->parse_form_data ();

($py_date = $results{'py_date'}) =~ s/\s.+// ;
$count     = $results{'count'};

####################################
#
# print out a basic here-doc to put
# up required HTML stuff
#
####################################
print <<EOF;
Content-type: text/html

<html>
<head>
<title>The Reservation Wizard</title>
</head>
<body.>
<h1>Seat Selection</h1>
EOF

####################################
#
# set up the shopping cart
#
```

```
####################################
$cartid = $results{'cartid'};
$cart = new Cart($cartid);
if ($cart->{'error'}) {
  print $cart->{'error'};
  exit;
}

####################################
#
# Add play date and number of people
# in the part to the cart.
#
####################################
$cart->additem("count", $count);
$cart->additem("py_date", $py_date);
$cart->writeitems;

####################################
#
# take the ODBC connection info and
# other persistent variables out of
# the cart.
#
####################################
$dsn      = $cart->getitem('DSN');
$user     = $cart->getitem('USER');
$passwd   = $cart->getitem('PASSWORD');
$py_id    = $cart->getitem('py_id');
$maxparty = $cart->getitem('maxparty');
$cu_id    = $cart->getitem('cu_id');
```

The interesting part of this script is how the problem of determining and displaying available seats is tackled. The performance date of the play is known and the number of seats the customer wants is known, as well. What remains is to determine where the customer will sit. The theater, being a dinner theater, seats its customers at tables (not database tables, the real, wooden thing!). There are several tables in a row and the food is served family style.

Fortunately, through the miracle of interactivity, the customers can have some say at which table their party sits. If it can be assumed that there are a finite number of rows, a finite number of tables in each row, and the same number of seats at each table, then this problem is actually quite simple. Fortunately, since this is a fictional system, I can make it up as I go along.

At the beginning of this chapter, you saw the definition for a table called RESERVE. In it, there was a customer id, a play id, a date, a table id, and a number of seats. Unlike the other ids, the table id does not refer to a table id somewhere in a table table (a table of tables? what is this world coming to?). Instead, tables are numbered, beginning with stage right. If you are standing on the stage, facing the tables, your right is stage right; if you are in the audience, it is the left. Now you know a lot about theater. The tables start with 001, and number from stage right to stage left, with the next row continuing from stage right until you hit the back wall of the theater.

In order to determine availability of seats, the following SQL `SELECT` is issued:

```
####################################
#
# Issue a select statement to find
# out which tables are assigned
# on the performance date that the
# user selected. This will also
```

```
# total up the number of seats
# assigned at each table.
#
####################################
$query = new NT::ODBC("DSN=$dsn;UID=$user;PWD=$password;");

if ($query->sql("SELECT re_table, SUM(re_seats) AS tot_seats
                    FROM reserve
                    WHERE re_py_id_  = $py_id
                    AND   re_sh_date = {d '$py_date'}
                    GROUP BY re_table")) {
  print $query->error;
  print "</body></html>";
  exit;
}
```

As always, if an error occurred, it is displayed and the script exits. This `SELECT` statement makes use of the `GROUP BY`. All of the rows in the table reserve are selected which have the re_py_id_ equal to the play the user selected way back in step one and the re_sh_date_ equal to the show date the user selected in the last step. Note the use of the ODBC date extension to ensure that the date string is evaluated as a date and not as a string. It takes the form YYYY—MM—DD.

The `GROUP BY` clause causes this `SELECT` statement to return only one row for each table, with a column called tot_seats. This column is the `SUM` of all the seats reserved for each table on that performance date. This is necessary, since several parties may reserve seats at each table.

This script is going to display a crude diagram of the theater. Each table will be represented and the user will have the option to select the table he or she wants to reserve via a hyperlink. However, tables which are already booked up, or which do not have enough seats to accommodate the users' party size, must not allow the hyperlink to appear. In order to determine how many seats are booked at each table, this script must perform a lookup based on the id of the table. Suppose the script were trying to determine how many seats were reserved at table 003. Right now, it's difficult to ascertain, because that information is stored in the results of the `SELECT` statement, which have not been read yet. What the script needs is an associative array indexed by table number, which contains the number of tables reserved, so the following expression

```
$assigned{'003'}
```

would yield the number of people already assigned to that table. Well, Perl makes this surprisingly easy to do.

```
####################################
#
# build a hash of all assigned tables,
# so we can tell them how many seats
# are left...
#
####################################
while ($query->fetchrow) {
  $assigned{$query->data('re_table')} = $query->data('tot_seats');
}
```

The familiar `while($query->fetchrow) { ... }` construct is used here, but with a twist. For each row in the result set, the associative array %assigned is updated, with $query->data(re_table) as the array index, and $query->data(tot_seats) as the value.

Everything is in place to draw the table diagrams. Before that happens, though, the user is prompted with a little information.

```
####################################
#
# a here-doc to prompt the user
#
####################################
```

```
print <<EOF;
Each "box" below shows a table. The first number is the table
number, and the second is the number of seats available
for the selected show. If you wish to reserve a particular table,
simply select one of the highlighted table numbers.<p>
<PRE>
F R O N T  O F  S T A G E    F R O N T  O F  S T A G E
EOF
```

Three critical variables are set up here:

```
####################################
#
# The variable $srows is the number
# of rows in the theater. The variable
# $scols is the number of tables in
# a row. $seatsper is the number of
# seats per table.
#
####################################
$srows    = 3;
$scols    = 5;
$seatsper = 6;
```

Here's where the fun begins. Two nested for loops are used here. The first, outer loop, iterates over each row in the theater. Within that loop, another loop iterates over each column in each row. When the inner loop is finished, the variables $table1 through $table6 contain all the ASCII graphics needed to display one row on the screen.

```
####################################
#
# the table "graphic" is made up of
# six rows of ASCII characters.
# It shows the table id, and the
```

```
# number of seats left at the table.
# If there are enough seats for the
# user to make a reservation, the table
# id is hyperlinked to the next page
# of the reservation wizard.
#
####################################
for ($rows = 1; $rows <= $srows; $rows++) {
  $table1 = '';
  $table2 = '';
  $table3 = '';
  $table4 = '';
  $table5 = '';
  $table6 = '';
  for ($cols = 1; $cols <= $scols; $cols++) {
    $table++;
    $tableno = sprintf("%03d", $table);
    $seats   =  sprintf("%02d", $seatsper - $assigned{$tableno});
    $table1 .= '+-----+      ';
    $table2 .= '|     |      ';
    $table3 .= '|TABLE|      ';

    if ($seats >= $count) {
      $cgidata = "reswiz05.pl?tableno=$tableno&cartid=$cartid";
      $table4 .= "| <a href=$cgidata>$tableno</a> |      ";
    } else {
      # don't add a link if the table doesn't have enough seats.
      $table4 .= "| $tableno |      ";
    }

    $table5 .= "| $seats   |      ";
    $table6 .= '+-----+      ';
```

```
    }
    print <<EOF;
  $table1
  $table2
  $table3
  $table4
  $table5
  $table6

  EOF
  }
```

At the beginning of each row, $table1 through $table6 are initialized to a blank string. As the script processes each column, the $table variable is incremented; this holds the table number. However, to make it nice and pretty, the variable $tableno will be used to display the number, prefixed with zeros for a total of three spaces. The `sprintf()` function, borrowed from C, lets you do this. This function, and its sibling, `printf()`, are used to generated formatted strings. They take multiple arguments, the template, and a list of values. Generally, the % (percent) symbol prefixes each value's position in the string. this example uses a formatted decimal value of three spaces with leading zeros. Since this is a rather rich function, you should visit your local C reference book for a good explanation of how to use the templates. The difference between `sprintf()` and `printf()` is that you can capture the value of `sprintf()` to a variable assignment, whereas `printf()` is used in the same way as `print()`.

The `sprintf()` function is also used in producing the number of seats available. In order to arrive at this number, the value of $tableno is used to index into %assigned. This data came directly from the `SELECT` statement; the number of seats per table ($seatsper) minus the number of seats assigned yields the number remaining.

Now comes the line-drawing part. ASCII graphics, however crude, provide an adequate rendering of a table. Each table will look something like this:

```
+-----+
|     |
|TABLE|
| 001 |
| 06  |
+-----+
```

The first number (001) is the table number and the second (06) is the number of seats available. The string needed to print this is contained in $table1 through $table6. Notice that six rows of text are needed for each table. This merely shows how the table will look upon the user's browser. If there are enough seats at a table for the customer's party, the table number is highlighted as a hyperlink. In order to accomplish this, the HTML code for each table with a hyperlink would look like:

```
+-----+
|     |
|TABLE|
| <a href=reswiz05.pl?tableno=001&cartid=0008205062650064>001</a> |
| 06  |
+-----+
```

However, tables which do not have enough seats are not displayed with this hyperlink. The expression $seats >= $count tests whether there are enough seats available. Since $table1 through $table6 are not printed out until all the columns have been processed, the .= operator is used, which *tacks* the values on to the end of each string, so $table1 through $table6 actually hold the whole row when they are displayed.

After the tables have been displayed, the terminated body and html tags are sent:

```
print <<EOF;
</body>
```

```
</html>
EOF
```

Figure 6.7 shows what the final document looks like.

Reservation Wizard: Step Five

Well, you're not out of the woods yet, but you're really close. With the users' click on their desired table, all of the information required to reserve a table is in hand. Everything except the table number is in the shopping cart; that information comes in via the CGI query and can be placed in the shopping cart.

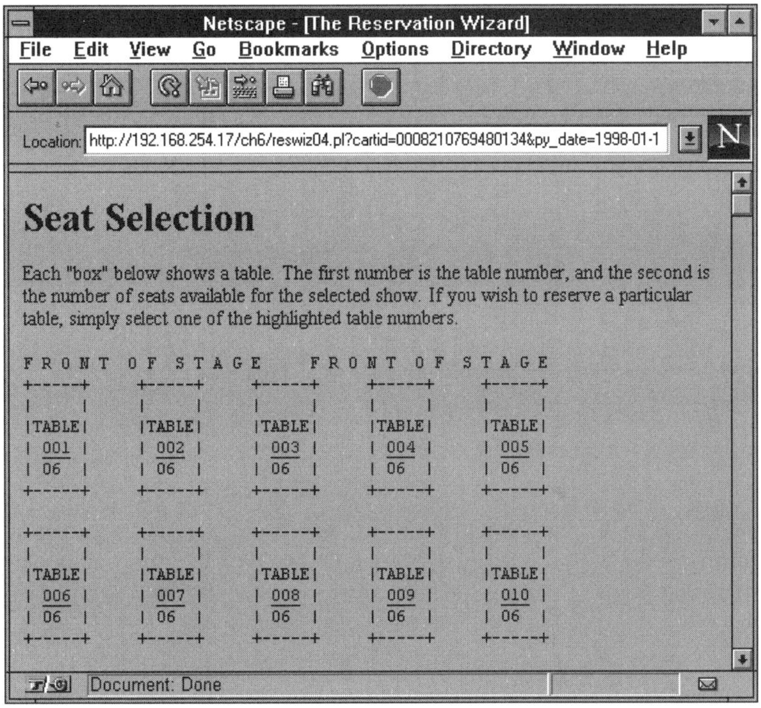

Figure 6.7 The final seat selection document.

```
# -*- Perl -*-
#
# Reservation Wizard: Page 5
#

use NT::ODBC;
use CGI_Lite;
use Cart;

###################################
#
# parse the results of the CGI query
#
###################################
$cgi = new CGI_Lite;
%results = $cgi->parse_form_data ();
$tableno = $results{'tableno'};

###################################
#
# print out a basic here-doc to put
# up required HTML stuff
#
###################################
print <<EOF;
Content-type: text/html

<html>
<head>
<title>Reservation Wizard</title>
</head>
<body>
```

```
<h1>Confirmation</h1>
<hr>
EOF

####################################
#
# set up the shopping cart
#
####################################
$cartid = $results{'cartid'};
$cart = new Cart($cartid);
if ($cart->{'error'}) {
  print $cart->{'error'};
  exit;
}

####################################
#
# Add play date and number of people
# in the part to the cart.
#
####################################
$cart->additem("tableno", $tableno);
$cart->writeitems;

####################################
#
# take the ODBC connection info and
# other persistent variables out of
# the cart.
#
####################################
```

```
$dsn      = $cart->getitem('DSN');
$user     = $cart->getitem('USER');
$passwd   = $cart->getitem('PASSWORD');
$py_id    = $cart->getitem('py_id');
$maxparty = $cart->getitem('maxparty');
$cu_id    = $cart->getitem('cu_id');
$count    = $cart->getitem('count');
$py_date  = $cart->getitem('py_date');
$py_name  = $cart->getitem('py_name');
```

The rest of this script is very, very simple. There is no ODBC query; the user is simply reminded of the options selected, such as the name of the play, the date, the table number, and size of the party. Then, the user is asked for the password. This is not the ODBC password, but the cu_passwd column from the CUST table.

```
print <<EOF;
You selected:<p>
<b>Play</b>: $py_name<p>
<b>Performance Date</b>: $py_date<p>
<b>Number in Party</b>: $count<p>
<b>Table Number</b>: $tableno<p>

<form action=reswiz06.pl method=post>
    <input type="hidden" name="cartid" value="$cartid">
    Enter your password: <input type="password" name="cu_passwd"><br>
    <input type="submit" value="Finish">
</form>
</body>
</html>
EOF
```

Figure 6.8 shows this page as displayed in the Netscape Navigator browser.

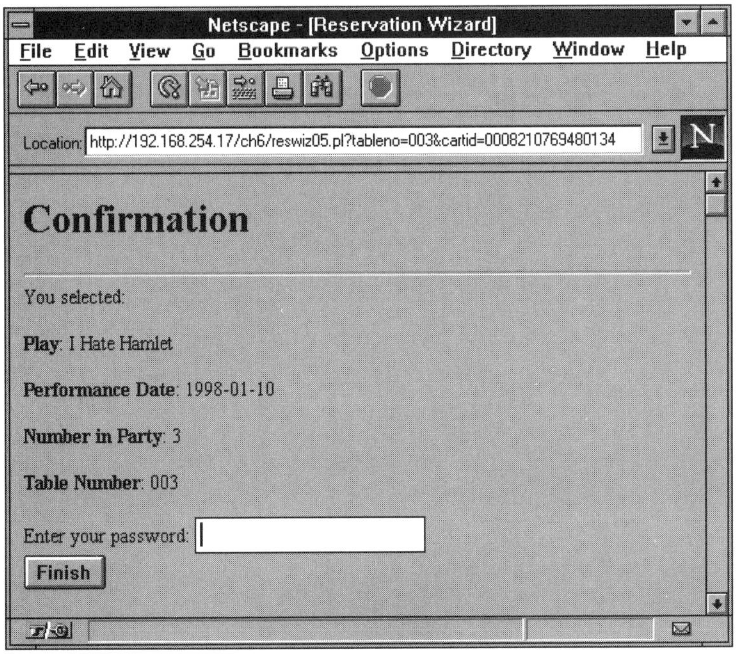

Figure 6.8 The confirmation page as shown in the Netscape Navigator browser.

Reservation Wizard: Step Six

Step six checks the password that the user typed; if it is correct, it inserts the reservation information into the reserve table and gives the user a warm, comforting message. The usual chores appear at the top of the script, except nothing new is put in the cart; everything is there. However, the $cu_passwd variable is pulled out of the CGI query. Also, the script tries to pull a new item out of the cart: 'attempts'. This should not be in the cart (yet); it is the number of unsuccessful attempts to provide the correct password. Users are given three chances with each cart. If they type the wrong password three times, they have to start over with a new cart. Also, a value called *finished* is looked for in the cart. This signals that this cart has already made its reservation and will prevent the user from hitting reload, which would cause multiple records to be added for the same reservation.

```
# -*- Perl -*-
#
# Confirmation page of the reservation wizard...
#

use CGI_Lite;
use NT::ODBC;
use Cart;

#####################################
#
# parse the results of the CGI query
#
#####################################
$cgi = new CGI_Lite;
%results = $cgi->parse_form_data ();
$cu_passwd = $results{'cu_passwd'};

#####################################
#
# here-doc syntax to print out the
# top part of the HTML document
#
#####################################
print <<EOF;
Content-type: text/html

<html>
<head>
<title>Reservation Wizard</title>
</head>
<body>
```

```
<h1>Reservation Wizard</h1>
<hr>
EOF


####################################
#
# set up the shopping cart
#
####################################
$cartid = $results{'cartid'};
$cart = new Cart($cartid);

if ($cart->{'error'}) {
  print $cart->{'error'};
  exit;
}

####################################
#
# take the ODBC connection info and
# other persistent variables out of
# the cart.
#
####################################
$dsn       = $cart->getitem('DSN');
$user      = $cart->getitem('USER');
$passwd    = $cart->getitem('PASSWORD');
$py_id     = $cart->getitem('py_id');
$maxparty = $cart->getitem('maxparty');
$cu_id     = $cart->getitem('cu_id');
$count     = $cart->getitem('count');
```

```
$py_date  = $cart->getitem('py_date');
$py_name  = $cart->getitem('py_name');
$tableno  = $cart->getitem('tableno');
$attempts = $cart->getitem('attempts');
```

The $attempts variable should be zero the first time this screen is entered. However, if three failed attempts have been made, the user is effectively "shut out."

```
###################################
#
# if they have met their retry
# attempts, don't let them go any
# further
#
###################################
if ($attempts > 3) {
  print "You have exceeded your number of password retry attempts.";
  exit;
}
```

The $finished variable should also be zero the first time this screen is entered. If the users have finished, they are told not to worry.

```
###################################
#
# if they have finished the
# reservation already, don't
# let them do it again
#
###################################
if ($finished) {
  print "You have already made this reservation.";
  print "Please contact the theater if you are having a problem.";
  exit;
}
```

If all is well, a new NT::ODBC object is instantiated. It will be used to issue two queries. The first selects all records in the CUST table where the cu_id is equal to the cu_id the user chose back in step two. There must only be one. A filter condition on the SELECT limits the results to those records which have a password equal to the $cu_passwd variable, which was pulled out of the CGI query.

```
####################################
#
# Check the user's password against
# the database
#
####################################
$query = new NT::ODBC("DSN=$dsn;UID=$user;PWD=$passwd;");
if ($query->sql("SELECT *
                      FROM cust
                      WHERE cu_id = $cu_id
                      AND cu_passwd = '$cu_passwd'")) {
  print $query->error;
  print "</body></html>";
  exit;
}
```

If the password doesn't match what is in the table, then the result set of that query will be empty and `$query->fetchrow()` will return a zero (false) value. If this is the case, the number of failed attempts ($attempts) is incremented, put in the cart, and written to disk. Then, the user is warned and told to go back to the last step and retry.

```
##################################
#
# If they entered a bad password,
# tell them, and exit
#
##################################
```

```
if (! $query->fetchrow()) {
  $attempts++;
  $cart->additem('attempts', $attempts);
  $cart->writeitems;
  print "Incorrect password.<p>";
  print "Please choose the back function of your browser to re-enter.";
  exit;
}
```

If the user entered the correct password, an SQL INSERT statement is issued, which puts the reservation information into the system. The *finished* value is added to the cart and the cart is written to disk, so subsequent reload attempts will not add extraneous records.

```
#################################
#
# insert the reservation and
# update the cart, so it knows
# that it's finished
#
#
#################################
if ($query->sql("INSERT INTO reserve
                    (re_cu_id_, re_py_id_, re_sh_date, re_table, re_seats)
                    VALUES($cu_id, $py_id, '$py_date', '$tableno', $count)"))
{
  print $query->error;
  print "</body></html>";
  exit;
} else {
  $cart->additem('finished', 1);
  $cart->writeitems;
}
```

```
print <<EOF;
Your table has been reserved.
</body>
</html>
EOF
```

That wraps up the reservation wizard. A number of new tricks were shown here. The shopping cart proved to provide a couple of nice features beyond form-to-form persistence. Step six actually demonstrates where persistence between the form and subsequent reloads of that form can be useful. Users are prevented from too many bad password attempts and the integrity of the system is protected against duplicate records. The reservation wizard should be a useful model as you attempt to develop data entry and query applications for your clients and users.

CHAPTER

7

REPORTING TECHNIQUES

The past two chapters have focused on getting data into your databases. At some point, it might be desirable to get data out of them. This chapter will examine some of the ways that you can build reports using Perl and ODBC.

Using Templates to Produce Simple Reports

You've already been introduced to template.pl, which allows you to define HTML templates for SQL SELECT statements. Chapter 4 contains many examples which will enable you to generate reports in this fashion.

Crosstab Reports

One of the more popular reports is the *crosstab* or *pivot* report. A crosstab takes normalized data and presents it in a pivoted fashion. Suppose, for example, that you have a collection of reservation information by city for all of the plays, which looks like this:

Play Name	City	Reservations
I Hate Hamlet	San Francisco	53
I Hate Hamlet	Warwick	1,500
I Hate Hamlet	Arctic	200
Our Town	San Francisco	20
Our Town	Warwick	1,178
Our Town	Arctic	200
Our Town	Providence	1,200
Steel Magnolias	Warwick	1,312
Steel Magnolias	Arctic	200
Steel Magnolias	Providence	1,156

Now, if you wanted to report the data in such a way that the city names were listed across the top, and there was one row for each play, the report would look like this:

Play Name	San Francisco	Warwick	Arctic	Providence
I Hate Hamlet	53	1,500	200	0
Our Town	20	1,178	200	1,200
Steel Magnolias	0	1,312	200	1,156

Since the city names have been "pivoted" from a vertical ordering (by row) to a columnar ordering, the data is said to have been pivoted. Such a report is also called a cross-tab. Since this is an awkward way to store data (see Chapter 3), it is not often that you will find a table designed this way—you need to go through some programmatic gymnastics to pivot the data.

xtab.pm: A Classy Way to Do Crosstabs

There is a Perl module on the CD-ROM that helps you perform crosstabs, and you are going to learn what it does and how to use it. There will be much mention of Perl references and objects, so if you feel shaky with this territory, then by all means reread some of the information about this subject in Chapter 5. If you still feel unsure, then read the Perl documentation pages *perlref* and *perlobj*. These are very good introductions to what might be one of the more complicated parts of the Perl language. The file is contained on the CD-ROM on \EG\xtab.pm.

The module xtab.pm contains a single package, coincidentally named xtab. After the package declaration, the NT:ODBC module is used, since each xtab object needs to execute a query.

```
# -*- Perl -*-
#
# xtab.pm
#
#
# a module for generating cross-tabulations from
# ODBC data sources
#
#
package xtab;

use NT::ODBC;
```

The xtab::new Method

The new method is invoked when you want to instantiate a new xtab object. It requires five parameters.

An SQL Query

This should be an SQL query which returns no more than three columns. It should have a group column, a pivot column, and naturally, a data column.

Here's an example which produces a result set similar to the table seen earlier in this chapter:

```
SELECT py_name, cu_city, SUM(re_seats) AS tot
              FROM reserve, plays, cust
              WHERE py_id = re_py_id_
                AND cu_id = re_cu_id_
              GROUP BY py_name, cu_city
```

This produces a result set where py_name + cu_city is unique; it holds every known combination of the two. The tot column contains the total number of reservations made for each play/city pair.

A Connection String

Hey! What's a connection string? You are now being initiated into the higher levels of the ODBC cabal. A *connection string* is a collection of values needed to connect to an ODBC data source. These strings generally contain elements that you have seen before, such as DSN, user id, and password. However, some ODBC drivers may support other elements; consult your driver documentation for more information.

The connection string is made up of one or more tag/value pairs, as in:

```
DSN=EXAMPLE;UID=bjepson;PWD=mypassword
```

You may have noticed this in earlier chapters; the values for data source name, user id, and password arrived via a CGI script and were sent to the new method of NT::ODBC in a connection string format.

A Pivot Column

The pivot column is the column that gets pivoted to read across the final report. In the previous example, this is the city name (cu_city).

A Data Column

This is the column that is used to fill in the "cells" of the crosstab. The tot column, which is a sum of reservation numbers, is the data column in the example.

A Group Column

The group column is the column which is used for each row in the crosstab. In the example, it is the play name. Here's an example of some code which will instantiate a new xtab object:

```
$query = "SELECT py_name, cu_city, SUM(re_seats) AS tot
              FROM reserve, plays, cust
              WHERE py_id = re_py_id_
                AND cu_id = re_cu_id_
              GROUP BY py_name, cu_city";
$dsn    = "EXAMPLE";
$crosstab = new xtab($query, "DSN=$dsn;", "cu_city", "tot", "py_name");
```

Here's the new method of xtab.pm:

```
sub new {

  my($class) = shift;

  my($self)  = {};
  bless($self);

  $self->{'query'}             = shift;
  $self->{'connection string'} = shift;
  $self->{'pivot column'}      = shift;
  $self->{'data column'}       = shift;
  $self->{'group column'}      = shift;

  $self;

}
```

As with other new constructors, this new method creates a reference to an anonymous hash with a local variable called $self. It is then blessed into a class and the five parameters are shifted into five properties of the object; query, connection string, pivot column, data column, and group column. Finally, $self (the reference to the anonymous hash, which is the instantiated xtab object) is returned to the calling program. Note that `return()` is not needed; the last value in the method is implicitly returned.

The xtab::doquery Method

The `xtab::doquery` method uses the properties assigned when the object is instantiated. The first thing it does is what any other virtual method does: It pulls a reference to the object off the parameter list with the `shift()` function. This allows you to have things like $self->{'connection string'} refer to the connection string of the correct xtab object. It's possible for you to have multiple instances of the xtab object, each with its own name. When you call `xtab::doquery` with something like `$myxtab->doquery`, the first parameter that is sent to this method is $myxtab, which contains a reference to the object instantiated with `$myxtab = new xtab(...)`.

```
sub doquery {

  my($self) = shift;
```

Now, all of the scalar variables and hashes which will be used in this method are declared local with the `my()` function:

```
  my($query, %pivot, %group, %rows, $pivot, $group);
```

An NT:ODBC object is instantiated, using the connection string property of this object. Then, the query property of this xtab object is passed to the NT::ODBC::sql method. If there's an error, it is assigned to the (previously nonexistent) error property of the xtab object:

```
  $query = new NT::ODBC($self->{'connection string'});
  if ($query->sql($self->{'query'})) {
    $self->{'error'} = $query->error;
  }
```

Now, each row in the result set can be processed in sequence:

```
# fetch each row in the result set
#
while ($query->fetchrow) {
```

The pivot column is the column that needs to be turned into a set of tabular values, going across the page. In the example seen earlier in this chapter, this would be the city name. This value is fetched from the query by passing the value of the pivot column property of the current xtab object to the data method of the $query object. This will return the value of that column for the current row. It is stored in the scalar variable $pivot:

```
###################################
#
# get the value of the pivot column
# this is the value that is used to
# generate the tabular columns
#
###################################
$pivot = $query->data($self->{'pivot column'});
```

The same is done for the group column; this is the column that is translated into the detail row of the resulting crosstab.

```
###################################
#
# get the value of the group by column
# This is the value that is used to
# generate the rows in the crosstab
#
###################################
$group = $query->data($self->{'group column'});
```

The value in the scalar variable $pivot is stored to a hash called %pivot by autoincrementing the value $pivot{$pivot}. Remember, Perl automagically grows hashes, so if you autoincrement $pivot{'Providence'} for the first time, it is set to one.

```
###################################
#
# this stores each $pivot value in
# the %pivot hash, for easy lookup
#
###################################
$pivot{$pivot}++;
```

The same is done for the $group variable:

```
###################################
#
# this stores each $group value in
# the %group hash, for easy lookup
#
###################################
$group{$group}++;
```

A reference is used to simulate a multidimensional array. the %rows hash (a.k.a. associative array) is a hash that contains another hash, indexed by $group. Each hash element contained in %rows is also a hash and each element in that hash contains the total number of reservations. So, in the previous example, the expression $rows{'Our Town'}{'Pawtucket'} would return the total number of reservations made from Pawtucket for the play "Our Town"

```
###################################
#
# the rows are stored in a hash
# which is indexed by the group
# value. Each hash element contains
```

```
    # a hash indexed by the pivot value,
    # and each element in that hash
    # contains the data value for the
    # column
    #
    ##################################
    $rows{$group}{$pivot} +=
      $query->data($self->{'data column'});

}
```

Finally, the %pivot and %group hashes are saved for posterity's sake. They are assigned to a hash, which is referenced as a property of the current object by %{$self->{'pivot'}} and %{$self->{'group'}}. Remember, $self is a scalar variable which contains a reference to an anonymous hash. This hash is created every time an xtab object is instantiated. This hash can contain scalar values, which can refer to scalar variables, hashes, or arrays of scalars. They can also contain scalar values.

```
##################################
#
# store the %pivot and %group
# hashes as properties of $self
#
##################################
%{$self->{'pivot'}} = %pivot;
%{$self->{'group'}} = %group;
```

The same thing happens with %rows; a reference to it is stored in the rows property. The return function makes sure that the entire %rows hash is returned to whatever called this method:

```
##################################
#
# return the rows to the calling
```

```
    # program. This may not be needed,
    # since xtab has a method for
    # displaying the crosstab
    #
    #####################################
    return (%{$self->{'rows'}}  = %rows);

}
```

Displaying the Crosstab: The xtab::html_table Method

The `xtab::html_table` method is invoked to print out the crosstab using an HTML table. This makes it easy to display the results of your crosstab and also can serve as a guide for creating a method that displays the data in other formats. This method requires a parameter: the title of the group column. The pivot columns are titled after the value of the pivoted data.

The `xtab::html_table` method first uses the shift function to pull the reference to the xtab object off the parameter array. The shift function is also used to get the header for the group column. The scalar variables $key, $value, and $table are declared to be local with the `my` function:

```
sub html_table {

    my ($self)   = shift;
    my ($header) = shift;
    my ($key, $value, $table);
```

Next, the table element is defined with the `<table>` tag. The entire table is stored in a variable called $table and is returned to the calling program. The header for the group column is added using a `th` element:

```
    #####################################
    #
    # Print out the <table> tag and the
```

```
# header for the grouping column
#
###################################
$table =  "<table border><th>$header</th>";
```

Each key in the %pivot hash is sorted and a `th` element containing each key is added to $table. This produces the pivoted columns as shown in the example and a newline is added, which will make the table more readable if the user were to use the View Source option of his or her browser:

```
###################################
#
# The keys to the  pivot hash are
# all of the pivot column values
# that are used in the crosstab.
#
# These are displayed as the tabular
# columns
###################################
foreach $key (sort keys %{$self->{'pivot'}}) {
  $table .= "<th>$key</th>";
}
$table .= "\n";
```

Next, two nested foreach loops are set up. The first loop goes through each group column (in the example, this is the name of the play). Before the second loop is entered, a `tr` (table row) element is started with the `<tr>` tag and the name of the play is added to the $table variable. This causes the play name to be printed at the left of each row and only once for each row.

```
###################################
#
# iterate over each key in the group
# hash. These are the key values for
```

```
# each row.
#
####################################
foreach $key (sort keys %{$self->{'group'}}) {

  ####################################
  #
  # column one of each row is the
  # key value
  #
  ####################################
  $table .= "<tr><td>$key</td>";
```

The second loop iterates over all of the pivot values. Notice that the hashes referenced in $self->{'group'} and $self->{'pivot'} are used for this purpose. Although the hash referenced in $self->{'rows'} contains all of these values, the pivot values for each play are limited to those which have a value. Zero values are not contained in there. Inside this loop, the expression ${$self->{'rows'}{$key}}{$_} * 1 returns the value for the current play and city. If it doesn't exist, it returns an undefined value. When this value is multiplied by one, it is forced into a numeric context and is displayed as zero, rather than blank.

```
  ####################################
  #
  # iterate over each key in the pivot
  # hash (the tabular columns)
  #
  ####################################
  foreach (sort keys %{$self->{'pivot'}}) {

    ####################################
    #
    # the value for each column is
```

```
        # retrieved from the rows hash,
        # which is, to all intents and
        # purpose, a multidimensional
        # hash indexed by group value
        # and the value of the tabular
        # column (pivot column)
        #
        # the value is multiplied by one
        # to force even blank (zero)
        # values into numeric context.
        #
        ##################################
        $value = ${$self->{'rows'}{$key}}{$_} * 1;
```

After the value has been obtained, it is then added to the table between a `td` (table data or cell) element:

```
        $table .= "<td>$value</td>";
      }
```

At the end of each row, the `</tr>` tag terminates the `tr` element:

```
      $table .= "</tr>\n";
    }
```

Finally, the table element itself is terminated with the `</table>` tag:

```
  $table .= "</table>\n";
 }
```

Here's an example script, which prints out the example data using xtab.pm (the script is located on the CD-ROM under \EG\CH7\xtab1.pl). First, it uses the xtab module and prints out a basic HTML document.

```
use xtab;


print <<EOF;
Content-type: text/html
```

```
<html>
<head>
<title>Sample Crosstab</title>
</head>
<body>
<h1>Sample Crosstab</h1>
<hr>
EOF
```

Next, the $query variable is populated with the value of a query, and xtab::new is called with the query, a connection string, the name of the pivot column, data column, and group column. You may need to change the connection string to specify whatever data source you are using. If it requires a user id and password, be sure to add the UID= and PWD= tag/value pairs.

```
$query = "SELECT py_name, cu_city, SUM(re_seats) AS tot
              FROM reserve, plays, cust
              WHERE py_id = re_py_id_
                AND cu_id = re_cu_id_
              GROUP BY py_name, cu_city";
$crosstab = new xtab($query, "DSN=EXAMPLE;", "cu_city", "tot", "py_name");
```

The `xtab::doquery` method is called; if it is successful (it returns a non-zero value on success), the `xtab::html_table` method is called with "Play" as the title column for py_name. Otherwise, an error message is printed.

```
if ($crosstab->doquery) {
  print $crosstab->html_table("Play");
} else {
print "yo";
  print "<b>An error has occurred:</b><p>";
  print $crosstab->{'error'}
}
```

Figure 7.1 shows the output of this script in the Netscape browser.

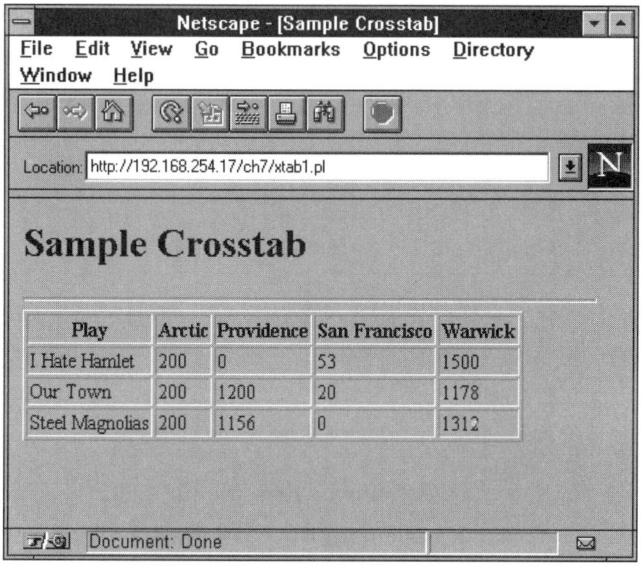

Figure 7.1 A crosstab sample.

Expanding Hierarchies

It's fairly common to see information presented in a hierarchical fashion. For example, when you open up the Windows File Manager (see Figure 7.2), the directory structure is shown in a hierarchical fashion. Similar views of data are available in the programs such as the Microsoft SQL Server Enterprise Manager.

Data that can be organized in this fashion is generally stored in a self-referential format. For example, in a disk's directory structure, each file's name is available, along with the name of the directory it is stored in. Since a directory is just a special sort of file, it also abides by the same conventions. Suppose the following directory structure:

```
\
        APPLICATIONS\
                VISICALC\
                        VISICALC.EXE
```

```
                    VISICALC.HLP
          TECO\
                    TECO.EXE
                    TECO.HLP
EMULATORS\
          PDP-10\
                    PDP-10.EXE
                    PDP-10.HLP
                    ITS\
                              ITS.EXE
                              ITS.HLP
```

Directories are denoted with a trailing \. It's possible to preserve the hierarchical aspect of this information by using a table with three columns. One of the columns is a unique key, which allows you to have duplicate file names in different directories (how many files named README do you have on your hard drive?). The other column is the name of the file or directory and the third column is a reference to the unique key of the directory that contains this file or directory. This is called a foreign key reference; in a relational data model, it usually refers to a primary key in another table. This type of table design is called self-referential, because some or all of the foreign key references point to the unique key of another record in the same table. Here's how the directory hierarchy could be organized.

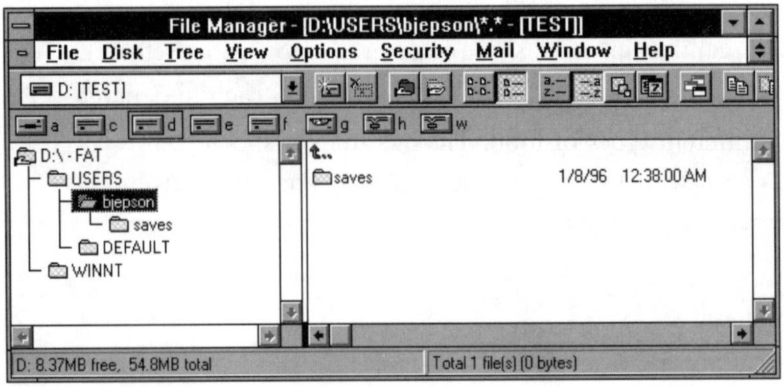

Figure 7.2 The Windows File Manager.

File ID	File Name	Parent Id
1	\	
2	APPLICATIONS\	1
3	VISICALC\	2
4	VISICALC.EXE	3
5	VISICALC.HLP	3
6	TECO\	2
7	TECO.EXE	6
8	TECO.HLP	6
9	EMULATORS\	1
10	PDP-10	9
11	PDP-10.EXE	10
12	PDP-10.HLP	10
13	ITS	10
14	ITS.EXE	13
15	ITS.HLP	13

The difficulty lies in trying to display this information to the user in a hierarchical fashion. The remainder of this chapter will showcase one possible approach, based on the Expanding Hierarchies example included in the Microsoft SQL Server Database Developer's Companion. That example is written in Transact-SQL, which is the native SQL of SQL Server. While the Perl solution differs in many ways, the same basic algorithm is used.

I will be departing from the Dinner Theater examples here; instead, this solution will be demonstrated with a simple example: a hierarchical database containing different types of food. The hierarchy is shown below:

```
Dairy
 Beverages
  Coffee Milk
  Whole Milk
  Skim Milk
```

```
      Cheeses
        Cheddar
        Stilton
        Swiss
        Gouda
        Muenster
    Beans and Nuts
      Beans
        Black Beans
        Kidney Beans
          Red Kidney Beans
          Black Kidney Beans
      Nuts
        Pecans
```

There are two top-level groupings in this simple, ovo-lacto vegetarian diet: "Dairy Products" and "Beans and Nuts." Each is further refined as the tree is descended. The table, FOOD, which follows, is included in the \DATA\DBF directory of the CD-ROM. A script to generate this table is included in \EG\CH7\FOOD.SQL.

fo_name	fo_id	fo_fo_id_
Food	001	NULL
Beans and Nuts	002	001
Beans	003	002
Nuts	004	002
Black Beans	005	003
Pecans	006	004
Kidney Beans	007	003
Red Kidney Beans	008	007
Black Kidney Beans	009	007
Dairy	010	001
Beverages	011	010

fo_name	fo_id	fo_fo_id_
Whole Milk	012	011
Skim Milk	013	011
Cheeses	014	010
Cheddar	015	014
Stilton	016	014
Swiss	017	014
Gouda	018	014
Muenster	019	014
Coffee Milk	020	011

The module outline.pm (located in \NTPERL\MODULES\outline.pm on the CD-ROM) can make short work of this problem. Although you can use it as a *black box*, I'll go over its internals now, and explain how you can deal with expanding a hierarchical database.

The outline::new Method

Like other modules, there is a package declaration, followed by the use NT::ODBC statement. This gives the outline module access to the NT::ODBC class, which will be used to instantiate an object, so a query can be executed.

```
# -*- Perl -*-
#
# OUTLINE.PM
#

package outline;
use NT::ODBC;
```

This is followed by the `outline::new` method, which is the constructor for this class. The class name is shifted off the parameter list (it is not explicitly used, but it has to be removed to get at the other parameters). The anonymous hash that represents an outline object is created and blessed into an object.

```
sub new {

    my ($class) =  shift;
    my $self={};
    bless $self;
```

The first four parameters are shifted off the parameter list. They are stored as properties of the outline object. The first parameter is the name of the table to query. The second is a comma-delimited column list. A substitution is bound to the assignment, which causes all spaces to be removed from the list of columns. The next parameter is the unique id of the row that you want to start building the tree from. If you were to specify 010 as this value, using the example FOOD data, then only the Dairy level and below would be selected. If you wanted to get all of the hierarchical tree, then you would use 001, the unique id of the Food row. The next parameter is a little curious. It is the path to a Perl script which can be used if you want to make the tree *active.* If you do this, then each item in the tree is presented as a hyperlink, with the Perl script specified as a target and the unique id of the selected item as a parameter.

```
    $self->{'table'}         = shift;
    ($self->{'column list'} = shift) =~ s/\s//g;
    $self->{'start id'}      = shift;
    $self->{'target'}        = shift;
```

The next three parameters are the data source, user id, and password, respectively. Once they are shifted off the parameter list, they are stored as a property called *connection string.*

```
    #################################
    #
    # Get the ODBC connection info
    # and store it.
    #
    #################################
```

```
my ($dsn, $user, $passwd);
$dsn    = shift;
$user   = shift;
$passwd = shift;
$self->{'connection string'} = "DSN=$dsn;UID=$user;PWD=$passwd";
```

If the items in the tree hierarchy are hyperlinked, the connection info will need to be preserved. For this reason, the next step sets up a cart and drops the connection string into it. The only other thing the target of the hyperlink will need is the id of the selected item; that will be a field in the CGI query.

```
################################
#
# Create a shopping cart and
# put the connection info in
# it.
#
################################
my ($cart) = new Cart;
$cart->additem("connection string", $self->{'connection string'});
$cart->writeitems;
$self->{'cartid'} = $cart->getitem('id');
```

The column list is now `split()` on the comma and stored in an array called @columns. There should be three columns in this list. The first is the unique id column, the second is the column containing the description of each item (the data column; this is what appears in the list), and the third is the parent id column. These are assigned to properties of the outline object.

```
my(@columns) = split(',', $self->{'column list'});
$self->{'id column'}        = $columns[0];
$self->{'data column'}      = $columns[1];
$self->{'parent id column'} = $columns[2];
```

After that is done, a reference to the newly instantiated object is returned.

```
    $self;
}
```

The outline::doquery Method

The `outline::doquery` method prepares, executes, and stores the results of the SQL query needed to process and display the hierarchical information. The first thing it does is to pull the reference to the current object off the parameter list. Then, it declares some variables local with the `my` function:

```
sub doquery {

    my $self = shift;

    my($sql, $query, @array);
```

After that, it uses the column list property to build an SQL SELECT statement. Since that list is comma-delimited, it can easily be used as the list of columns in an SQL SELECT statement. Obviously, the table name is a required portion of the SQL SELECT statement. The variable $sql is defined, with the column list and table properties of the current outline object interpolated in the correct places.

```
    ##########################
    #
    # The sql query needed to
    # build the tree diagram
    # needs only the three
    # columns in the column
    # list property
    #
    ##########################
    $sql = "SELECT $self->{'column list'} FROM $self->{'table'}";
```

Now that an SQL SELECT statement is ready and waiting, our old friend NT::ODBC is called into action, and the query is executed. If there was failure, the error message is stored in the error property and the method returns a zero value to the calling program.

```
##########################
#
# Use NT::ODBC to issue
# the query.
#
##########################
$query = new NT::ODBC("$self->{'connection string'}");
if ($query->sql($sql)) {
  $self->{'error'} = $query->error;
  return 0; # return failure
}
```

If the query went without an error, then the method did not return. In order to have the query results in the format needed to generate the tree diagram, the results will be stored in an array. This will be an array of scalars, with one element for each row in the result set. Each element in the array is a reference to a hash. This hash contains the values of each column for that row, indexed by column name. This is accomplished by first creating an array of column names by calling NT::ODBC::fieldnames. Then, as each row is fetched using NT::ODBC::fetchrow, each field value is retrieved using the `NT::ODBC::data` method:

```
##########################
#
# Create an array with
# all the columnnames.
#
##########################
my(@columns) = $query->fieldnames;
```

```
##########################
#
# Create an array of each
# row in the table. Each
# array element contains
# a reference to a hash.
# this hash is indexed by
# column name and contains
# the value of each column
# for that row.
#
##########################
while ($query->fetchrow) {
  foreach (@columns) {
  $array[$recno]{$_} = $query->data($_);
  }
  $recno++;
}
```

Finally, the array which contains the results is stored as the data property in the current object and a value indicating success is returned:

```
##########################
#
# Store the array which
# contains all the rows
# as a property in this
# object.
#
##########################
@{$self->{'data'}} = @array;

1; # return success

}
```

The outline::tree Method

This is the method which processes the data obtained in the `doquery` method. It turns the data into a hierarchical tree diagram, which can be displayed in your browser, and looks quite nice. It is recommended that it be enclosed within the pre element, since the tree structure is defined using spaces as padding; the indent helps to identify nesting depth.

This method first pulls the reference to the outline object off the parameter list. Then, the data property of the object is dereferenced to get the array containing the results of the query issued in the `doquery` method:

```
sub tree {

  my $self = shift;

  my (@array) = @{$self->{'data'}};
```

After that, a whole slew of variables are declared local with the my function:

```
  my ($level, $line, $parent, $pad,
      $current, %stack, $levelFound, $index,
      $item, $id, $cartid, $url, @children);
```

The algorithm used to traverse the tree is non-recursive, which means, unlike many such algorithms, it does not need to invoke itself for each successive level. In order to keep track of the nesting depth, a variable called $level is initialized to one. When tree skips down a level, it is incremented. When it skips up, it is decremented. When this variable goes down to zero, the tree is finished:

```
  $level = 1;
```

An associative array named %stack is used to keep track of all pending items. This associative array has the unique key of each item as its key; the value referred to by that key is the nesting level of that item. When an item has been processed, its value in %stack is set to 0, and if it has any children (other records which are grouped under it), they are added to %stack, with the next higher level as their value. The first item's id is added to %stack, with its level equal to one.

```
# this non-recursive algorithm requires the use of a
# stack in order to process each element. After each
# element is processed, it is removed from the stack
# (actually, the value of the hash that represents
# the item is set to 0), and its children on the next
# level are added to the stack. Then it starts all over
# again until we run out of elements.
#
$stack{ $self->{'start id'} } = 1;
```

A `while {...}` construct is set up, which continues as long as `$level` is nonzero:

```
# $level starts out at 1. Every time we run out of items
# to process at the current level (if $levelFound == 0)
# $level is decremented. If we get to 0, we have run out of
# items to process, and can call it quits.
#
while ($level) {
```

The stack is traversed until an item can be found on the stack whose level is equal to $level. If none is found, the flag variable $levelFound remains set to 0. If it was found, $current is set to the id of that item. This is used to perform lookups into the @array, which holds the results of the query performed in `doquery`.

```
    # search the stack for an item whose level matches
    # $level.
    #
    $levelFound = 0;
    foreach $index (keys %stack) {
      if ($stack{$index} == $level) {
```

```
        # if we have found something whose level is equal
        # to $level, set the variable $current so we can
        # refer to it later. Also, set the flag $levelFound
        #
        $current = $index;
        $levelFound = 1;
        last;

      }
    }
```

As long as something was found to be processed at the current level, the item is added to the tree diagram variable, $value. If not, the $level variable is decremented.

```
    # if we found something at the current level, its id will
    # be in $current, so let's process it. Otherwise, we drop
    # through this, decrement $level, and if $level is not 0,
    # start the process over again.
    #
    if ($levelFound) {
```

In order to locate the row whose unique id matches the value of $current, each record is checked.

```
      $reccount = $#array;
      ######################################
      #
      # loop through the array of rows until
      # we find the record with the id that
      # matches $current. This is the id of
      # the item we pulled off of $stack
      #
      ######################################
```

```
for ($i = 1; $i <= $reccount; $i++) {

if ($array[$i]{$self->{'id column'}} eq $current) {
```

When it is found, some padding is added to the front of it, which causes it to be indented depending upon how deeply nested it is.

```
################################
# add some padding; $level * 2
# spaces, which creates the
# nice hierarchical indent.
#
################################
$value .= ' ' x ($level * 2);
```

Then, the data column property is used to look up the value to use as the label and the shopping cart id is stored to a local variable.

```
################################
#
# the data column is used to get
# $item, which is the label in
# the tree diagram.
#
# The cartid property is the id
# of the shopping cart that was
# created in the new method
#
################################
$item   = $array[$i]{$self->{'data column'}};
$cartid = $self->{'cartid'};
```

Now, the label can be added to the $value variable, which holds the entire tree. If there was a target specified, it is used, along with the id of the item, and the cart id, to create a URL which calls a script. There's a type of string notation that you haven't seen yet: it's the qq[...] notation. When you want to include the " (double-quote) within a double-quoted string, you can choose whatever string delimiter you want. Trick is, you have to choose a delimiter that you're not using in the string. If you're lucky, you will (as I have done in the following example) choose a bracketing pair of delimiters, such as (), [], {}, or <>. If you can't use those, you have to use the "same character fore and aft," to quote the perlop man page. The first delimiter must be prefixed with qq, and the last one must appear where the double quote would normally appear.

```
    ###############################
    #
    # if the calling program defined
    # a target script, define this
    # item on the tree as a hyperlink.
    # include variables for id and
    # cartid.
    #
    # Otherwise, just add the item
    # as it is.
    #
    ###############################
    if ($self->{'target'}) {
      $url    = "$self->{'target'}?id=$current&cartid=$cartid";
      $value .= qq[<a href="$url">$item</a>\n];
    } else {
      $value .= "$item\n";
    }
    last;
  }


  }
```

The current item's value in the %stack associative array is set to 0.

```
$stack{$current} = 0;
```

Next, the entire result set is processed; any rows whose parent ids are equal to the row that was just processed ($current) are added to the stack, with a level of $level + 1:

```
#################################
#
# add all the children (if any)
# of the current item to the stack
#
###############################
$reccount = $#array;
for ($i = 1; $i <= $reccount; $i++) {

  if ($array[$i]{$self->{'parent id column'}} eq $current) {
    $stack{$array[$i]{$self->{'id column'}}} = $level + 1;
    $children[$level] = 1;
  }

}
```

If we were able to find rows to process on this level, the $level variable is incremented; the process starts over. If there were no rows found on this level, the $level variable is decremented. This continues until $level reaches zero.

```
      $level++ ;
    } else {
      $level—;
    }

  }
  $value;
}
```

Putting It All Together

Here's a sample Perl script which will create a hierarchical view of the FOOD table:

```
use outline;


# instantiate a new outline object
$outline1 = new outline('FOOD', 'fo_id,fo_name,fo_fo_id_', '001',
                   'getfood.pl', 'EXAMPLE', '', '');



# put up a basic html document
print <<EOF;
Content-type: text/html

<html>
<head>
<title>Sample Outline</title>
</head>

<body>
<h1>Sample Outline</h1>
</body>
<pre>
EOF

# execute the query. If it succeeds,
# print out the tree diagram
if ($outline1->doquery) {
  print $outline1->tree;
} else {
  print $outline1->{'error'};
}
```

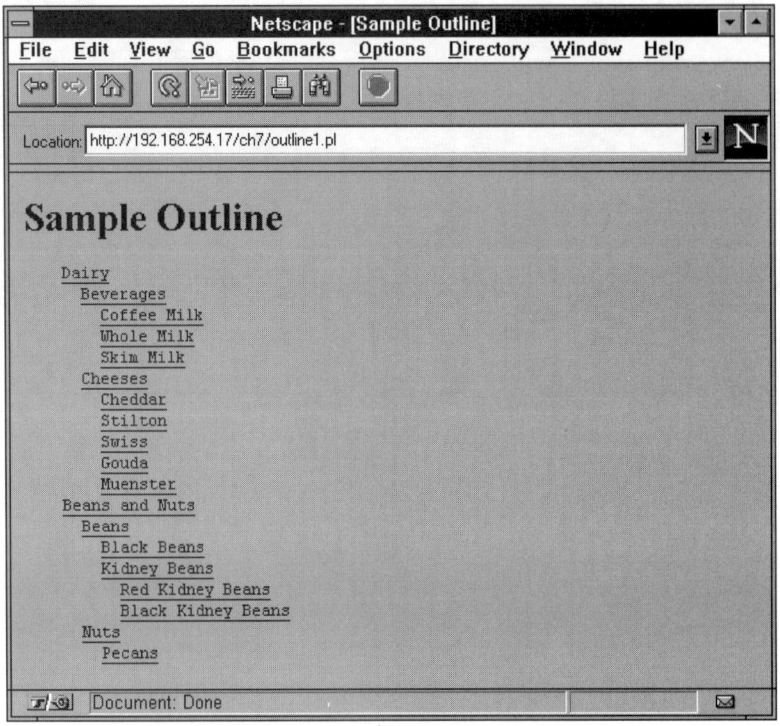

Figure 7.3 The food hierarchy.

It is located on the CD-ROM in /EG/CH7/outline1.pl. It can be called from your Web browser with no parameters. Figure 7.3 shows how it will look in the Netscape Navigator product. The script creates an active tree diagram, which will link to the getfood.pl script, also contained in the same directory. That script brings up a detailed description of the selected food item, as shown in the following:

```
use NT::ODBC;

use CGI_Lite;

use Cart;


####################################

#

# Parse the CGI query and get the
```

```
# id of the selected food
#
####################################
$cgi = new CGI_Lite;
%results = $cgi->parse_form_data ();
$id     = $results{'id'};

####################################
#
# put up an HTML document header
#
####################################
print <<EOF;
Content-type: text/html

<html>
<head>
EOF

####################################
#
# set up the shopping cart and get
# the connection string from it.
#
####################################
$cartid = $results{'cartid'};
$cart = new Cart($cartid);
if ($cart->{'error'}) {
  print $cart->{'error'};
  exit;
}
$connstring = $cart->getitem("connection string");
```

```
####################################
#
# Instantiate a new NT::ODBC object
# and execute a query that retrieves
# the row from food whose fo_id
# matches $id
#
####################################
$query = new NT::ODBC($connstring);
if ($query->sql("SELECT fo_name, fo_desc FROM food WHERE fo_id = '$id'")) {
  print $query->error;
  exit;
}

####################################
#
# fetch the row and print out the
# name and description of the food
#
####################################
$query->fetchrow;
$fo_name = $query->data('fo_name');
$fo_desc = $query->data('fo_desc');

print <<EOF;
<title>$fo_name</title>
</head>

<body>
<h1>$fo_name</h1>
<hr>
$fo_desc
```

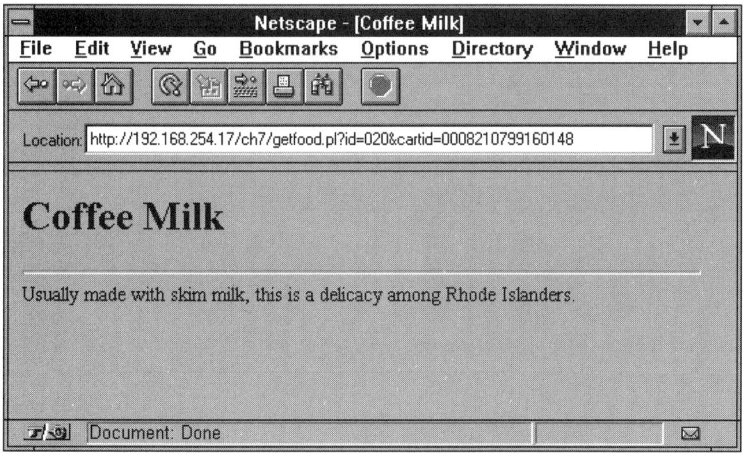

Figure 7.4 Results when "Coffee Milk" is clicked in the tree diagram.

```
</body>
</html>
EOF
```

Figure 7.4 shows the results of this script when the user clicks on "Coffee Milk" in the tree diagram.

You have seen examples of how to generate some of the more complicated type of reports. Hopefully, even if you do not need to use any of these specific routines, they will serve as inspiration for solving other complicated tasks.

CHAPTER

8

OTHER ISSUES

Generating Static HTML Documents

The bulk of this book has been concerned with giving users live access to data by using CGI scripts. It may not always be necessary or desirable to allow World Wide Web users to have live access to your data. There are several situations where this may be the case. For example, if you do not need to allow users to perform transactions on-line, it is not necessary to provide the interactive services that CGI scripts offer.

Also, advanced CGI scripts can be compute-intensive and every business may not have the resources to supply a high-end server. Some businesses may not want to put a server on-line and may rely on an inexpensive arrangement with an Internet Service Provider to have Web space on another computer. Others may have an http server running on an operating system other than Windows NT, and thus cannot take advantage of the examples in the other chapters.

Irrespective of these circumstances, it is still possible to leverage the power of Windows NT, Perl, and ODBC. Rather than dynamically creating content with CGI scripts, you can write Perl scripts that build HTML documents from the databases. These documents can be saved as files on your computer, then uploaded to your Web server. Whenever substantial changes occur in your databases, you can go through this process again. The following examples assume that you have copied the \EG subdirectory from the CD-ROM to someplace on your hard drive. Since the example scripts write files to the disk, you cannot run them from the CD-ROM.

Brian's On-Line Book Collection

Fortunately, I have a perfect example up my sleeve for this problem. It just so happens that I have a book collection that I'd like to showcase on the Web. My home pages are located on a UNIX box; therefore, I can't easily apply the techniques shown in previous chapters. Nevertheless, I have the book information in three databases and I even have some scans of the book covers. What I'd like to do is write a Perl script or two that will generate the HTML documents; then I can upload them to the Web server via ftp.

The tables are contained on the CD-ROM in the \DATA directory, along with the other example tables (A Microsoft Access database is contained in \DATA\ACCESS\EXAMPLE.MDB, FoxPro/dBase tables are in \DATA\DBF, and an install script is included in \DATA\MSSQL for SQL Server). The database structures are very simple.

BOOK

Column	Type	Width	Description
bo_name	char	40	Book Name
bo_au_id_	float		Author Id
bo_pu_id_	float		Publisher Id

BOOK Continued

Column	Type	Width	Description
bo_image	char	12	Filename of book's cover image
bo_id	float		Book Id

AUTHOR

Column	Type	Width	Description
au_fname	char	25	Author's first name
au_lname	char	25	Author's last name
au_id	float		Author Id

PUBLISH

Column	Type	Width	Description
pu_name	char	30	Publisher Name
pu_id	float		Publisher Id

Generate the Documents

Two scripts will be used to generate the documents. The first, byauth.pl, is located on the CD-ROM under \EG\CH8\byauth.pl. It generates the main list of books, organized by author. This script is rather run-of-the-mill, as far as Perl scripts go. Unlike other scripts in the book, however, this one only makes use of the NT::ODBC module. There is no need for Cart or CGI_Lite:

```
# -*- Perl -*-
#
#
```

```
#####################
#
# use the ODBC module
#
#####################
use NT::ODBC;
```

Once this has been done, an NT::ODBC object is instantiated and used to perform a query. You should replace the data source name (EXAMPLE) with whatever data source you are actually using. In this script, you will need the name of all the authors and every book they wrote. This SELECT statement will retrieve one row for each book the author wrote and will include the title and id of the book. If an error occurred, the error is not printed as part of the HTML document, but is printed to STDERR as part of a `die()` function. There's no need to print an error message in the document, since that is really a function needed by CGI scripts, because they are susceptible to system and data quality conditions. Once you have put an HTML document on-line, the only thing you need to worry about is failure on the part of the server:

```
##################################
#
# Issue a query to get all authors
# and the books associated with
# them.
#
##################################
$query = new NT::ODBC("DSN=EXAMPLE;");
$sql   = "SELECT au_fname, au_lname, bo_name, bo_id, au_id
              FROM author, book
              WHERE bo_au_id_ = au_id
              ORDER BY au_lname, au_fname";
if ($query->sql($sql)) {
  die ("Couldn't execute query: " . $query->error);
}
```

In Chapter 2, you learned how to open a file for reading. In this example, you'll see how to open a file for writing. Note that this will completely overwrite any existing filename byauth.htm. The byauth.htm file is opened under the filehandle BYAUTHOR or the script dies with an error message:

```
##################################
#
# Open the byauth.htm file; this
# will contain authors and titles
# in a definition list format
#
##################################
open (BYAUTHOR, ">byauth.htm") || die "Could not open html file.";
```

The next step is to print out the first part of the HTML document. There is no need for a Content-type indicator, since this document is not created by a CGI script. You will notice that there is a <dl> tag in the body element. The list of authors and books will be handled as a definition list, with the author name appearing as a definition term (heralded with the <dt> tag) and each book appearing as a definition (the <dd> tag). From here to the end of the script, all print statements are redirected to the BYAUTHOR filehandle, by including the filehandle after the print statement.

```
##################################
#
# Print out an HTML document
#
##################################
print BYAUTHOR <<EOF;
<html>
<head>
<title>Brian Jepson's Books</title>
</head>

<body>
```

```
<h1>Brian Jepson's Books</h1>
<hr>
<dl>
EOF
```

The `NT::ODBC::fetchrow` method is called to get each row and the `NT::ODBC::data` method is called to get values for each column. As this is done, the values are assigned to Perl variables whose names correspond to the column names.

```
##################################
#
# fetch each row, and copy the
# data into Perl variables
#
##################################
while ($query->fetchrow) {

   $au_fname = $query->data('au_fname');
   $au_lname = $query->data('au_lname');
   $au_id    = $query->data('au_id');
   $bo_id    = $query->data('bo_id');
   $bo_name  = $query->data('bo_name');
```

Within the definition list, it is only necessary to print out the name of each author once. In order to track whether each author has been printed, the associative array %seen is used. This contains the number of books that have been printed for each author; the keys to this array are the authors' ids. If $seen{$au_id} is undefined or zero, then that author has not been *seen* by the program, and his name must be printed out.

```
   ##############################
   #
   # %seen contains the count of
   # books that each author has.
```

```
# if it's undefined, this
# author's books have not
# been displayed. If this is the
# case, then print out the
# author's name as a <dt>
# (a definition term) and
# increment the value in %seen
#
##############################
if (! $seen{$au_id}) {
  print BYAUTHOR "<dt>$au_fname $au_lname\n";
  $seen{$au_id}++;
}
```

After we are finished with this script, the next script you will see is books.pl. It will generate one html document for each book. The first four characters of each document name will be "book" (how appropriate) and the last four will be the id of the book, padded with zeros. The `sprintf()` function is used to do the padding, with the %04d template (the value, $bo_id, is inserted here, formatted to four spaces, padded with zeros on the left). The replacement that occurs within a `sprintf()` function is similar to regular Perl variable interpolation, except it is formatted to fit a template.

```
##############################
#
# The script, books.pl, will
# generate one html document for
# each book. The document name
# is 'book' plus the book id,
# which is padded on the left
# with up to three zeros, so
# book id 10 would be:
```

```
#     book0010.htm
#
################################
$href = sprintf("book%04d.htm", $bo_id);
```

Now, the book's title can be displayed as the text of a hyperlink. This hyperlink contains an href to the document name previously generated. This loop continues for each book.

```
################################
#
# print each book as definition
# data under the author's name
# it should be a hyperlink to
# the document which describes
# the book.
#
################################
print BYAUTHOR qq[    <dd><a href=$href>$bo_name</a>\n];

}
```

When this is done, the HTML document is completed and the file can be closed.

```
################################
#
# finish out the HTML document
# and close the file
#
################################
print BYAUTHOR <<EOF;
</dl>
</body>
</html>
```

```
EOF

close (BYAUTHOR);
```

In order to execute this script, you may issue the command

```
perl byauth.pl
```

and the files will be created in your current directory.

Figure 8.1 shows what the document will look like in the Netscape Navigator Web browser.

The second script that is used here creates an HTML document for each book. It's called books.pl, and appears on the CD-ROM under \EG\CH8\books.pl. This script is very similar to the one just shown, with a few differences noted.

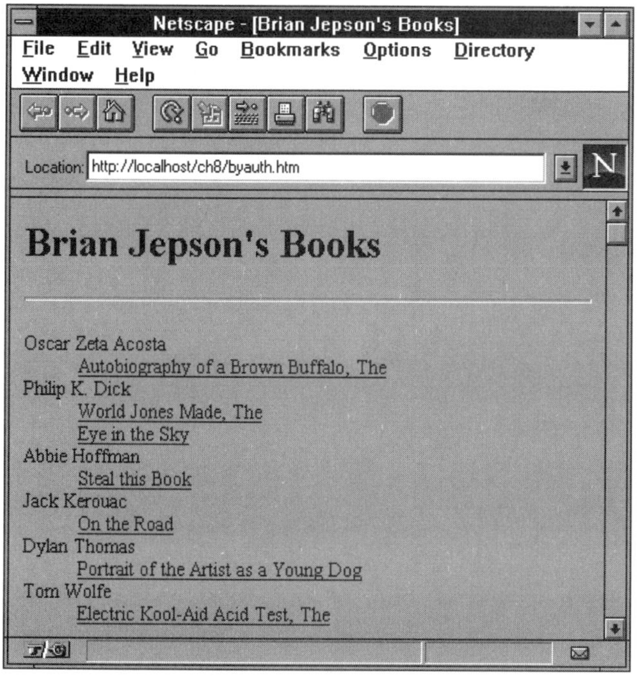

Figure 8.1 A static HTML document.

```
# -*- Perl -*-
#
#

#####################
#
# use the ODBC module
#
#####################
use NT::ODBC;

##################################
#
# Issue a query to get all books
# and all author information,
# publisher information, and
# book information associated with
# them.
#
##################################
$query = new NT::ODBC("DSN=EXAMPLE;");
$sql   = "SELECT au_fname, au_lname, bo_name,
                 bo_image, pu_name, bo_id
              FROM author, book, publish
              WHERE bo_au_id_ = au_id
                AND bo_pu_id_ = pu_id
              ORDER BY au_lname, au_fname";
if ($query->sql($sql)) {
  die ("Couldn't execute query: " . $query->error);
}

##################################
```

```
#
# fetch each row, and copy each
# value into Perl variables
#
##################################
while ($query->fetchrow) {

  $au_fname = $query->data('au_fname');
  $au_lname = $query->data('au_lname');
  $bo_name  = $query->data('bo_name');
  $bo_id    = $query->data('bo_id');
  $bo_image = $query->data('bo_image');
  $pu_name  = $query->data('pu_name');

  ##################################
  #
  # determine the name of the HTML
  # file, using the book's id.
  # See byauth.pl for more info
  # on this.
  #
  ##################################
  $file = sprintf("book%04d.htm", $bo_id);

  ##################################
  #
  # open the file corresponding to
  # the book. die if it fails
  #
  ##################################
  open(BOOK, ">$file") || die "Couldn't open $file";
```

```
  #################################
  #
  # print a complete html document
  # that file, showing the title
  # an image of the book, along
  # with the author and publisher
  #
  #################################
  print BOOK <<EOF;
<html>
<head>
<title>$bo_name</title>
</head>

<body>
<img src="images/$bo_image" align=left>
<h1>$bo_name</h1>
<hr>
<address>by $au_fname $au_lname</address>
<address>Published by $pu_name</address>
</body>
</html>
EOF

  #################################
  #
  # close the file
  #
  #################################
  close(BOOK);

}
```

In order to execute this script, you may issue the command

```
perl books.pl
```

and the files will be created in your current directory. Figure 8.2 shows what one of these documents will look like in the Netscape Navigator Web browser.

Uploading the Documents to a UNIX-based Web Server

Now that you've generated these files, you need to upload them to your World Wide Web directory on a UNIX box. The exact location of your Web pages will vary, but mine is under my home directory, in a subdirectory called www. When I use ftp to log into my account, I start out in my home directory. You may need to contact your system administrator to find the location of your Web page directory. Here's the ftp session that I used to upload my files to conan.ids.net, the UNIX machine where my Web pages are stored. These files can be accessed via the URL.

```
http://conan.ids.net/~bjepson/byauth.htm
```

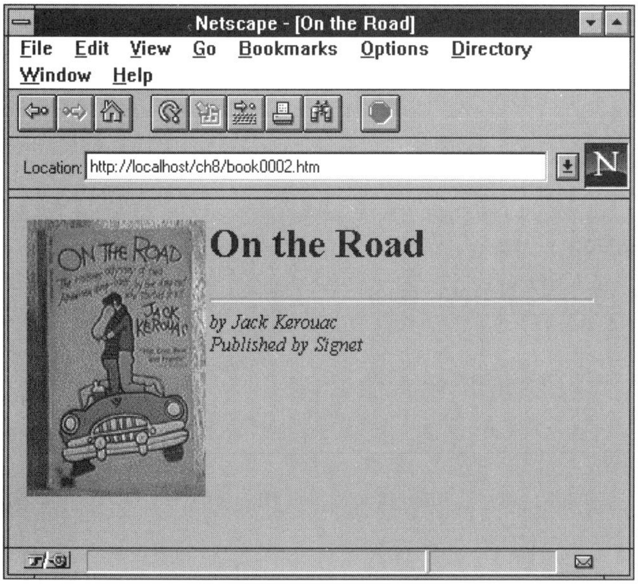

Figure 8.2 One of the static HTML documents.

In the following example, commands that I typed are in bold.

```
W:\eg\ch8>ftp conan.ids.net
Connected to conan.ids.net.
220 conan FTP server (SunOS 4.1) ready.
User (conan.ids.net:(none)): bjepson
331 Password required for bjepson.
Password: [Type a password here]
230 User bjepson logged in.
```

After I log in, I need to change directory—using the `cd` command—to my World Wide Web data directory:

```
ftp> cd www
250 CWD command successful.
```

I then need to issue the `mput` (put multiple files) command with a wildcard expression (`*.htm`); this will upload all files which have the .htm extension. Note that I must answer y (for yes) to each file.

```
ftp> mput *.htm
mput book0005.htm? y
200 PORT command successful.
150 ASCII data connection for book0005.htm (155.212.99.10,1171).
226 ASCII Transfer complete.
293 bytes sent in 0.06 seconds (4.88 Kbytes/sec)
mput book0006.htm? y
200 PORT command successful.
150 ASCII data connection for book0006.htm (155.212.99.10,1172).
226 ASCII Transfer complete.
229 bytes sent in 0.04 seconds (5.72 Kbytes/sec)
mput book0003.htm? y
200 PORT command successful.
150 ASCII data connection for book0003.htm (155.212.99.10,1173).
226 ASCII Transfer complete.
```

```
245 bytes sent in 0.02 seconds (11.67 Kbytes/sec)
mput book0007.htm? y
200 PORT command successful.
150 ASCII data connection for book0007.htm (155.212.99.10,1174).
226 ASCII Transfer complete.
244 bytes sent in 0.02 seconds (12.20 Kbytes/sec)
mput book0002.htm? y
200 PORT command successful.
150 ASCII data connection for book0002.htm (155.212.99.10,1175).
226 ASCII Transfer complete.
227 bytes sent in 0.04 seconds (5.67 Kbytes/sec)
mput book0001.htm? y
200 PORT command successful.
150 ASCII data connection for book0001.htm (155.212.99.10,1176).
226 ASCII Transfer complete.
284 bytes sent in 0.06 seconds (4.73 Kbytes/sec)
mput book0004.htm? y
200 PORT command successful.
150 ASCII data connection for book0004.htm (155.212.99.10,1177).
226 ASCII Transfer complete.
268 bytes sent in 0.03 seconds (8.93 Kbytes/sec)
mput byauth.htm? y
200 PORT command successful.
150 ASCII data connection for byauth.htm (155.212.99.10,1178).
226 ASCII Transfer complete.
658 bytes sent in 0.04 seconds (16.45 Kbytes/sec)
```

Then, I need to make a directory to hold the images and transfer them as well. These are located in the directory \EG\CH8\IMAGES. In order to do this, I need to make a directory on conan called images, and change directory (cd) into it:

```
ftp> mkdir images
257 MKD command successful.
```

```
ftp> cd images
250 CWD command successful.
```

I also must issue the `lcd` command (local change directory) to make sure that I am in the images directory under the \EG\CH8 directory:

```
ftp> lcd images
Local directory now W:\eg\ch8\images
```

Since the image files must be transmitted in binary mode, I need to issue the `bin` (which specifies binary transfer mode) and `hash` commands. Since the image files are likely to be slightly larger than the HTML files, I can use the `hash` command, which causes a # mark to appear for every 2,048 bytes that are transferred, just so I can see how much has been sent.

```
ftp> bin
200 Type set to I.
ftp> hash
Hash mark printing On (2048 bytes/hash mark).
ftp> mput *.jpg
mput eye.jpg? y
200 PORT command successful.
150 Binary data connection for eye.jpg (155.212.99.10,1179).
##
226 Binary Transfer complete.
5930 bytes sent in 0.06 seconds (98.83 Kbytes/sec)
mput acosta.jpg? y
200 PORT command successful.
150 Binary data connection for acosta.jpg (155.212.99.10,1180).
##
226 Binary Transfer complete.
7547 bytes sent in 0.29 seconds (26.02 Kbytes/sec)
mput electric.jpg? y
200 PORT command successful.
```

```
150 Binary data connection for electric.jpg (155.212.99.10,1181).
##
226 Binary Transfer complete.
6424 bytes sent in 0.06 seconds (107.07 Kbytes/sec)
mput jones.jpg? y
200 PORT command successful.
150 Binary data connection for jones.jpg (155.212.99.10,1182).
##
226 Binary Transfer complete.
6735 bytes sent in 0.04 seconds (168.38 Kbytes/sec)
mput dog.jpg? y
200 PORT command successful.
150 Binary data connection for dog.jpg (155.212.99.10,1183).
##
226 Binary Transfer complete.
7894 bytes sent in 0.06 seconds (131.57 Kbytes/sec)
mput steal.jpg? y
200 PORT command successful.
150 Binary data connection for steal.jpg (155.212.99.10,1184).
##
226 Binary Transfer complete.
7562 bytes sent in 0.11 seconds (68.75 Kbytes/sec)
mput onroad.jpg? y
200 PORT command successful.
150 Binary data connection for onroad.jpg (155.212.99.10,1185).
###
226 Binary Transfer complete.
8390 bytes sent in 1.89 seconds (4.43 Kbytes/sec)
ftp> quit
221 Goodbye.

W:\eg\ch8>
```

And that's all there is to it. You'll need to go through these steps each time you regenerate the documents.

Uploading the Documents to a VMS-based Web Server

It just so happens that I also have an account on a VAX, which is running VMS as its operating system. Although there are a lot of UNIX boxen (plural of box) on the Internet, there are also a lot of VAXen (plural of VAX) on the Internet. The way that directories are dealt with is slightly different than that of UNIX. For one, you may need to specify a volume name (this is a logical organization of disk space, used much in the same way as driver letters under MS-DOS, OS/2 and Windows NT) when specifying directories. The directory separator is . (a period) instead of a \ (backslash) under MS-DOS or a / (forward slash) under UNIX. You will need to know the directory where your World Wide Web files are located. This can be obtained from your system administrator.

Here's the ftp session I used to upload my files to a VAX machine. These files can be accessed via the URL.

```
http://ids.net/~bjepson/byauth.htm
```

In the following example, commands that I typed are in bold.

```
W:\eg\ch8>ftp ids.net
Connected to ids.net.
220 ids.net MultiNet FTP Server Process 3.3(14) at Sun 7-Jan-96
11:03AM-EST
User (ids.net:(none)): bjepson
331 User name (bjepson) ok. Password, please.
Password: [Type a password here]
230 User BJEPSON logged into $WORKSPACE:[BJEPSON] at Sun 7-Jan-96 11:03AM-EST,
job 10bb.
```

After logging in, I `cd` (change directory) to the volume (DKA500) and directory (BBS.USERDIRS.BJEPSON.WWW) where my home pages are stored.

```
ftp> cd DKA500:[BBS.USERDIRS.BJEPSON.WWW]
250 Connected to DKA500:[BBS.USERDIRS.BJEPSON.WWW].
```

Now, it's simply a matter of issuing the `mput` (put multiple files) command with a wildcard expression (`*.htm`); this will upload all files which have the .htm extension. Note that I must answer y (for yes) to each file.

```
ftp> mput *.htm
mput book0005.htm? y
200 Port 4.61 at Host 155.212.99.10 accepted.
150 ASCII Store of DKA500:[BBS.USERDIRS.BJEPSON.WWW]BOOK0005.HTM;1 started.
226 Transfer completed.  293 (8) bytes transferred.
293 bytes sent in 0.05 seconds (5.86 Kbytes/sec)
mput book0006.htm? y
200 Port 4.62 at Host 155.212.99.10 accepted.
150 ASCII Store of DKA500:[BBS.USERDIRS.BJEPSON.WWW]BOOK0006.HTM;1 started.
226 Transfer completed.  229 (8) bytes transferred.
229 bytes sent in 0.04 seconds (5.72 Kbytes/sec)
mput book0003.htm? y
200 Port 4.63 at Host 155.212.99.10 accepted.
150 ASCII Store of DKA500:[BBS.USERDIRS.BJEPSON.WWW]BOOK0003.HTM;1 started.
226 Transfer completed.  245 (8) bytes transferred.
245 bytes sent in 0.03 seconds (8.17 Kbytes/sec)
mput book0007.htm? y
200 Port 4.64 at Host 155.212.99.10 accepted.
150 ASCII Store of DKA500:[BBS.USERDIRS.BJEPSON.WWW]BOOK0007.HTM;1 started.
226 Transfer completed.  244 (8) bytes transferred.
244 bytes sent in 0.03 seconds (8.13 Kbytes/sec)
mput book0002.htm? y
200 Port 4.65 at Host 155.212.99.10 accepted.
150 ASCII Store of DKA500:[BBS.USERDIRS.BJEPSON.WWW]BOOK0002.HTM;1 started.
226 Transfer completed.  227 (8) bytes transferred.
227 bytes sent in 0.01 seconds (22.70 Kbytes/sec)
```

```
mput book0001.htm? y
200 Port 4.66 at Host 155.212.99.10 accepted.
150 ASCII Store of DKA500:[BBS.USERDIRS.BJEPSON.WWW]BOOK0001.HTM;1 started.
226 Transfer completed.  284 (8) bytes transferred.
284 bytes sent in 0.03 seconds (9.47 Kbytes/sec)
mput book0004.htm? y
200 Port 4.67 at Host 155.212.99.10 accepted.
150 ASCII Store of DKA500:[BBS.USERDIRS.BJEPSON.WWW]BOOK0004.HTM;1 started.
226 Transfer completed.  268 (8) bytes transferred.
268 bytes sent in 0.02 seconds (13.40 Kbytes/sec)
mput byauth.htm? y
200 Port 4.68 at Host 155.212.99.10 accepted.
150 ASCII Store of DKA500:[BBS.USERDIRS.BJEPSON.WWW]BYAUTH.HTM;1 started.
226 Transfer completed.  658 (8) bytes transferred.
658 bytes sent in 0.03 seconds (21.93 Kbytes/sec)
```

I also need to transfer over the images. These are located in the directory \EG\CH8\IMAGES. In order to do this, I need to make a directory on the VAX called images and change directory (`cd`) into it.

```
ftp> mkdir images
257 "DKA500:[BBS.USERDIRS.BJEPSON.WWW.IMAGES]" Directory created
ftp> cd images
250 Connected to DKA500:[BBS.USERDIRS.BJEPSON.WWW.IMAGES].
```

I also must issue the `lcd` command (local change directory) to make sure that I am in the images directory under the \EG\CH8 directory.

```
ftp> lcd images
Local directory now W:\eg\ch8\images
```

Before I use `mput` to transfer the files, I issue the `bin` (which specifies binary transfer mode, required for transferring binary data) and `hash` commands. Since the image files are likely to be slightly larger than the HTML files, I can use the `hash` command to see a mark for every 2,048 bytes that are transferred; this allows me to get a vague idea of how much time is remaining in the transfer.

```
ftp> bin
200 Type I ok.
ftp> hash
Hash mark printing On (2048 bytes/hash mark).
ftp> mput *.jpg
mput eye.jpg? y
200 Port 4.71 at Host 155.212.99.10 accepted.
150 IMAGE Store of DKA500:[BBS.USERDIRS.BJEPSON.WWW.IMAGES]EYE.JPG;1 started.
##
226 Transfer completed.  5930 (8) bytes transferred.
5930 bytes sent in 0.05 seconds (118.60 Kbytes/sec)
mput acosta.jpg? y
200 Port 4.74 at Host 155.212.99.10 accepted.
150 IMAGE Store of DKA500:[BBS.USERDIRS.BJEPSON.WWW.IMAGES]ACOSTA.JPG;1
started.
##
226 Transfer completed.  7547 (8) bytes transferred.
7547 bytes sent in 0.05 seconds (150.94 Kbytes/sec)
mput electric.jpg? y
200 Port 4.77 at Host 155.212.99.10 accepted.
150 IMAGE Store of DKA500:[BBS.USERDIRS.BJEPSON.WWW.IMAGES]ELECTRIC.JPG;1
started.
##
226 Transfer completed.  6424 (8) bytes transferred.
6424 bytes sent in 0.10 seconds (64.24 Kbytes/sec)
mput jones.jpg? y
200 Port 4.78 at Host 155.212.99.10 accepted.
150 IMAGE Store of DKA500:[BBS.USERDIRS.BJEPSON.WWW.IMAGES]JONES.JPG;1 started.
##
```

```
226 Transfer completed.  6735 (8) bytes transferred.
6735 bytes sent in 0.07 seconds (94.86 Kbytes/sec)
mput dog.jpg? y
200 Port 4.79 at Host 155.212.99.10 accepted.
150 IMAGE Store of DKA500:[BBS.USERDIRS.BJEPSON.WWW.IMAGES]DOG.JPG;1 started.
##
226 Transfer completed.  7894 (8) bytes transferred.
7894 bytes sent in 0.06 seconds (131.57 Kbytes/sec)
mput steal.jpg? y
200 Port 4.80 at Host 155.212.99.10 accepted.
150 IMAGE Store of DKA500:[BBS.USERDIRS.BJEPSON.WWW.IMAGES]STEAL.JPG;1 started.
##
226 Transfer completed.  7562 (8) bytes transferred.
7562 bytes sent in 0.05 seconds (151.24 Kbytes/sec)
mput onroad.jpg? y
200 Port 4.83 at Host 155.212.99.10 accepted.
150 IMAGE Store of DKA500:[BBS.USERDIRS.BJEPSON.WWW.IMAGES]ONROAD.JPG;1
started.

###
226 Transfer completed.  8390 (8) bytes transferred.
8390 bytes sent in 2.06 seconds (4.07 Kbytes/sec)
ftp> quit
221 QUIT command received. Goodbye.

W:\eg\ch8>
```

That's all there is to it. Each time you regenerate the documents, you will need to go through these steps.

Miscellaneous Issues

The remainder of this chapter is concerned with issues for those who need to configure the EMWAC http server to log in as a specific user. There are a lot of reasons why you might want to do this. For example, you may wish to use ODBC against a networked single-tier data source, such as a FoxPro data source located on a computer other than the Web server. The techniques used herein are especially useful to those, who for one reason or another, do not use ODBC 2.5 or greater, and thus cannot take advantage of a system data source; they must configure a data source for each user. Also, for those who use SQL Server in integrated security mode (SQL Server takes login information from Windows NT), this is required.

The Windows NT User Manager

The first thing you must do is create a user. This can be accomplished by starting the Windows NT User Manager, which should be located in the Administrative tools group of the Windows NT Program Manager. Figure 8.3 shows the main screen of the Windows NT User Manager. In order to add a new user, select the New User... option from the User menu. This will cause the New User dialog box to appear. In this example, I will use the name wwwuser. You should type this into the Username field, and also supply a password in both the Password and Confirm Password field. Take care to memorize the password. It may be advantageous to check the User Cannot Change Password

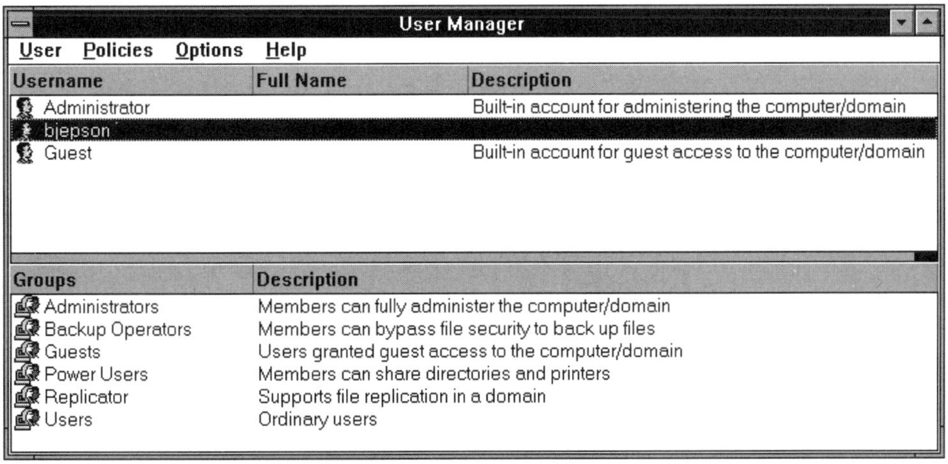

Figure 8.3 The main screen of the Windows NT User Manager.

and Password Never Expires checkboxes, as you will rarely log in interactively under this username, and therefore won't see any warnings about password expiration. Checking the Password Never Expires checkbox will only allow members of the administrator group to change the password. As with any other user, you should change this user's password frequently. If you do so, you must re-enter the password into the service start-up options dialog. This process is outlined in the following section. Figure 8.4 shows the New User dialog box.

Configuring HTTPS to Log in as a User

Now that you've managed to add the user, you need to configure HTTPS to log in as that user. Start the control panel, and double-click on the Services applet. From within this applet, double-click on EMWAC HTTP Server. If you are using another Web server product, this process will differ. If the EMWAC HTTPS server does not appear in the list of services, it has not been installed correctly. Please see the documentation for the HTTPS server for information on installing it.

Once you have double-clicked on the EMWAC HTTPS server item in the Services list, the Service dialog box will appear, as shown in Figure 8.5. Type in the name of the user that you created in the previous step and also the pass-

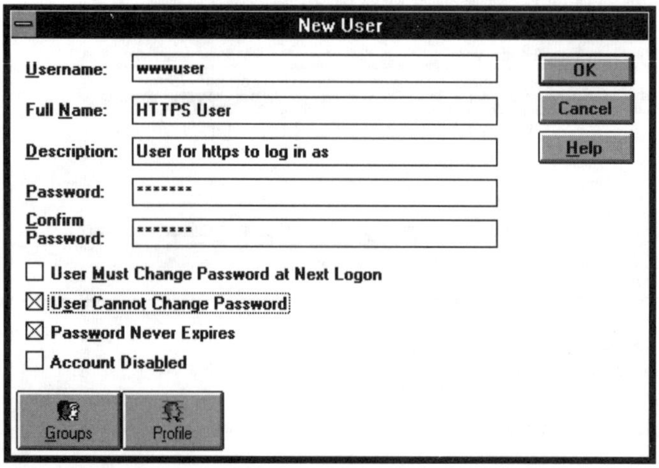

Figure 8.4 The New User dialog box.

word (you must type the password into the Password and Confirm Password fields). As the service is configured to log in as that user, a dialog appears, announcing that that user has been granted the Log On As A Service right.

Log in as the User

Before HTTPS can do much with the account, you may need to log in as that user and set any required paths. At this point, you can also configure ODBC data sources, if you are using a version of ODBC which does not support system data sources.

You must first select Logoff . . . from the Program Manager's File Menu, then go through the Windows NT logon sequence; but this time, log in with the user name and password created earlier. At this point, if you installed Windows NT over a Windows 3.x installation, you may be asked if you want to migrate the WIN.INI and SYSTEM.INI settings over to that user's account. You can choose OK for this option, as it might be needed for running certain programs as that user in the future.

Configuring Permanent Drive Mappings and Data Sources

Once you have logged in as that user, you will need to map a drive. In my test environment, I want to map drive X: to the share BOOKCD on the

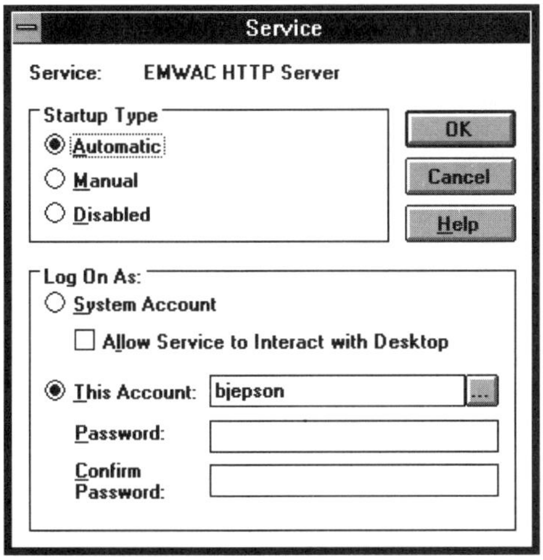

Figure 8.5 The Server dialog box.

server OSCAR. This contains a writeable copy of the CD's contents; I can map this drive with the command:

```
net use X: \\OSCAR\BOOKCD /PERSISTENT:YES
```

The /PERSISTENT:YES flag causes the drive mapping to be remembered each time the user logs in. If you need to configure a data source for that particular user, you can go into the ODBC manager and set up a data source for that user. The process is similar to that outlined in Chapter 3, except you will add the data source from the first screen, rather than selecting the System Data Source screen. For systems with older versions of the ODBC driver manager, there is no System Data Source screen and this is the only way to configure the data sources.

Now that you have configured a mapping to the networked drive, you may use network drive letters in path specifications for data sources. Figure 8.6 shows the setup dialog for a FoxPro data source which uses a network drive in the data source.

This chapter has covered some of the miscellaneous issues involved with World Wide Web database development. As more arise, they will be added to the FAQ devoted to this book:

```
http://www.ids.net/~bjepson/www-database/FAQ.html
```

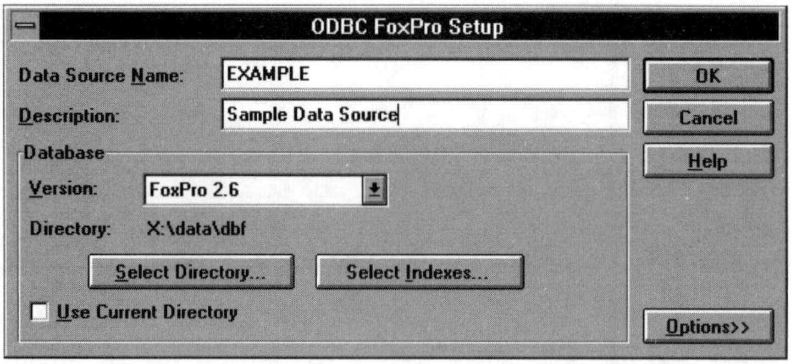

Figure 8.6 The FoxPro setup dialog box.

CHAPTER

9

WRAP-UP

Most of this book has been dedicated to showing you what can be done with a small part of the existing set of freely redistributable tools available for Windows NT. Since innovations occur constantly in the realm of free software (I claim that they occur faster than in commercial software), I am going to gaze into my crystal ball and tell you what (in my not so humble opinion) the future holds.

Perl and DBI

There is an effort under way to provide a standardized means of accessing databases from Perl. The DBI project, led by Tim Bunce (Tim.Bunce@ig.co.uk) provides an architecture-neutral method of accessing databases from Perl. If you think it sounds a lot like ODBC, then you are right! DBI *is* a lot like ODBC. Further, it has recently taken a turn and will soon be reengineered as an ODBC-based solution.

At the time of this writing, the Windows NT version of Perl is an incomplete port of its UNIX-based counterpart. Since Perl is more "at home" on UNIX, and certainly very prevalent and popular there, it should come as no surprise that most of the Perl goodies start out on UNIX. If they can be made to run on Windows NT or Windows 95, they will make their way "down" to us Windows NT and Windows 95 users. DBI is one of those goodies. Like ODBC, DBI, in its present incarnation, has something akin to a driver manager, which is called the Module Handler. In order to access a specific database, DBI also requires database drivers, just as ODBC does.

Like many tools on UNIX, DBI is available for free. All of the functionality is accessed through a Perl module, so anyone with Perl knowledge can use it. However, most of the functionality provided by the Module Handler and each driver is implemented through a *loadable module*. Loadable modules are portions of code that are loaded on demand by Perl. These are very similar to Windows DLLs; on Windows NT and Windows 95, these modules are implemented as .PLL files, which are more or less .DLL files. As with many products, including Perl itself, the road from UNIX to Windows NT is full of complications. For one, the standard Windows NT C compiler, Microsoft Visual C++, cannot compile UNIX applications "out of the box." However, even across widely different versions of UNIX, source code for programs can usually be compiled by merely modifying a Makefile, which is a roadmap for a program called `make`. This program determines which components of a program need to be compiled and also runs the C compiler, eventually spitting out a completed executable program. It can also be used, as is the case with DBI and the DBI drivers, to run a series of tests on the compiled code and make sure that it was built correctly. Finally, it can be used to install the program (and any libraries required by the program) on your system.

A lot of UNIX tools are distributed freely. Many of these are distributed under the terms of the GNU General Public License, which is a standard license on everything that comes out of the Free Software Foundation, an organization dedicated to providing free software (as the name implies). The software they distribute is known as GNU Software. GNU stands for GNUs Not UNIX, one of the many recursive acronyms you will come across. Many other people have chosen to use this license, which allows the author to hold the copyright, but places few restrictions on the user. Perl itself is distributed under the terms of this license as well as another license, the Artistic License. One of the requirements of the General Public License is that the source code must be made available freely. This is very important on UNIX, as there are many flavors of UNIX running on different architectures and it is often necessary to compile the source code on your machine. Further, even the same implementation of UNIX, or a UNIX-compatible operating system, can vary enough from installation to installation, that it is advantageous to recompile certain programs on each individual machine on which you plan to install it.

One of the toolsets (or toolchains, as some like to call them) that makes it possible to easily build programs on various flavors of UNIX is the Free Software Foundation's GNU C compiler and related utilities. This provides a freely redistributable toolchain for building software on UNIX and UNIX-like platforms. Most of the source code distributions of GNU software include a `configure` script, which probes your system for GNU versions or other versions of programs typically found in the GNU toolchain. In addition to determining which components are installed, some small programs are compiled in order to see how your C compiler handles certain tasks. Once it has determined that your computer has the software needed to build the program, it generates a Makefile, which can then be used with the `make` utility. Unfortunately, the components packaged with Microsoft's Visual C++ are not compatible with the `configure` script. As a result, `configure` cannot be used to automatically generate Makefiles for Visual C++. Typically, once the GNU C compiler and the rest of the toolchain have been ported to a target platform, compiling the rest of the plethora of free software becomes trivial.

As mentioned previously, at present it is not very easy to port a UNIX application to Windows NT or Windows 95. The good folks at Hip Communications (http://info.hip.com) have done an excellent job of transcending the difficulties of porting from UNIX to Windows NT and Windows 95. However, their job may soon get a lot easier (and the jobs of folks who port such programs as GNU EMACS, Tcl/Tk, and Ghostscript to Windows NT and Windows 95). Steve Chamberlain (sac@cygnus.com) of Cygnus Software has spearheaded an effort to port GNU C and the entire GNU toolchain to Windows NT. This effort is known as the gnu-win32 project, and includes such programs as `bash` (the FSF's shell, which replaces command.com and cmd.exe), `awk` (a pattern matching language), `sed` (a stream editor), and `bison` (a parser generator). This effort is very far along; the latest beta UNIX distribution of Perl (5.002) has been successfully compiled using an early version of this toolchain. However, the Windows NT- and Windows 95-specific bells and whistles are lost in this process, as the distribution of Perl which is being developed by Hip Communications, Inc. includes many features which have not been incorporated into the UNIX distribution. On the flip side, the Windows NT and Windows 95 versions of Perl lack many of the features found in the UNIX distribution, which is due to inadequacies on the part of Microsoft's Visual C++ toolkit as well as to the Windows NT and Windows 95 operating systems. The developers at Hip Communications, Inc. have done an excellent job of transcending these inadequacies. Since the goal of the Cygnus port of GNU C is to transcend the same differences that are holding back the port of Perl to Windows NT and Windows 95, one can only hope that the Perl distribution for Windows NT can be migrated to the GNU C compiler.

In addition to making the jobs of those who port Perl to Windows NT and Windows 95 easier, migrating the distribution over to GNU C will make a lot of other things very easy. For example, the DBI loadable module and the DBI drivers compile cleanly under GNU C. If Perl for Windows NT and Windows 95 were compiled under GNU C using the results of the gnu-win32 project, then it would be possible to seamlessly integrate it with the DBI extensions also compiled under GNU C.

As previously mentioned, DBI is going to be reimplemented as an ODBC-based solution. A free ODBC driver manager exists for UNIX, which was developed by Ke Jin (kejin@lithium.empress.com) of Empress Software. It's called iODBC, which should not be confused with Lee Fesperman's IODBC.EXE, which is a freely redistributable command line ODBC tool for Windows NT and Windows 95. As DBI moves towards an ODBC-based solution, you will probably see the DBI developers working closely with Ke Jin to integrate iODBC with the Perl DBI loadable module.

Since the DBI Module Handler is a C program compiled as a Perl extension, it will need to be linked to Ke Jin's ODBC driver manager, also written in C. When the gnu-win32 project is completed, it will be possible to build Perl, Ke Jin's iODBC, and the various DBI components from the UNIX source distribution. Although Microsoft sells an ODBC SDK (Software Development Kit) as part of the Microsoft Developer's Network, Ke Jin's iODBC is freely available and works with a freely available C compiler. If Windows NT and Windows 95 developers can have access to a freely redistributable, fully functional UNIX development toolchain, then the 32-bit Windows world will no longer be isolated from UNIX. This means that Windows users and developers can begin to enjoy the software that has made the lives of UNIX users and developers easy for years.

As the gnu-win32 project nears completion, Windows NT and Windows 95 developers and users will soon reap the benefits of the work being performed by the likes of Tim Bunce and Ke Jin. It should soon be possible for users and developers who have nothing but a computer running a copy of Windows 95 or Windows NT to do large-scale, robust database development in Perl without having to buy another piece of software. Here's a breakdown of Free Software currently available for Windows NT and Windows 95.

GNU C and Related Utilities

This is the gnu-win32 project, which was previously mentioned. It contains the programs and libraries necessary to build applications from UNIX source distributions on Windows NT and Windows 95. The programs and supporting files can be downloaded from

```
ftp://ftp.cygnus.com/pub/gnu-win32/latest/
```

and the project's Web page is

```
http://www.cygnus.com/misc/gnu-win32/
```

Perl

If you've gotten this far in the book, you should know what Perl is! But for those of you who don't, it's Larry Wall's interpreted systems language. The source code (for UNIX) can be found on (among other locations):

```
ftp://ftp.cis.ufl.edu/pub/perl/CPAN/src/5.0/
```

As of this writing, you will not be able to build Perl "out of the box" with gnu-win32. This is likely to change by the time the book falls into your hands. However, Sven Verdoolaege (skimo@dns.ufsia.ac.be) has managed to compile Perl from the UNIX sources using the gnu-win32 toolchain.

```
ftp://dns.ufsia.ac.be/pub/perl/
```

Of course, only the Perl that we've been using all along in this book works with the book's examples. So, unless you are experimenting with other database connectivity options, such as DBI, you will want the Hip Communications port of Perl 5 to Windows NT and Windows 95.

```
ftp://ntperl.hip.com/ntperl/
```

GNU EMACS

GNU EMACS is the extensible, self-documenting, real-time text editor of the Free Software Foundation. It supports a subset of Common Lisp, which can be used to extend the power of the editor. It also supports syntax coloring and *intelligent* editing modes for a variety of programming languages. GNU EMACS for Windows NT and Windows 95 can be found on

```
ftp://june.cs.washington.edu/pub/ntemacs/latest/
```

and the Web page describing the status of this port can be found on:

```
http://www.cs.washington.edu/homes/voelker/ntemacs.html
```

iODBC Driver Manager

Ke Jin's iODBC provides a free UNIX-based ODBC driver manager. It can be found on

```
ftp://ftp.mcqueen.com/pub/dbperl/other/iODBC
```

along with the nntp ODBC driver, which allows you to use nntp news servers as ODBC data sources.

Java and ODBC

If you've been paying much attention to the media, you will have been exposed to some of the hype surrounding Java. Hopefully, this section of the chapter will demystify Java. Java is a product of Sun Microsystems and some parts of it are distributed freely. It is a programming language with many object-oriented features. It is said to be an *embeddable language*, meaning software vendors can embed support for it within their products. For those of you who have used Microsoft's OLE, this should be nothing new. However, Java code can be passed from a server on the Internet to a client workstation and executed in any application which supports Java. The bits of code that get passed around are called *applets*. Rather than running as machine code compiled for your particular architecture, Java runs in a *virtual machine*, which has its own set of instructions called *Java bytecode*. In order to supply Java support on a given architecture, such as an Intel-based Windows NT platform, the Java virtual machine needs to be ported to that platform. Once the virtual machine and all of the glue that hooks into the operating system has been ported, you can embed Java support into software targeted for that architecture. Because of this, Java is said to be *architecture-neutral*. At the time of this writing, Java support is available on a variety of architectures, including Windows NT and Windows 95 running on Intel processors.

What does this mean to the average Internet user? Lots. The introduction of Java marks one of the first of many steps that the software industry will be taking towards seamless integration of the desktop with the Internet. Think about your desktop now. When you want to *surf* the Internet, you need to start up a Web browser, Telnet client, or a gopher or ftp session. As more Internet bandwidth is available—and as personal Internet access becomes more common—it will be possible to "Internet-enable" many common applications, such as spreadsheets and word processors. With Java (or a similar embeddable language, such as Python), you will be able to include executable content in your documents. For example, imagine that you are putting together a report which includes economic information on a particular region, such as Providence, Rhode Island. Suppose also, that a colleague in your field has developed a Java applet that displays a graph based on economic data from that region and the data is updated daily. Perhaps the applet not only displays a graph, but also would let you access some of the properties of that graph, such as the data on which the graph is based. It would be a simple matter of embedding it in your word processing document and writing a macro which updates your facts and figures that are included within the body of the document.

How does all of this relate to ODBC? Well, as more World Wide Web developers come to rely on the inclusion of data sources in their Web documents, they will also want to hang on to that type of functionality when they start working with Java.

Unfortunately, there exists much debate as to how Java applets should communicate with an ODBC data source. Because CGI scripts execute on a remote server, there's really no question as to how to implement ODBC connectivity in Perl CGI scripts. Since the Perl script executes on a remote server, it's easy to establish a method to allow that script to have access to the data source; the data source can reside on that server or one close by. Further, the data source itself does not need to be exposed to the outside world in order to get this to happen. The only process that needs access to the data source is the Perl script. You don't have to contend with many users directly accessing and manipulating the data source from a wide variety of machines. However, since Java applets execute on a client machine, allowing that applet to have access to an ODBC data source on one of your computers results in a compromise; in order for a remotely executing ODBC-enabled Java applet to have access to the data on your machine, you need to provide the same level of security (or lack thereof) that would allow someone running another remote ODBC-enabled application, such as Excel or Powerbuilder, to access your data source.

However, there may be certain situations where you want everyone to have access to your data. Imagine that some day, some government decides that it would be rather keen to deploy a system on the Internet that provides detailed census data. In order to do this, they install a copy of SYBASE or Microsoft SQL Server on the Internet and install nothing but this data and the required system databases on it. Wisely, they decide not to put any proprietary or confidential information on it. Further, they decide to supply an ODBC-enabled Java applet that allows folks to generate a graph based on the data. The Java applet will connect to the data source on the Internet and generate the graph. Since the database server is also on the Internet, it provides an additional benefit. Internet users wishing to query the data using the query tool of their choice may do so. If they want to use Powerbuilder, FoxPro, or Excel, they all have that option.

Another complexity added by introducing any sort of client-side executable is that of configuration management. Any user who wants to use an ODBC-enabled Java applet will have to, at a minimum, install a driver manager and at least one driver. Fortunately, since an ODBC connection string can include enough information to make a connection, users may not have to configure a data source for each driver. Also, ODBC is starting to become more commonplace; many Microsoft products include the ODBC driver manager and several drivers, as does Solaris 2.5. In any case, as users' needs become more complex, a certain amount of that configuration management becomes their responsibility. For many applications, Java will be a simple point-and-click operation. However, as users begin hooking into proprietary data sources, they may need to do a little configuration on their end.

Ke Jin of Empress Software is presently tackling this issue. One of the challenges in a project such as this involves the question of how to implement ODBC within Java. Although Java is architecture-neutral, it provides a means of developing native methods, which are programs written in a language such as C or C++ that can be called from Java. The benefit of native methods is that they enable the Java developer to write code that takes advantage of a specific architecture's features, but they sacrifice cross-platform functionality. For example, a native method developed to use Windows NT's ODBC Driver Manager would have to be recompiled on Solaris to work with their ODBC driver manager. Since most, if not all, vendor-supplied drivers are C libraries or shared libraries under UNIX and DLLs, using native methods is the most practical means of accomplishing ODBC with Java until and unless, as Ke Jin says, "all database vendors provide their proprietary layers as pure Java . . . [which] requires a new standard."

Microsoft Internet Information Server, ODBC, and Perl

As odd as it may seem, Microsoft is a late arrival in the business of Web servers for Windows NT. Their Internet Information Server, formerly known as Gibraltar, will be available by the time this book falls into your hands. Although it is one of the latest arrivals, it includes many features that make it attractive to those developing Web sites on Windows NT. In addition to a Web server, the Internet Server also includes FTP and Gopher services. It also has integrated security with Windows NT; you can administer security on your Web site down to the file level with the same tools that you use to assign permissions on Windows NT. It also supports SSL (Secure Socket Layer), and IP address-level security; groups of IP addresses can be denied or granted access to Internet services on a particular machine.

Starting with build 103 of Perl for Win32, a separate, DLL-based version of Perl has been included in the release. This DLL can communicate with the Microsoft Internet Information Server using the Internet Server API (ISAPI). ISAPI allows developers to extend the Microsoft Internet Information Server with their own code.

Also, the Internet Information Server supplies a component called the Internet Database Connector, which functions a lot like the HTML templates seen in Chapter 4. This uses a DLL called HTTPODBC.DLL. Rather than one .TPL file, as shown in the templates which use template.pl, HTTPODBC.DLL uses two files: the Internet Database Connector (*.IDC) files and HTML extension (*.HTX) files. The .IDC files include ODBC connection information, as well as a pointer to the .HTX file, which serves as a template for the HTML file to generate.

The Internet Information Server appears to be a robust and extensible system for deploying information. Although it is appearing late in the game, it seems that it will provide some features not yet seen in Web servers on Windows NT.

CHAPTER

10

JIVE: A TOOL FOR ODBC-ENABLED HTML DOCUMENTS

The author of IODBC (the 32-bit command-line ODBC tool), Lee Fesperman, has released a new, freely redistributable tool called Jive. Jive is a powerful HTML scripting language with ODBC capability. As of this writing, versions for Windows NT and Windows 95 are available; it compiles on Linux and SunOS 4.1.x (it probably compiles on other UNIXes, but these are the only two that I've tested so far). On UNIX, Jive is linked against Ke Jin's iODBC driver manager (not to be confused with IODBC, also by Lee Fesperman). Ke Jin's iODBC driver manager is freely redistributable, and can be obtained on one of the following sites:

```
ftp://ftp.demon.co.uk/pub/perl/db/other/iODBC/
ftp://ftp.uu.net/pub/database/perl-interfaces/other/iODBC
ftp://ftp.mcqueen.com/pub/dbperl/other/iODBC/
```

Lee Fesperman's Jive is included on the CD-ROM in the directory \JIVE. Source is included, as well as executables for Windows NT and Windows 95 running on Intel processors. See the included \EG\DEFAULT.HTM file for a link to instructions on how to build Jive on UNIX.

Jive commands are embedded directly into HTML text as extensions and Jive is referenced as a CGI executable. As of this writing, Jive only works with the CGI POST method, but by the time this book falls into your hands, it should understand the GET method. Consequently, all of the examples in this chapter use HTML forms with a POST method, even where a URL might be more appropriate. The GET method will utilize a full URL, such as

```
http://localhost/jive.exe/page=ch10/plays.jiv
```

whereas the POST method pipes the CGI query data directly to the script or executable. The executable, JIVE.EXE, should be copied into your https data directory. If you installed the examples from the CD-ROM onto your hard drive and set that directory as the https data directory, this is already done for you, since JIVE.EXE is also included on the CD-ROM under \EG. See Appendix C for more information on installing the examples from the CD-ROM.

I'm going to revisit some of the templates shown in Chapter 4, and show you how easy it is to rewrite them using Jive. Keep in mind that because I am a thirty-sixth degree Yakmeister, I am privy to many things that you aren't. Consequently, I am working with a pre-release version of Jive; by the time you get a copy of this book, not only will I be halfway to Mars (you think I'm kidding!!!), but some things might have changed with the way Jive works. As a result, the support site for this book will be updated by my minions to include any addenda, such as changes in the Jive language. The support site is located on:

```
http://www.ids.net/~bjepson/www-database/
```

Web Page to Call Jive

As previously mentioned, the pre-release version of Jive which I am using requires use of the POST method. Because of this, you will use an HTML document which contains a form to link to the Jive executable. Here's the document, which is on the CD-ROM under \EG\CH10\plays.htm:

```
<html>
<head>
<title>City Nights Dinner Theatre</title>
</head>

<body>
Welcome to the City Nights Dinner Theatre home pages. We've
just started to put some of our information on line,
starting with a searchable index of performances:<p>

<hr>

<form action=/jive.exe method=post>
   <input type=hidden name=page   value=ch10/plays.jiv>
   <input type=submit name=submit value="See All Plays">
</form>
```

As you can see, it's a very simple HTML document. It looks a lot like the plays.htm document used in Chapter 4. The executable, JIVE.EXE, resides in the root of the https data directory, which is why there is a trailing / before the name of the executable. The page variable tells Jive where to find the HTML document. Since this HTML document includes Jive extensions, it has a different extension: .jiv. Jive is executed in the https document root; thus, it needs the path name to the HTML document, ch10/plays.jiv. Figure 10.1 shows how this document will appear in the Netscape Navigator Web browser.

Simple Jive Document

Jive reads in the HTML document referenced in the page CGI variable. This document can contain Jive extensions, which are enclosed in curly

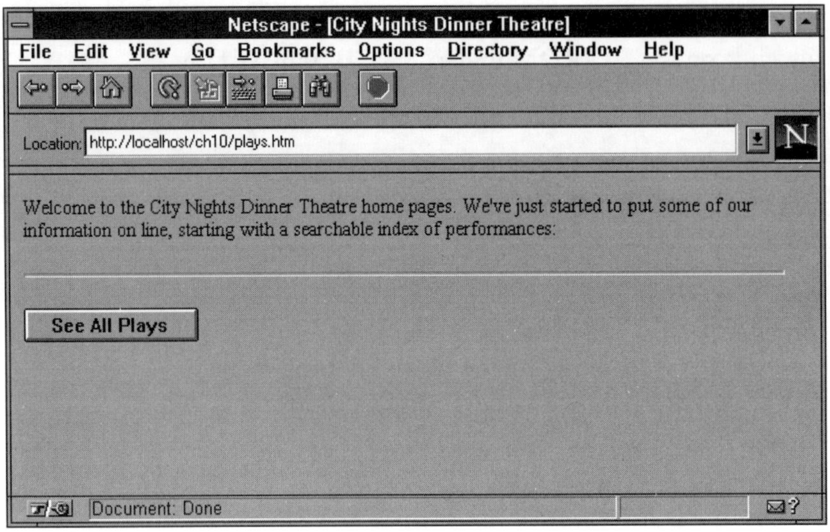

Figure 10.1 An HTML document with links to Jive.

braces {}. I'm going to take you step-by-step through the plays.jiv document, located on the CD-ROM in \EG\CH10\plays.jiv.

The first thing needed is the familiar content-type identifier. You may not need to include this in later releases of Jive, but it is required here. After that, the document head is printed out.

```
Content-type: text/html


<html>
<head>
<title>List of all plays</title>
</head>
```

Next, the <body> tag is displayed, with a pointer to an image located in the images subdirectory, off of the https document root.

```
<body background=/images/bgmask.gif>
```

Then, a header (<h1>) is printed, followed by a table (<table>), and table headers (<th>) for play name and performance dates are also printed.

```
<h1>List of all plays</h1>
<table border><th>Name</th><th>First Performance Date</th>
```

Before Jive can execute a query, a Jive extension must be included which connects to an ODBC data source. This should be a fully qualified connection string. If you are connecting to a data source which requires no username or password, then you only need to include the DSN tag (you may need to change this to access one of your installed data sources).

```
{connect 'DSN=EXAMPLE;'}
```

Jive allows you to define a block of repeated HTML code. This is enclosed between a `SELECT` statement extension and the `{end}` keyword. You can label each result set by including a label with a semicolon before the `SELECT` statement. `SELECT` statements may be broken up across multiple lines.

```
{results:select py_name, py_id, min(sh_date) AS start
            from plays, shows
            where sh_py_id_ = py_id
            group by py_id, py_name}
```

All of the HTML code from the `SELECT` statement to the `{end}` keyword is repeated for each record. You may include columns from the result set by enclosing the column name in curly braces {}. If you used a label for the result set, you should qualify the column name by including the label followed by a period before the column name (label.column_name). The following HTML will print out a table row (<tr>) with three table columns (<td>), one of which contains a form. The form includes a hidden variable (page) for the name of the Jive-enhanced document (ch10/cast.jiv) and a hidden variable called py_id, which will be given the value of the column py_id in the result set. Also, a submit button is included, with the label "See Cast." When the form is displayed, the user can click on the "See Cast" button to call cast.jiv:

```
<tr>
<td>{results.py_name}</td>
```

```
    <td>{results.start}</td>
    <td>
    <form action=/jive.exe method=post>
      <input type=hidden name=page   value=ch10/cast.jiv>
      <input type=hidden name=py_id  value={py_id}>
      <input type=submit name=submit value="See Cast">
    </form>
    </td>
    </tr><br>
```

In order to signify the end of the repeating block, the `{end}` keyword appears, followed by the tags needed to terminate the table, as well as the `body` and `html` elements:

```
{end}

</table>
<hr>
</body>
</html>
```

Figure 10.2 shows how this document will appear in the Netscape Navigator Web browser.

Another Jive Document

Let's take a look at the cast.jiv document. This is a lot like the previous one, except it pulls in a variable from the CGI query and uses it in the `SELECT` statement:

```
Content-type: text/html

<html>
<head>
<title>List of Players</title>
</head>
```

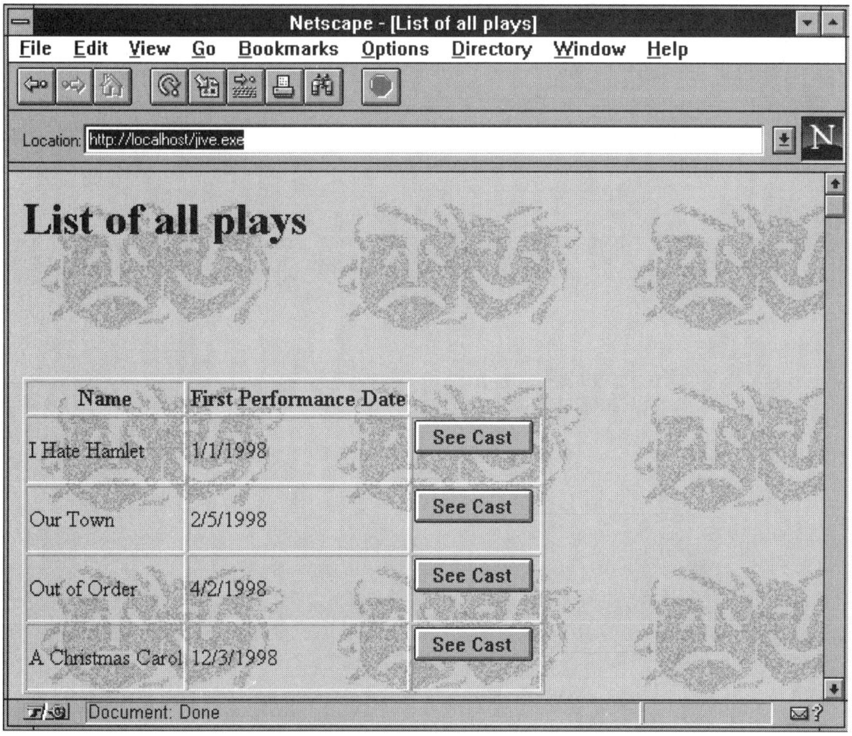

Figure 10.2 A list of all plays produced by Jive.

```
<body>
<h1>List of Players</h1>
```

This document was loaded as a link from the document generated by plays.jiv; plays.jiv passed a CGI variable with the value of the play id: py_id. The input extension is used to read this in from the CGI query. The `int` keyword ensures that the variable py_id is initialized as integer:

```
{input int py_id}
```

Next, a connection is established, then the `SELECT` statement is issued. Note the use of the :variable syntax within the `SELECT` statement. This causes the variable to be inserted into the `SELECT` statement with the proper delimiters (Jive takes care of this for you!).

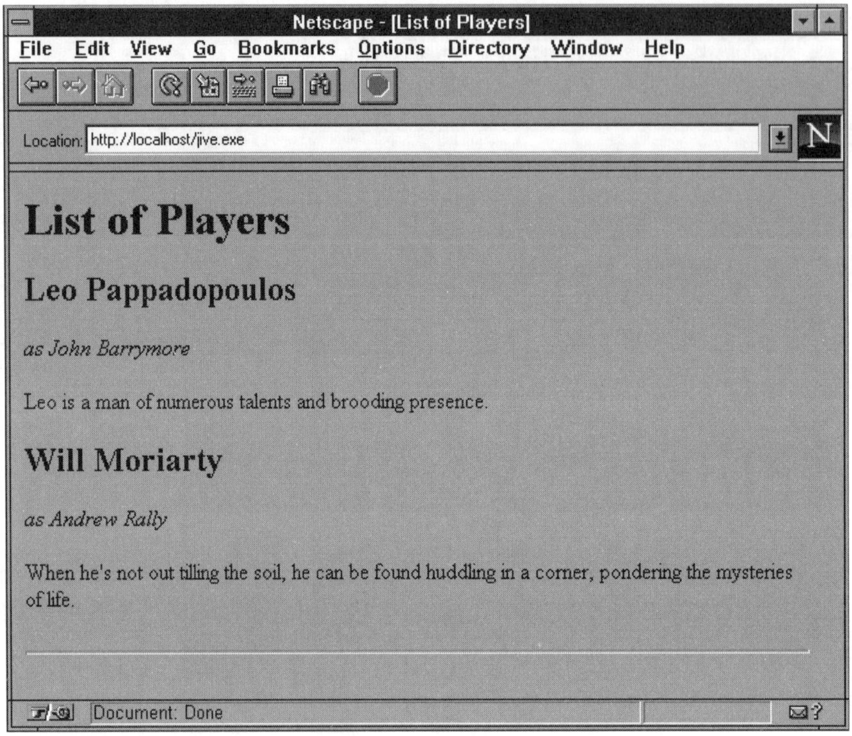

Netscape - [List of Players]
File Edit View Go Bookmarks Options Directory Window Help
Location: http://localhost/jive.exe
List of Players
Leo Pappadopoulos
as John Barrymore
Leo is a man of numerous talents and brooding presence.
Will Moriarty
as Andrew Rally
When he's not out tilling the soil, he can be found huddling in a corner, pondering the mysteries of life.
Document: Done

Figure 10.3 A list of players produced by Jive.

```
{connect 'DSN=EXAMPLE;'}
{results:select py_name, pl_fname, pl_lname, pp_name, pl_bio
            from players, plays, pyplxr
            where pp_pl_id_ = pl_id
            and   pp_py_id_ = py_id
            and   py_id = :py_id}
```

Next, the results of the query are turned into HTML. A player's first and last name is displayed, along with the name of the person he or she portrays, followed by a small biography. Then, the `{end}` keyword appears and the rest of the document is printed.

```
<h2>{results.pl_fname} {results.pl_lname}</h2>
<address>as {results.pp_name}</address><br>
```

```
  {results.pl_bio}<p>
{end}

<hr>
</body>
</html>
```

Figure 10.3 shows how this document will appear in the Netscape Navigator Web browser.

Jive is a fast, elegant, and simple means of connecting World Wide Web users to your ODBC databases. Although Jive is a small language, there is a lot that you can do with it. The fact that it is cross-platform makes it all the more attractive. I've only scratched the surface as far as what can be done with Jive; you may want to consult the Jive documentation (in HTML format), which is included on the CD-ROM in JIVE\JIVE.ZIP. The documentation includes a full programmer's reference with example code.

APPENDIX

A

TEMPLATE.PL INTERNALS

In Chapter 4, you were introduced to template.pl, a Perl script which allows you to create dynamic documents based on a single SQL `SELECT` statement. This appendix will walk through each line of template.pl and explain how it works. Template.pl is located on the CD-ROM under \eg\ch4.

A Word about eval()

This script uses a Perl function called `eval` to force variable interpolation on a string expression. For example, if your script were to read in the line

```
This is my little HTML document. Written by me, $myname
```

and assign it to `$_`, and the variable $myname were to have the value Brian Jepson, then executing the line

```
print eval(qq["$_"]);
```

would print out

```
This is my little HTML document. Written by me, Brian Jepson
```

The `eval()` function treats its argument as a Perl program, executes it, and returns the value of the last expression in the program. The `qq` operator is used, which allows you to specify alternate delimiters for double quotes. In this case, the left (`[`) and right (`]`) brackets are used. It is necessary to nest double quotes in this case, since `eval` takes a string expression as an argument, then evaluates the value contained within the string. The value of

```
qq["$_"]
```

is:

```
"This is my little HTML document. Written by me, $myname"
```

Since a double-quoted string allows for variable interpolation, when qq["$_"] is evaluated, it replaces $myname with its value.

Inside Template.pl

Template.pl is a component of an ODBC connectivity toolkit I distributed some time ago. It was released under the GNU General Public License, like Perl. This information is included in the header of the program:

```
# -*- Perl -*-
#
# template.pl
#
# Copyright 1995, Brian C. Jepson
#                  (bjepson@conan.ids.net)
#
# This program is free software; you can redistribute it and/or modify
# it under the terms of the GNU General Public License as published by
# the Free Software Foundation; either version 2 of the License, or
```

```
# (at your option) any later version.
#
# This program is distributed in the hope that it will be useful,
# but WITHOUT ANY WARRANTY; without even the implied warranty of
# MERCHANTABILITY or FITNESS FOR A PARTICULAR PURPOSE.  See the
# GNU General Public License for more details.
#
# You should have received a copy of the GNU General Public License
# along with this program; if not, write to the Free Software
# Foundation, Inc., 675 Mass Ave, Cambridge, MA 02139, USA.
#
#
```

Like many of the examples in the book, the NT::ODBC and the CGI_Lite are used, in order to provide access to the classes contained therein:

```
use NT::ODBC;
use CGI_Lite;
```

Next, a CGI_Lite object is instantiated and its method `parse_form_data()` is invoked to parse the results of the CGI query

```
#########################
#
# Parse the CGI data
#
#########################
$cgi = new CGI_Lite;
%results = $cgi->parse_form_data();
```

Among the CGI query variables is the name of the template. The variable name is TEMPLATE and case is significant. This value can be accessed from the %results hash with the expression `$results{'TEMPLATE'}`. Here, it is stored to the variable $file, then used as an argument to `open()`, in order to open the template file for reading. If an error occurs, the

`CGI_Lite::return_error()` method is invoked, which causes CGI programs to report errors gracefully.

```
#########################
#
# open the named template
# file
#
#########################
open (TEMPLATE, "<$file") ||
  $cgi->return_error("", "File Open Error", "Could not open $file: $!");
```

Now, it's time to read in information from the template. The first component included in the template is the SQL `SELECT` statement. It is terminated by a `;` (semicolon) and the last `if (/;$/)` statement causes the while loop to terminate when this line is encountered. As each line of the SQL is read in, it is chopped (this removes trailing newlines), and appended to the $sql variable:

```
#########################
#
# extract the SQL Statement
# from the template
#
#########################

while (<TEMPLATE>) {
  chop;
  $sql .= $_;
  last if (/;$/);
}
```

Now the script can strip off that trailing semicolon:

```
$sql =~ s/;$//;
```

Each key in the `%results` hash corresponds to one of the CGI query variables. The next segment of code will iterate over each of those keys; for each key (except the DSN, USER, and PASSWORD), it will define a Perl variable with the name and value of the CGI variable. This is done so that the variables can be interpolated into the SQL statement, or even components of the template, such as the header.

```
##############################
#
# process each CGI variable
#
##############################
foreach $key (keys %results) {

  if ($key ne 'DSN' && $key ne 'USER' && $key ne 'PASSWORD') {
```

The variables are defined by creating a string value consisting of a valid Perl assignment, such as $variable = “value”. Then, it is evaluated using the `eval()` function, which causes the assignment to occur. Note the use of the qq[ ] delimiters (this is an alternate method of including double quotes) are used, since you cannot nest double-quotes.

```
     #########################
     # create a variable with
     # the same name as the
     # CGI variable; each
     # variable can be interpolated
     # into the SQL statement
     # or into the template itself.
     #
     #########################
     $assignment = qq[\$$key = "$results{$key}"];
     eval($assignment);
  }
}
```

Now, the $sql variable is evaluated, which allows for variable interpolation to occur, so any CGI query variables which were previously defined are not incorporated into the SELECT statement.

```
#########################
# evaluate the SQL variable,
# forcing interpolation on
# any variables which
# correspond to the variables
# we created above...
#
#########################
$sql = eval(qq["$sql"]);
```

In order to make the ODBC connection, the data source name, username, and password must be extracted from the CGI query. These values are assigned to the variables $dsn, $user, and $password, respectively.

```
#########################
#
# get the data source name,
# user name, and password
#
#########################
$dsn      = $results{'DSN'};
$user     = $results{'USER'};
$password = $results{'PASSWORD'};
```

The values needed to generate a connection string have been extracted, and the SQL `SELECT` statement is ready to go. Now, the NT::ODBC object must be instantiated and the `NT::ODBC::sql` method is invoked to execute the query. If there was an error, the `CGI_Lite::return_error` method is invoked to display it in an HTML-friendly way.

```
#########################
#
# Issue the SQL Statement.
```

```
# If there was an error,
# print it out within an
# HTML document.
#
#########################
$query = NT::ODBC->new("DSN=$dsn;UID=$user;PWD=$password;");
if ($query->sql($sql)) {
  $error = $query->error;
  $cgi->return_error("", "ODBC Error", "SQL Error: $error: $!");
}
```

Next, a special variable, called $persist, is created. This contains a URL-ready version of the data source name, username, and password. It can be embedded in the template if the template developer needs to connect one template to another via a URL. It is also useful if the developer needs to call another CGI script which needs the ODBC connection information. Note that spaces are translated to addition `(+)` symbols; the addition symbol represents spaces within the CGI query portion of a URL. They can be automatically translated to spaces by `CGI_Lite::parse_form_data` when it decodes them in another script.

```
($persist = "DSN=$dsn&USER=$user&PASSWORD=$password") =~ s/ /+/g;;
```

Now, the header, body, and footer of the template can be read into the variables $head, $template, $footer, respectively. The process is similar to the one used to read in the SQL Statement; each component is terminated by a `;` (semicolon), which is removed from the component as it is assigned to its respective variable.

```
#########################
#
# Read in each component
# of the HTML template,
# starting with the header,
# and progressing to the
# body of the template and
```

```
# the footer. Each component
# is separated by a ;
#
########################
while (<TEMPLATE>) {
   ($head .= $_) =~ s/;$//;
   last if (/;$/);
}

while (<TEMPLATE>) {
   ($template .= $_) =~ s/;$//;
   last if (/;$/);
}

while (<TEMPLATE>) {
   ($footer .= $_) =~ s/;$//;
   last if (/;$/);
}

close(TEMPLATE);
```

The `eval()` function is used, with $head included as a parameter. It is evaluated as a double-quoted string and must itself be included within a double-quoted string. In order for the users' browsers to understand the results of this script, the content-type identifier is printed, and then the variable $head is displayed.

```
############################################
#
# Execute an eval on the $head, and print it.
# since no rows have been fetched, it's really
# only useful to include CGI form variables
# in the header for evaluation
#
############################################
```

```
$head = eval(qq["$head"]);
print "Content-type: text/html\n\n";
print $head;
```

The template header has been displayed; now the body of the template must be displayed. Remember that for each row in the result set, the body of the template is displayed. In order for this to occur, each row must be fetched using `NT::ODBC::fetchrow()`:

```
########################
#
# fetch each row in the
# result set, and evaluate
# the body of the template
# for each row
#
########################
while ($query->fetchrow) {
```

For each row, a variable is defined with the same name of the column and assigned the value of that column. The results of `NT::ODBC::fieldnames` is a list, that can be iterated over with the `foreach` construct. Then, the `NT::ODBC::data` method is invoked with the name of the column as a parameter and is assigned to the variable $fvalue. Note that any single quotes are converted to an escape sequence `\'`, which will preserve the quote when the variable assignment takes place. The assignment expression is included within double quotes, so if $f (the column name) were equal to 'co_name', and $fvalue (the column value for the current row) were equal to 'Brian Jepson', then $assignment would be equal to:

```
co_name = 'Brian Jepson'
```

When that expression is used as an argument to the `eval()` function, it is evaluated as Perl code and the variable co_name is defined, and assigned a value. This happens for each row in the result set, so the variable is redefined each time through.

```
########################
#
# define a Perl variable
# for each column name,
# consisting of its value
# for the current row.
#
########################
foreach $f ($query->fieldnames) {
  ($fvalue = $query->data($f)) =~ s/'/\\'/g;
  $assignment = "\$$f = '$fvalue'";
  eval($assignment);
}
```

The template body can contain explicit references to the variables previously created. If the template contains something like

```
Collector name: $co_name
```

then, for each row, when it is evaluated, the $co_name is replaced within the template with the value of that column for the current record:

```
  ########################
  #
  # eval the template body,
  # which interpolates the
  # value of any of the
  # fields
  #
  ########################
  $html = eval(qq["$template"]);
  print $html;

}
```

Finally, `eval()` is used on the $footer, variable; it is printed and template.pl is finished!

```
##############################################
#
# Execute an eval on the $footer, and print it.
#
##############################################
$footer = eval(qq["$footer"]);


print $footer;
```

This script has various applications and can be especially powerful when templates are linked to each other or custom scripts. You will probably find template.pl more than adequate for your reporting needs and may put it to use in other areas.

APPENDIX

B

ABOUT ODBC EXTENSIONS FOR PERL-WIN32

The examples in this book rely on the existence of ODBC extensions to Perl. These extensions were written by Dan DeMaggio (dmag@umich.edu) and consist of a .PLL file and a Perl module. The .PLL file is a Perl extension, which was written in C and compiled. A .PLL file is a .DLL file with a different extension and can be dynamically loaded by Perl which gives you the ability to call its functions within Perl scripts or modules.

Installing ODBC.PLL

The ODBC.PLL file is located on the CD-ROM in the directory \MODULES\AUTO\NT\ODBC. It should be installed under your Perl installation. Under the top-level Perl directory, there is a subdirectory called Lib. This contains another directory, called auto. All of the dynamically loaded extensions go somewhere under this directory. Another subdirectory, NT, is where older

Windows NT extensions (the newer ones use the directory Win32), such as ODBC.PLL are stored. Each extension is given its own subdirectory, so, if your Perl installation is in C:\NTPERL, then ODBC.PLL should be copied to `C:\NTPERL\Lib\auto\NT\ODBC\ODBC.PLL`.

Installing ODBC.pm

The Perl module ODBC.PM provides the developer with a friendly programmatic interface for using the functions in ODBC.PLL. This should be installed in the NT directory under the Perl Lib directory. Newer modules are installed under Win32; NT::ODBC will probably be migrated over to the new directory structure. If your Perl installation is in C:\NTPERL, then ODBC.PM should be copied to C:\NTPERL\Lib\NT\ODBC.PM. The module can then be used in your program as NT::ODBC.

Using ODBC.pm

ODBC.PM has a few easy-to-use methods which provide the developer with access to the functionality of ODBC.PLL. These are included in the NT::ODBC object. In order to have access to any of these methods, you must include the line

```
use NT::ODBC;
```

in your Perl script or module.

The NT::ODBC:new() method

This method is the NT::ODBC constructor. It is used when creating a new instance of an NT::ODBC object. You must include a connection string as an argument. The simplest version of a connection string has the DSN tag, along with a value, such as:

```
DSN=EXAMPLE;
```

Other connection strings can contain a username or password:

```
DSN=EXAMPLE;UID=bjepson;PASSWORD=xyzzy;
```

Other tags are supported in connection strings. See the driver-specific help or documentation for more information. Here's an example of how the `NT::ODBC::new` method could be invoked:

```
$sql = NT::ODBC->new("DSN=EXAMPLE;");
```

Once you have issued this, $sql (or whatever variable you use) will contain a reference to the object you just created.

The NT::ODBC:sql() method

This method allows you to issue SQL statements against the data source you connected to with the `NT::ODBC::new` method. This method takes a single argument, the SQL statement:

```
$sql->sql("SELECT * FROM collect")
```

If the `NT::ODBC::sql` method returns a non-zero value, which is the ODBC error code, then an error occurred. For those of you uncomfortable with the following syntax

```
if ($sql->sql("SELECT * FROM collect")) {
    print $sql->error, "\n";
    exit();
}
```

you can safely replace this with

```
$sql->sql("SELECT * FROM collect");
if ($sql->error) {
    print $sql->error, "\n";
    exit();
}
```

The NT::ODBC:fieldnames() method

After you have executed the query, the `NT::ODBC::fieldnames` method can be used to get the list of column names in the result set. This value can be processed with the `foreach` construct or processed like an array.

```
@fieldnames = $sql->fieldnames;
```

will populate the array @fieldnames with the name of each column.

```
print join("\n", $sql->fieldnames);
```

will join the list value returned by $sql->fieldnames, separating each element by a newline.

```
foreach ($sql->fieldnames) {
      print "$_\n";
}
```

will process each item in the list value returned by $sql->fieldnames and print the value followed by a newline.

The NT::ODBC:fetchrow() method

This method will retrieve the first row in the query's result set, with each successive call retrieving the next row. Since it returns a true (1) value as long as rows remain to be processed, you can use the while operator to fetch all rows:

```
while ($sql->fetchrow) {
    $count++;
    print "row number $count\n";
}
```

The NT::ODBC:data() method

Where does each row go when you call the `NT::ODBC::fetchrow` method? It goes into a buffer area that must be read with the `NT::ODBC::data` method. This method must be invoked with the name of a column as an argument, which can be conveniently gotten from `NT::ODBC::fieldnames`, as follows (remember, the `foreach` construct sticks each value from $sql->fieldnames into $_):

```
while ($sql->fetchrow) {
    foreach ($sql->fieldnames) {
      $value = $sql->data($_);
      print "$_: $value\n";
    }
}
```

The NT::ODBC:error() method

This method is used to retrieve the text of any error that may have occurred. As shown in the `NT::ODBC::sql` example, if this method evaluates to logical true (non-zero, non-blank), you know an error has occurred:

```
$sql->sql("SELECT * FROM collect");
if ($sq3001->error) {
    print $sql->error, "\n";
    exit();
}
```

NT::ODBC contains all the necessary functionality to query ODBC data sources. However, as time goes on, more functionality may be added to it, including methods to retrieve certain properties of tables, columns, and databases. Keep your Web browser tuned to

```
http://www.ids.net/~bjepson/www-database/
```

for updates and other information.

APPENDIX

C

SUGGESTED CONFIG FOR YOUR WEB SERVER

Hardware

Determining the best configuration for a Web Server can be tricky. It goes without saying that you should get a system which exceeds the minimum requirements for Windows NT. Although a Pentium is ideal, this author has had tremendous success with a 120 Megahertz 486. The bare minimum memory requirement is 16 Megabytes; if you can procure a machine with 32 Megabytes or more, all the better. For those of you not using advanced disk performance techniques such as those provided by certain RAID levels, it is highly recommended that you configure your system to place its virtual memory files on an infrequently used physical disk. I have two hard drives installed in my computer: a 1.2 Gigabyte drive, which contains all of my software and data files, and a 340 Megabyte drive, which contains Linux on one partition, with about 80 Megabytes available to Windows NT solely for virtual memory. This ensures that while your system is loading large tables into memory, it is not simultaneously reading and writing to the same physical disk.

If you are using a database server product, it is advantageous to put the server on a different computer than the Web server. This can provide incredible performance benefits. You will need to configure your ODBC data sources appropriately to connect to the database server.

File/Directory Structure

With all of the functionality visited in this book, there's a lot of software to install! I'll go over one potential scenario for installing this software on a single computer. I will also revisit the installation steps outlined in earlier chapters, keeping it together here under one single reference source.

What's on the CD-ROM?

The CD-ROM contains several pieces of software needed to assemble a working WWW site. The use of each program is explained throughout the book.

1. *Utility Programs*. These include free info-zip unzip utility, GNU zip (gzip), and GNU tar (tar). These will be used to extract files from archives on disk.
2. *Example Scripts and Web Pages*. The example scripts and Web pages from various chapters are included on the CD-ROM.
3. *The EMWAC https Web Server Version 0.99*. This is a Web server which can be installed on any Windows NT machine. It supports Perl CGI scripts, among other things.
4. *Perl for Win32 Build 105*. Perl is a general purpose systems language written by Larry Wall. It was ported to Windows NT and Windows 95 by Hip Communications. The port was sponsored by Microsoft.

5. *Support Scripts, Modules, and Extensions.* These include Dan DeMaggio's ODBC extensions to Perl, Shishir Gundavaram's CGI_Lite.pm, and other supporting code for the examples in the book.
6. *IODBC.* IODBC is a 32-bit console application, written by Lee Fesperman, which allows you to execute ODBC queries from a command prompt.

What Is Freeware/Shareware?

Freeware is software that is distributed by disk, through BBS systems and the Internet, free. There is no charge for using it, and can be distributed freely as long as the use it is put to follows the license agreement with it.

Shareware (also known as user supported software) is a revolutionary means of distributing software created by individuals or companies too small to make inroads into the more conventional retail distribution networks. The authors of Shareware retain all rights to the software under the copyright laws while still allowing free distribution. This gives the user the chance to freely obtain and try out software to see if it fits his needs. Shareware should not be confused with Public Domain software even though they are often obtained from the same sources.

If you continue to use Shareware after trying it out, you are expected to register your use with the author and pay a registration fee. What you get in return depends on the author, but may include a printed manual, free updates, telephone support, and so on.

Hardware/Software Requirements

The programs included on the CD-ROM will run on any machine which meets the minimum requirements for Windows NT. You should be running Windows NT to use these programs. You must also have TCP/IP installed in order to use the examples.

You should also have 32-bit ODBC and the ODBC driver manager installed. 32-bit ODBC is supplied with a variety of products, such as Microsoft Office for Windows NT, Microsoft Office 95, Microsoft Visual FoxPro, Microsoft Visual Basic, and others.

Installing the Software

All of the instructions below assume you are running Windows NT and have administrative privileges on the computer.

Utility Programs

The utility programs (gzip.exe, tar.exe, and unzip.exe) are contained in the \UTIL directory on the CD-ROM. These files should be copied to a directory on your local computer. This directory should be referenced in your System Path setting. You may modify your System Path setting on Windows NT by double-clicking on the System applet in the Control Panel. See your Windows NT manuals or on-line help for more information.

Example Scripts and Web Pages

1. Choose and make a directory to install the scripts in. C:\HTTP might not be a bad idea, since it is the HTTPS default data directory:

```
C:\USERS\DEFAULT>mkdir C:\http
```

2. Change directory into the directory you just made:

```
C:\USERS\DEFAULT>cd C:\http
```

3. Extract the scripts from the .TGZ archive on the CD-ROM under \EG\EG.TGZ. You will need to have installed the utility programs in the previous step (this assumes that your CD-ROM drive is drive G:):

```
C:\HTTP>gzip -d -c G:\EG\EG.TGZ 1 tar xvf -
```

EMWAC https

1. Binary-only distributions of EMWAC https are included on the CD-ROM in the \HTTPS directory. Choose from one of the following:

HSALPHA.ZIP	EMWAC https version .99 for DEC Alpha processors
HSI386.ZIP	EMWAC https version .99 for Intel 386 or above processors
HSMIPS.ZIP	EMWAC https version .99 for MIPS processors
HSPP.ZIP	EMWAC https version .99 for PowerPC processors

2. Make a directory into which to install htpps. Example:

```
C:\USERS\DEFAULT>mkdir C:\WIN32APP\HTTPS
```

3. Change directory into that directory. Example:

```
C:\USERS\DEFAULT>cd C:\WIN32APP\HTTPS
```

4. Extract the files from the CD-ROM drive. Example (this assumes that your CD-ROM drive is drive G:):

```
C:\WIN32APP\HTTPS>unzip -d G:\HTTPS\HSI386.ZIP
```

5. Move the HTTPS.EXE,HTTPS.CPL, and HTTPS.CPL, and HTTPS.HLP files to your %SYSTEMROOT%\SYSTEM32 directory:

```
C:\win32app\https>move https.exe %SYSTEMROOT%\SYSTEM32
        1 file(s) moved

C:\win32app\https>move https.cpl %SYSTEMROOT%\SYSTEM32
        1 file(s) moved

C:\Win32app\https>move https.hlp %SYSTEMROOT%\SYSTEM32
        1 file(s) moved
```

6. Install the HTTPS software with the following command:

```
C:\win32app\https>https -install
```

7. You may start the software with the following command:

```
C:\win32app\https>net start https
```

To specify that the https service starts up each time the system is booted, you may set its startup options in the Services applet from the Windows NT control panel. When you have run the Services Applet, look for "EMWAC HTTP Server", click on the Startup. . . button, and set its Startup type to "Automatic."

If you installed the examples from the previous section into a directory other than C:\HTTPS, you should stop the https server with:

```
C:\win32app\https>net stop https
```

Then, you can change the https data directory by opening the HTTP Server applet in the Control Panel, and entering the name of the desired directory into the Data Directory field. Then, you should restart the server with:

```
C:\win32app\https>net start https
```

Testing HTTPS

To test the installation after you have started the https web server, you should start your favorite browser. Then, open the URL:

```
http://localhost/README.htm
```

If this fails, try:

```
http://127.0.0.1/README.htm
```

or

```
http://x.x.x.x/README.htm
```

where x.x.x.x is the IP address of your computer. If you are still having trouble, examine the documentation that was included with the EMWAC HTTP Server.

Perl for Win32

1. Using the unzip utility provided, unzip the 105-I86.ZIP file included on the CD-ROM in the \NTPERL directory. If you are using a PowerPC, MIPS, or ALPHA-based Windows NT system, choose from one of the following files in the \NTPERL directory:

   ALPHA.ZIP Perl 5.001 for DEC Alpha processors

   MIPS.ZIP Perl 5.001 for MIPS processors

   PPC.ZIP Perl 5.001 for PowerPC processors

   If you must use one of these versions of Perl, you should follow the special instructions for using IODBC as an alternate ODBC interface, which is included in Appendix F. Appendix F is included as an HTML document along with the examples. You will find a link to it from the README.htm file you loaded in the previous section.

   The zip file includes a top-level directory, so you can install it from the directory above where you wish it to reside. Example (assuming that your CD-ROM is drive G:):

```
C:WIN32APP>unzip -d G:\NTPERL\105-I86.ZIP
```

2. Enter the Perl5 directory that was created with the unzip command:

```
C:WIN32APP>CD perl5
```

3. Execute the INSTALL.BAT script and follow the prompts.

```
C:WIN32APP\perl5>INSTALL.BAT
```

Testing the Perl5 Installation

1. Reboot your computer and log back in to Windows NT.
2. Change directory to the ntt\directory below where you installed Perl:

```
C:\USERS\DEFAULT>CD\WIN32APP\perl5\ntt
```

3. Run the regression tests. Since the Perl5 port is still "in progress", you may fail on one or two tests:

```
C:\WIN32APP\perl5\ntt>test.bat
```

IODBC

IODBC.EXE and IODBC16.EXE (for 16-bit data sources) can be found on the CD-ROM in the \IODBC directory. Both files should be copied to a directory on your local computer. This directory should be referenced in your System Path setting. You may modify your System Path setting on Windows NT by double-clicking on the System applet in the Control Panel. See your Windows NT manuals or on-line help for more information.

Testing the IODBC Installation

In order to test IODBC, you can execute it with the /S (data source name), /U (user name, if necessary), /P (password, if necessary). You must know the name of an ODBC data source that is installed on your computer. Refer to the documentation that came with ODBC or the on-line help for information on installing and configuring data sources. If you know the name of a data source (I am using "EXAMPLE" below), and you do not need to supply a user name and password, you can start IODBC with the following command:

```
IODBC/S "EXAMPLE"
```

If you need to supply a user name and password (such as for Microsoft SQL Server or Oracle), you should use the following syntax, substituting your username and password:

```
IODBC/S "EXAMPLE"/U "USERNAME"/P "PASSWORD"
```

Support Scripts, Modules, and Extensions

1. Change directory into the Lib\directory below the Perl for Win32 installation:

```
C: \USERS\DEFAULT>CD\WIN32APP\perl5\Lib
```

2. Extract the scripts from the .TGZ archive on the CD-ROM under\MODULES\MODULES.TGZ. You will need to have installed the utility programs in the first step (this example assumes that your CD-ROM drive is drive G:):

```
C: \WIN32APP\perl5\Lib>gzip-d-cG: \MODULES\MODULES.TGZ|tar xvf-
```

User Assistance and Information

The software accompanying this book is being provided as is without warranty or support of any kind. Should you require basic installation assistance, or if your media is defective, please call our product support number at (212) 850-6194 weekdays between 9 AM and 4 PM Eastern Standard Time. Or, we can be reached via e-mail at: wprtusw@jwiley.com. For a list of Frequently Asked Questions, and other information, you may also visit the Web site which is devoted to this book at:

```
http://www.ids.net/~bjepson/www-database/
```

To place additional orders or to request information about other Wiley products, please call (800) 879-4539.

As you continue working with Perl and CGI, you will no doubt want to expand your horizons. There exists a cornucopia of Perl scripts and modules on CPAN, the Comprehensive Perl Archive Network. CPAN contains about 120 Megabytes of data at last count and should be "the only Perl archive you will ever need," as stated in the README.

Although the master CPAN site is ftp://ftp.funet.fi/pub/languages/perl/CPAN/, you can get a list of all the mirror sites from http://www.perl.com/perl/CPAN/CPAN.html. Of particular interest to you will be the modules subdirectory, which contains the meat of the archive. The modules/by-module subdirectory contains many directories, CGI and HTML perhaps being the most pertinent to readers of this book. Nevertheless, poke around before you write something. Chances are, someone has already written it! If not, hopefully, you will see fit to release it to the Perl community if you do write it. Hopefully, you will also include the following language, which lets everyone use it (including me!) without restriction:

```
This code is Copyright (C) <Your Name Here> <Year>. All rights reserved.  This
code is free software; you can redistribute it
and/or modify it under the same terms as Perl itself.
```

APPENDIX

D

ODBC SQL REFERENCE

ODBC provides a rich set of SQL statements for your use. Most of the examples in the book used the `SELECT`, `INSERT`, or `UPDATE` statements. This appendix will cover many of the ODBC SQL statements that you may find useful. Remember that certain data sources, such as SQL Server and Oracle, have their own SQL dialect that is similar to that of ODBC. For this reason, you should make sure that you have reference materials available for that specific data source if you want to write driver-specific SQL.

Minimum, Core, and Extended Grammars

An ODBC driver can provide support for some or all of the *ODBC SQL grammar*. There are three levels of conformance, *Minimum*, *Core*, and

Extended. To determine which level is supported by the driver you are using, you should consult the help file or documentation which accompanies the driver. The help file for a particular driver can be accessed by clicking on the Help button in the Driver Setup Dialog which comes up when you add a data source for that driver with the Add Data Source dialog. Different SQL statements are available depending upon the *conformance level* of the driver; the description of each SQL statement in this appendix is accompanied by its conformance level. If an SQL statement is available in a lower level (starting with Minimum), it will be available in the higher levels, as well. Some components of certain SQL statements are only available with higher conformance levels.

Conventions

Certain conventions are used in each statement's description. For example, items enclosed in greater than or less than signs <> indicate components which will be explained in greater detail in the section titled SQL Components, such as:

```
<select list>
<table name>
```

Items enclosed in braces `[]` are optional components of the syntax, such as:

```
SELECT <select list>
    FROM <table name>
    [WHERE <search condition list>]
```

The previous example indicates that the

```
WHERE <search condition list>
```

component is optional.

An ellipsis . . . indicates elements which may repeat. For example,

```
SELECT <select list>
```

```
    FROM <table name>
    [WHERE <search condition list>]
    [GROUP BY <column name>[, <column name>]...]
```

This indicates that you may continue adding column names to the GROUP BY clause until you exceed the driver's limit, if any.

A pipe symbol | indicates alternate components. In the following example

```
CREATE [UNIQUE] INDEX <index name>
    ON <table name>
    (<column name> [ASC | DESC]
     [, <column name> [ASC | DESC]]...)
```

either ASC or DESC may be used, but not both.

The {} curly braces are used to group alternate components in cases where it may not be immediately clear how they are grouped. For example, the following grouping

```
INSERT INTO <table name>
    [(<column name> [, <column name>]...)]
    { <query specification> | VALUES (<expression> [, <expression>]...)}
```

tells you that the alternating components separated by the | symbol are limited to <query specification> and VALUES clause.

SQL Statements

ALTER TABLE

Conformance Level: Core

This adds one or more columns to the structure of a table within your data source. The value of the column for each row which existed before you added the column is set to NULL.

```
ALTER TABLE <table name>
    ADD <column name> <data type>
    | ADD (<column name> <data type> [, <column name> <data type>]...)
```

Examples are:

```
ALTER TABLE collect
   ADD co_height int

ALTER TABLE collect
   ADD (co_height int, co_width int)
```

CREATE INDEX

Conformance Level: Core

This creates a named index on one or more columns in a table.

```
CREATE [UNIQUE] INDEX <index name>
   ON <table name>
   (<column name> [ASC | DESC]
    [, <column name> [ASC | DESC]]...)
```

You can add an index to a table, which can cause certain statements, particularly those with a `WHERE` clause, to potentially run faster. You may specify one or more columns for the index. Each column may be indexed ascending or descending by specifying one of the optional `ASC` or `DESC` keywords. Certain ODBC drivers will respect the usage of the `UNIQUE` keyword. If an index is created as unique, any attempt to enter duplicate values in the table for the columns named in the index will generate an error.

An example is:

```
CREATE UNIQUE INDEX ix_name
   ON collect
   (co_name ASC)
```

CREATE TABLE

Conformance Level: Minimum

This creates a table.

```
CREATE TABLE <table name>
   (<column element> [, <column element>]...)
```

A column element may either be a column definition

```
<column name> <data type>
    [DEFAULT <expression>]
    [<column constraint> [, <column constraint>]...]
```

or a table constraint definition.

```
  UNIQUE (<column name> [, <column name>]...)
| PRIMARY KEY (<column name> [, <column name>]...)
| CHECK (<search condition>)
| FOREIGN KEY (<referencing column list>)
  REFERENCES <referenced table>  (<referenced column list>)
```

The simplest column element is a column name and a data type, as shown in the following CREATE TABLE statement (the column elements are shown in bold).

```
CREATE TABLE people
    (pe_name char (10),
     pe_shoesize int,
     pe_IQ int)
```

A column element may also have a `DEFAULT` clause, which specifies a value to be used when a row is inserted, but the column name is not included in the insert. Here's an example:

```
CREATE TABLE people
    (pe_name char (10),
     pe_shoesize int DEFAULT 8,
     pe_IQ int)
```

A column constraint definition can consist of any of the following clauses:

```
NOT NULL
| UNIQUE
| PRIMARY KEY
| REFERENCES <referenced table> (<referenced column list>)
| CHECK <search condition>
```

A column may have multiple constraint definitions. The NOT NULL clause specifies that that column must be assigned a value on an insert and cannot be changed to a NULL. A NULL is the absence of any value and can cause undesirable (but predictable) behavior in queries. The UNIQUE clause specifies that no two rows in the table may have the same value for the column; the PRIMARY KEY clause specifies that that column is the primary key for the table.

The REFERENCES clause allows the developer to specify declarative referential integrity. If you have two or more tables which are linked to each other by primary and foreign keys, such as:

```
CREATE TABLE collect
    (co_name char (25),
     co_id int)
CREATE TABLE cart
    (ca_name char (25),
     ca_id int)
CREATE TABLE cartxref
    (cx_ca_id_ int,
     cx_co_id_ int,
     cx_quant int)
```

In this example, collect is linked to cartxref on co_id = cx_co_id_, and cart is linked to cartxref on ca_id = cx_ca_id_. If your data source supports it, you can explicitly declare this relationship by defining the tables this way:

```
CREATE TABLE collect
    (co_name char (25),
     co_id int PRIMARY KEY)
CREATE TABLE cart
    (ca_name char(25),
     ca_id int PRIMARY KEY)
CREATE TABLE cartxref
    (cx_ca_id_ int REFERENCES cart (ca_id),
     cx_co_id_ int REFERENCES collect (co_id),
     cx_quant int)
```

Certain data sources can utilize this declarative referential integrity. It can be useful in situations where a user might try to delete rows in the cart table while there are related rows in the cartxref table. The declarative referential integrity can aid in cascading the deletions to the cartxref table or blocking them entirely.

The CHECK clause can be used to prevent insertions based on certain criteria. You can supply a search condition as the argument to the CHECK clause:

```
CREATE TABLE cartxref
    (cx_ca_id_ int,
     cx_co_id_ int,
     cx_quant int CHECK (cx_quant >= 0))
```

This above CHECK constraint would prevent you from entering negative values for cartridge quantities.

A table constraint definition is used to define certain table-wide attributes. The UNIQUE clause is used to specify a column or series of columns the values of which, taken collectively, must be unique for a given row. For example, if the columns co_name and co_age are defined with a UNIQUE clause such as:

```
UNIQUE (co_name, co_age)
```

then no two rows may have the same age and name. Attempting to insert 'Brian Jepson' as the co_name and 28 as the co_age into more than one row will generate an error. The PRIMARY KEY clause enforces the same criteria, but the column(s) are listed in the system data dictionary as the primary key for that table.

The CHECK clause in a table constraint definition is used to reject INSERTs based on certain criteria. For example, the following table definition will reject any attempt to INSERT a person whose IQ is less than his or her shoe size.

```
CREATE TABLE people
    (pe_name char (10),
```

```
pe_shoesize int,
pe_IQ int,
CHECK (pe_IQ > pe_shoesize))
```

The `FOREIGN KEY` clause allows you to specify one or more columns for a foreign key reference, as seen in the column constraint `REFERENCES`. The example seen earlier could be rewritten with the `FOREIGN KEY` clause as shown:

```
CREATE TABLE cartxref
    (cx_ca_id_ int,
     cx_co_id_ int,
     cx_quant  int,
     FOREIGN KEY (cx_ca_id_) REFERENCES cart (ca_id),
     FOREIGN KEY (cx_co_id_) REFERENCES collect (co_id))
```

DELETE

Conformance Level: Minimum

This deletes rows matching a search condition.

```
DELETE FROM <table name>
    [WHERE <search condition>]
```

With a search condition, the `DELETE` statement deletes all rows matching the search condition. Without a search condition, it deletes all records. For example:

```
DELETE FROM cartxref
    WHERE cx_quant = 0
```

This example deletes all rows in the cartxref table which have a zero quantity.

DROP INDEX

Conformance Level: Core

This drops (removes) an index.

```
DROP INDEX <index name>
```

or

```
DROP INDEX <index name> ON <table name>
```

Some drivers require that you specify the name of the table to which the index belongs. For example:

```
DROP INDEX ix_name
   ON collect
```

DROP TABLE

Conformance Level: Minimum

This drops (removes) a table.

```
DROP TABLE <table name>
```

Caution: this will permanently remove a table! For example:

```
DROP TABLE collect
```

INSERT (Minimum)

Conformance Level: Minimum

This inserts a single row into a table.

```
INSERT INTO <table name>
   [(<column name> [, <column name>]...)]
   VALUES (<expression> [, <expression>]...)
```

The `INSERT` statement will insert a row into the named table and will populate each column specified with the corresponding value. If values are supplied for all columns in the physical order in which they are defined, the column names are not needed. For example:

```
INSERT INTO cartxref
   (cx_ca_id_, cx_co_id_, cx_quant)
   VALUES (1, 1, 1)
```

INSERT (Core)

Conformance Level: Core

This inserts one or more rows into a table.

```
INSERT INTO <table name>
```

```
[(<column name> [, <column name>]...)]
{ query-specification| VALUES (<expression> [, <expression>]...)}
```

Instead of a VALUES clause, you may also supply a query specification (see the SELECT statement) which returns a result set that can be inserted into the table. For each column in the INSERT statement, there must be a corresponding column in the SELECT statement which makes up the query. For example:

```
INSERT INTO summary
   (su_name, su_quant)
   SELECT co_name, SUM(cx_quant)
      FROM collect, cartxref
      WHERE cx_co_id_ = co_id
      GROUP BY co_name
```

SELECT

Conformance Level: Minimum, Core

This retrieves a selected set of columns from one or more tables where rows match a specified search condition.

```
SELECT [ALL | DISTINCT] <select list>
   FROM <table reference list>
   WHERE <search condition list>
   [ORDER BY    <column designator> [ASC | DESC]
             [, <column designator> [ASC | DESC]]...]
```

The Select List

A select list consists of one or more expressions, which can optionally be followed by an AS clause. The AS clause specifies the name of the column to use in the result set.

```
<expression> [AS <result column name>]
```

An expression can simply be a column name:

```
SELECT co_name
   FROM collect
```

The AS clause can be used to rename the column in the result set:

```
SELECT co_name AS name
   FROM collect
```

An expression can also be any valid expression in the ODBC SQL syntax.

```
SELECT pl_fname + ' ' + pl_lname AS fullname
   FROM players
```

You may also use the * (asterisk) character to specify that all columns from all tables are to be included.

```
SELECT *
   FROM players
```

The ALL and DISTINCT keywords

The ALL keyword (this is assumed if neither ALL nor DISTINCT is supplied) retrieves all rows from the result set, regardless of duplicates. The DISTINCT keyword will eliminate duplicate rows, that is, each row will have a unique value for all columns in a result set which uses the DISTINCT clause. The ALL and DISTINCT clauses do not modify one particular column. They affect all columns in the result set; there may only be one ALL or DISTINCT clause per SELECT statement. If you wanted a list of all unique last names in the players table, you could issue this SELECT statement:

```
SELECT DISTINCT pl_lname
   FROM players
```

The WHERE Clause

The WHERE clause allows you to specify various filter criteria. A WHERE clause requires a search condition list. Each search condition should return a Boolean true or false value and may be separated by AND or OR. A search condition may take several forms. The following predicates are available in drivers which conform to the minimum grammar:

```
  <expression> <comparison operator> <expression>
| <expression> LIKE <pattern value>
| <column name> IS [NOT] NULL
```

The Comparison Predicate of the WHERE Clause

The comparison predicate is quite simple. You must supply an expression on both sides of the comparison; each row that the comparison evaluates to true is selected:

```
SELECT *
    FROM cartxref
    WHERE cx_quant < 10
```

This example selects all rows which have a quantity of less than 10. You may combine comparison predicates with the AND or OR clause.

```
SELECT *
    FROM cartxref
    WHERE cx_quant < 10
        OR cx_quant > 100
```

This example selects all rows which either have a quantity of less than 10 or greater than 100. The comparison predicate is also used to join one or more tables. In order to ensure that you get the collector name lined up with the correct cartridge ids, you must join cartxref to collect with the expression cx_co_id_ = co_id:

```
SELECT *
    FROM cartxref, collect
    WHERE cx_quant < 10
    AND   cx_co_id_ = co_id
```

This above example will select all rows from cartxref for which the quantity is less than 10. All of the columns from collect are included, but only those rows for which co_id is equal to the cx_co_id_ on cartxref will be selected. That makes sure that cartridge assignments are retrieved with the correct collector name.

The Like Predicate of the WHERE Clause

The `LIKE` predicate is similar to the comparison, except that the right-hand side of the expression must be a pattern value. A pattern value is a string literal which can contain wildcard characters. Within a pattern value, the character `%` (percent) will match zero or more occurrences of any character, and the character _ (underscore) will match one single character:

```
SELECT *
   FROM cartxref, collect
   WHERE cx_quant < 10
   AND   cx_co_id_ = co_id
   AND   co_name LIKE 'B%'
```

This will select all cartridge assignments and collector names for which the quantity is less than 10 and the collector's name starts with the letter B.

The NULL Predicate of the WHERE Clause

The `NULL` predicate is used to include or exclude all rows based on whether a particular column is NULL or not. A column is said to be NULL if it contains no value; a blank value (zero or the empty string) is not considered NULL. This will select all cartridge assignments which have no quantity assigned, rather than zero:

```
SELECT *
   FROM cartxref, collect
   WHERE cx_quant IS NULL
```

Core Grammar WHERE Predicates

In addition to the previous predicates, the following predicates are available to drivers conforming to the core grammar.

```
<expression> BETWEEN <expression> AND <expression>
| EXISTS ( <subquery> )
| <expression> [NOT] IN (subquery)
| <expression> <comparison operator> {ALL | ANY} <subquery>
```

The Between Predicate of the WHERE Clause

The BETWEEN predicate allows you to specify values which fall between a specific range:

```
SELECT *
   FROM cartxref
   WHERE cx_quant BETWEEN 10 AND 100
```

The Exists Predicate of the WHERE Clause

The EXISTS predicate allows you to specify a subquery (another SQL SELECT) and only evaluates to true if there is at least one row returned by the subquery. This is often used with a correlated subquery. A correlated subquery is a SELECT statement which contains references to fields contained in tables other than the tables included in that SELECT's table list:

```
SELECT co_name
   FROM collect
   WHERE EXISTS
      (SELECT *
         FROM cartxref
         WHERE cartxref.cx_co_id_ = collect.co_id)
```

This SELECT statement correlates the subquery to the top-level query on cartxref.cx_co_id_ = collect.co_id. Note that the collect table is not included in the subquery's table list.

The In Predicate of the WHERE Clause

The IN predicate is used to compare values in one query with values in a subquery. It allows you to select all rows for which a given expression's value is (or is not) contained within another query.

```
SELECT ca_name
   FROM cart
   WHERE ca_id IN
```

```
        (SELECT cx_ca_id_
            FROM cartxref
            WHERE cx_quant > 10)
```

This example will select all cartridge names whose ids can be found in the subquery, which selects all cartridge ids which have a quantity greater than 10 assigned to a collector. This can be restated as

```
SELECT DISTINCT ca_name
   FROM cart, cartxref
   WHERE ca_id = cx_ca_id_
   AND cx_quant > 10
```

The `DISTINCT` clause is needed because there may be more than one cartridge/collector assignment which exceeds 10 in quantity for a particular cartridge. Typically, `IN` clauses which use the `NOT` keyword cannot be restated as previously shown.

```
SELECT ca_name
   FROM cart
   WHERE ca_id NOT IN
       (SELECT cx_ca_id_
           FROM cartxref
           WHERE cx_quant > 10)
```

This query will select only those cartridges which have no collector/cartridge assignment such that one collector owns 10 of the cartridges. So, if collector A owns 12 of the Missile Command cartridges, and collector B owns 2, the Missile Command cartridge is excluded. However, the following query will not exclude this cartridge, because at least one record will be found which is less than 10; so, modifying the query to not use a subquery does not work, even if you reverse the quantity filter condition.

```
SELECT DISTINCT ca_name
   FROM cart, cartxref
   WHERE ca_id = cx_ca_id_
   AND cx_quant <= 10
```

The Subquery Comparison Predicate of the WHERE Clause

The subquery comparison predicate performs a similar function, but can be used with the comparison operator. The `ANY` keyword specifies that the comparison must evaluate to true for any of the rows in the subquery. The following `SELECT` will retrieve all collector names who have at least one cartridge, the quantity of which is equal to that of any quantity of any cartridge owned by T. Johnson.

```
SELECT DISTINCT co_name
   FROM cartxref, collect
   WHERE cx_co_id_ = co_id
   AND cx_quant = ANY
       (SELECT cx_quant
           FROM cartxref, collect
           WHERE cx_co_id_ = co_id
           AND co_name = 'T. Johnson')
```

The `ALL` keyword specifies that the comparison must evaluate to true for all of the rows in the subquery. The following `SELECT` will retrieve all collector names who have at least one cartridge, the quantity of which is greater than that of any quantity of any cartridge owned by T. Johnson.

```
SELECT DISTINCT co_name
   FROM cartxref, collect
   WHERE cx_co_id_ = co_id
   AND cx_quant > ALL
       (SELECT cx_quant
           FROM cartxref, collect
           WHERE cx_co_id_ = co_id
           AND co_name = 'T. Johnson')
```

The ORDER BY Clause

The `ORDER BY` clause allows you to specify how the `SELECT` statement is to order its results. You can optionally specify `ASC` or `DESC` to control whether the results are ordered for that column ascending or descending. You may specify the name(s) of the column(s) to order by, as in

```
SELECT cx_co_id_, cx_ca_id_
    FROM cartxref
    ORDER BY cx_co_id_, cx_ca_id_
```

or you may specify an integer value for each column's position in the result set.

```
SELECT cx_co_id_, cx_ca_id_
    FROM cartxref
    ORDER BY 1, 2
```

Core Grammar Extensions to the SELECT Statement

In addition to Core grammar WHERE clauses, several other SELECT statement clauses are supported by the Core grammar.

```
SELECT [ALL | DISTINCT] <select list>
    FROM <table reference list>
    WHERE <search condition list>
    [GROUP BY <column name> [, <column name>]...]
    [HAVING <search condition>]
    [UNION <subquery>]
    [ORDER BY    <column designator> [ASC | DESC]
              [, <column designator> [ASC | DESC]]...]
```

The GROUP BY Clause

The GROUP BY clause is used to generate summary values. You are allowed to choose which columns are used to produce distinct values by which the summary values are generated. For example, to see a sum total of all cartridges owned by each collector, you could issue:

```
SELECT co_name, SUM(cx_quant)
    FROM collect, cartxref
    WHERE cx_co_id_ = co_id
    GROUP BY co_name
```

This will produce one record for each collector, followed by a column containing the sum total of all cartridges that the collector owns. You can also use an aggregate function without the GROUP BY clause.

```
SELECT SUM(cx_quant)
   FROM cartxref
```

This will give you the sum of all carts owned. The HAVING clause works in conjunction with the aggregate functions. To get a sum total of all cartridges owned by each collector, but only for those collectors having more than two, you could use the following select statement:

```
SELECT co_name, SUM(cx_quant)
   FROM collect, cartxref
   WHERE cx_co_id_ = co_id
   GROUP BY co_name
   HAVING SUM(cx_quant) > 2
```

The following aggregate functions are available:

AVG()	Average of values
COUNT()	Count of records which match criteria
MIN()	Minimum value
MAX()	Maximum value
SUM()	Sum of values

The UNION Clause

The UNION clause allows you to combine one or more queries into a result set. The number of columns and data types of each corresponding column must match or an error will result. Here's a UNION which combines the minimum number of any given cart and maximum number of any given cartridge owned by each collector.

```
SELECT co_name,
       'MAX' AS type,
       MAX(cx_quant)
```

```
    FROM collect, cartxref
    WHERE cx_co_id_ = co_id
    GROUP BY co_name
    UNION
    SELECT co_name,
           'MIN' AS type,
           MIN(cx_quant)
      FROM collect, cartxref
      WHERE cx_co_id_ = co_id
      GROUP BY co_name
```

UPDATE

Conformance Level: Minimum

This updates columns within a table.

```
UPDATE <table name>
   SET   <column name> = {<expression> | NULL}
       [,<column name> = {<expression> | NULL}]...
   WHERE <search condition>
```

The `UPDATE` statement is used to update the values of certain columns within a table. You can specify which columns to update using a search condition, which follows the same criteria as the `WHERE` clause of the `SELECT` statement. You may specify any number of columns to update and may include an expression to assign to those columns or `NULL`.

Examples are: To change the spelling of a single name within the collector table

```
UPDATE collect
   SET co_name = 'Brian Jepson'
   WHERE co_id = 2
```

To uppercase all of the names within the collector table

```
UPDATE collect
   SET co_name = {fn UCASE(co_name)}
```

ODBC Scalar Functions

In the last example (the `UPDATE` statement), you saw the use of the `UCASE` function to uppercase a value. In general, ODBC scalar functions, such as `UCASE`, should be enclosed in the *ODBC Extended Escape delimiters*, `{and}`. The `fn` keyword tells ODBC that a function name is expected. This ensures that even if the ODBC driver's syntax for a particular function differs, you can use the ODBC scalar function name, without having to modify your code for each driver. This makes it easier to write cross-platform code.

String Functions

ASCII(<string>)

This function returns as an integer value, the ASCII code of the leftmost character of the argument <string>:

```
SELECT {fn ASCII(co_name)}
    FROM collect
```

CHAR(<integer>)

The CHAR function returns the character that has the ASCII value specified in <integer>:

```
SELECT {fn CHAR(co_id + 64)}
    FROM collect
```

CONCAT(<string1>, <string2>)

CONCAT returns a single string value which is the result of concatenating the arguments <string1> and <string2>:

```
SELECT {fn CONCAT(pl_fname, pl_lname)}
    FROM players
```

INSERT(<string1>, <integer1>, <integer2>, <string2>)

This replaces <integer2> characters within <string1>, starting at the character position represented by <integer1>. The first character position is 1. The value of <string2> is inserted as a replacement string:

```
SELECT {fn INSERT(pl_fname, 2, 4, pl_lname)}
    FROM players
```

LCASE(<string>)

This function returns the lowercased string value of <string>:

```
SELECT {fn LCASE(pl_lname)}
    FROM players
```

LEFT(<string>, <integer>)

The LEFT function returns a string consisting of the <integer> leftmost characters from <string>:

```
SELECT {fn LEFT(pl_fname, 3)}
    FROM players
```

LENGTH(<string>)

This returns an integer value consisting of the number of characters in <string>, ignoring any trailing blanks:

```
SELECT {fn LENGTH(pl_fname)}
    FROM players
```

LOCATE(<string1>, <string2> [, <integer>)

This returns the offset in <string2> of the first occurrence of <string1>. You may optionally supply a position to begin searching, with <integer>.

```
SELECT {fn LOCATE('on', pl_lname)}
    FROM players
```

LTRIM(<string>)

This function returns a string consisting of the <string> with leading blanks removed:

```
SELECT {fn LTRIM(pl_fname)}
    FROM players
```

REPEAT(<string>, <integer>)

REPEAT returns a string composed of <string> repeated <integer> times:

```
SELECT {fn REPEAT(pl_fname, 2)}
   FROM players
```

REPLACE(<string1>, <string2>, <string3>)

This returns a string created by replacing all occurrences of <string2> within <string1> with <string3>:

```
SELECT {fn REPLACE(pl_fname, 'e', 'o')}
   FROM players
```

RIGHT(<string>, <integer>)

This function returns a string consisting of the <integer> rightmost characters from <string>:

```
SELECT {fn RIGHT(pl_fname, 3)}
   FROM players
```

RTRIM(<string>)

The RTRIM function returns a string consisting of the <string> with trailing blanks removed:

```
SELECT {fn RTRIM(pl_fname)}
   FROM players
```

SUBSTRING(<string>, <integer1>, <integer2>)

This returns a substring of <string> which begins at <integer1> position within <string> and continues for <integer2> characters:

```
SELECT {fn SUBSTRING(pl_fname, 3, 3)}
   FROM players
```

UCASE(<string>)

This returns the uppercased string value of <string>:

```
SELECT {fn UCASE(pl_lname)}
   FROM players
```

Numeric Functions

ABS(<numeric>)

ABS returns the absolute value of the integer or float value specified by <numeric>:

```
SELECT {fn ABS(profit_loss)}
    FROM portfolio
```

ACOS(<float>)

This function returns the arccosine of the value specified by <float> expressed as an angle in radians:

```
SELECT {fn ACOS(roof_angle)}
    FROM dimensions
```

ASIN(<float>)

This returns the arcsine of the value specified by <float> expressed as an angle in radians:

```
SELECT {fn ASIN(roof_angle)}
    FROM dimensions
```

ATAN(<float>)

ATAN returns the arctangent of the value specified by <float> expressed as an angle in radians:

```
SELECT {fn ATAN(roof_angle)}
    FROM dimensions
```

ATAN2(<float1>, <float2>)

The ATAN2 function returns the arctangent of the x and y coordinates specified by <float1> (x) and <float2> (y), expressed as an angle in radians:

```
SELECT {fn ATAN(point_x, point_y)}
    FROM dimensions
```

CEILING(<numeric>)

This returns the smallest integer which is greater than or equal to the float or integer value expressed by <numeric>:

```
SELECT {fn CEILING(roof_angle)}
    FROM dimensions
```

COS(<float>)

This returns the cosine of the value specified by <float> expressed as an angle in radians:

```
SELECT {fn COS(roof_angle)}
    FROM dimensions
```

EXP(<float>)

EXP returns the exponential value of the value specified by <float>:

```
SELECT {fn EXP(length * width * height)}
    FROM dimensions
```

FLOOR(<numeric>)

This returns the largest integer which is less than or equal to the float or integer value expressed by <numeric>:

```
SELECT {fn FLOOR(roof_angle)}
    FROM dimensions
```

LOG(<float>)

This returns the natural logarithm of the value expressed by <float>:

```
SELECT {fn LOG(roof_angle)}
    FROM dimensions
```

MOD(<integer1>, <integer2>)

Modulus arithmetic returns the remainder of <integer1> divided by <integer2>:

```
SELECT {fn MOD(length, height)}
    FROM dimensions
```

PI()

This returns the constant floating-point value of pi:

```
SELECT {fn PI() * (radius * radius)}
    FROM dimensions
```

RAND([<integer>])

The RAND function returns a pseudo-random floating-point value, optionally seeding the random number generator with the value of <integer>:

```
SELECT {fn RAND(co_id)}
    FROM collect
```

SIGN(<numeric>)

SIGN returns the sign (1, 0, or -1) of the integer or float value specified by <numeric>:

```
SELECT {fn SIGN(profit_loss)}
    FROM portfolio
```

SIN(<float>)

SIN returns the sine of the value specified by <float> expressed as an angle in radians:

```
SELECT {fn SIN(roof_angle)}
    FROM dimensions
```

SQRT(<float>)

This returns the square root of the value specified by <float>:

```
SELECT {fn SQRT(length + width + height)}
    FROM dimensions
```

TAN(<float>)

This returns the tangent of the value specified by <float> expressed as an angle in radians:

```
SELECT {fn TAN(roof_angle)}
    FROM dimensions
```

Date and Time Functions

CURDATE()

This returns the current date, expressed as a date value:

```
SELECT {fn CURDATE()}, co_name
    FROM collect
```

CURTIME()

This returns the current time, expressed as a time value:

```
SELECT {fn CURTIME()}, co_name
    FROM collect
```

DAYOFMONTH(<date>)

This function returns the day of the month of <date>. It is expressed as an integer value between 1 and 31:

```
SELECT {fn DAYOFMONTH(sh_date)}, sh_py_id_
    FROM shows
```

DAYOFWEEK(<date>)

This function returns the day of the week of <date>. It is expressed as an integer value between 1 and 7. Sunday is represented by 1:

```
SELECT {fn DAYOFWEEK(sh_date)}, sh_py_id_
    FROM shows
```

DAYOFYEAR(<date>)

The DAYOFYEAR function returns the day of the year of <date>. It is expressed as an integer value between 1 and 366:

```
SELECT {fn DAYOFYEAR(sh_date)}, sh_py_id_
    FROM shows
```

HOUR(<time>)

This returns the hour of the time value <time>, expressed as an integer between 0 and 23:

```
SELECT {fn HOUR({fn CURTIME()})}, co_name
   FROM collect
```

MINUTE(<time>)

This returns the minute of the time value <time>, expressed as an integer between 0 and 59:

```
SELECT {fn MINUTE({fn CURTIME()})}, co_name
   FROM collect
```

MONTH(<date>)

This returns the month of <date>. It is expressed as an integer value between 1 and 12:

```
SELECT {fn MONTH(sh_date)}, sh_py_id_
   FROM shows
```

NOW()

This returns the current date and time, expressed as a timestamp value:

```
SELECT {fn NOW()}, co_name
   FROM collect
```

QUARTER(<date>)

QUARTER returns the quarter of <date>. It is expressed as an integer value between 1 and 4:

```
SELECT {fn QUARTER(sh_date)}, sh_py_id_
   FROM shows
```

SECOND(<time>)

This returns the second of the time value <time>, expressed as an integer between 0 and 59:

```
SELECT {fn SECOND({fn CURTIME()})}, co_name
   FROM collect
```

WEEK(<date>)

This function returns the week number of <date>. It is expressed as an integer value between 1 and 53:

```
SELECT {fn WEEK(sh_date)}, sh_py_id_
   FROM shows
```

SQL Components

This section describes each component available within the various SQL statements. Each includes an example, where the component is shown in **bold**.

<column designator>

This is the name of a column, or an integer representing the position of a column, in a `SELECT` statement; for example:

```
SELECT co_name, co_id
   FROM collect
   ORDER BY 1, co_id
```

<column element>

See the documentation for CREATE TABLE.

<column name>

A valid column name (usually alphanumeric); for example:

```
SELECT co_name FROM collect
```

<comparison operator>

This is an operator which returns a true or false (Boolean) value. Several comparison operators are available:

x = y	x is equal to y
x <> y	x is not equal to y
x > y	x is greater than y
x < y	x is less than y

x >= y	x is greater than or equal to y
x <= y	x is less than or equal to y

The comparison operator can compare an expression, which may consist of any combination of column names, literal values, or other operators. Examples are:

```
SELECT *
    FROM cartxref
    WHERE cx_quant < 10
```

This example selects every record from the cartxref table where the quantity is less than 10.

```
SELECT pe_name
    FROM people
    WHERE pe_IQ > (pe_shoesize * 2)
```

This example selects every record from the people table where the person's IQ is greater than his or her shoe size multiplied by 2.

<data type>

This is any one of the data types supported by your ODBC driver and can include optional column width;

for example:

```
CREATE TABLE collect
    (co_id float,
     co_name char (40))
```

<expression>

Any well-formed combination of column names, operators, literal values, and scalar functions; for example:

```
SELECT cx_co_id_
    FROM cartxref
    WHERE SQRT(cx_quant * 8) = 18
```

<index name>

The name of an index.

```
CREATE INDEX ix_name
    ON collect
    (co_name)
```

<pattern value>

A string value used for pattern matches. See the documentation for the SELECT statement.

<query specification>

This is a valid SQL SELECT statement and this can be embedded in other statements, such as INSERT.

```
INSERT INTO summary
    (su_name, su_quant)
    SELECT co_name, SUM(cx_quant)
        FROM collect, cartxref
        WHERE cx_co_id_ = co_id
        GROUP BY co_name
```

<referenced column list>

See documentation for CREATE TABLE.

<referenced table>

See <table name>.

<referencing column list>

See documentation for CREATE TABLE.

<search condition>

This is an expression used to filter results in a query. It can consist of literal values as well as column names. The keywords AND and OR can be used, as well; for example:

```
SELECT cx_co_id_
   FROM cartxref
   WHERE cx_quant > 10
```

See the documentation on the SELECT statement for more information.

<search condition list>

This is one or more search conditions, joined with the AND or OR keywords. See the documentation on the SELECT statement for more information.

<table name>

This is the name of a table within your data source; for example:

```
SELECT * FROM collect
```

<table reference list>

This is a list of tables within a SELECT statement. It may consist of table names or view names. Each table or view name is separated by a comma. The . (dot) notation, as in the following example, allows you to explicitly state to which table a certain column belongs.

```
SELECT collect.co_name, cartxref.cx_quant
   FROM collect, cartxref
   WHERE cartxref.cx_co_id_ = collect.co_id
```

Also, a *local alias* may be included in the table reference list, which allows you to specify an alternate table name within the query.

```
SELECT a.co_name, b.cx_quant
   FROM collect a, cartxref b
   WHERE b.cx_co_id_ = a.co_id
```

INDEX

T

CUSTOMER NOTE:

IF THIS BOOK IS ACCOMPANIED BY SOFTWARE, PLEASE READ THE FOLLOWING BEFORE OPENING THE PACKAGE.

This software contains files to help you utilize the models described in the accompanying book. By opening the package, you are agreeing to be bound by the following agreement:

This software product is sold as is without warranty of any kind, either expressed or implied, including but not limited to the implied warranty of merchantability and fitness for a particular purpose. Neither Wiley nor its dealers or distributors assumes any liability of any alleged or actual damages arising from the use of or the inability to use this software. (Some states do not allow the exclusion of implied warranties, so the exclusion may not apply to you.)